MILITARY ARCHITECTURE
IN MEDIEVAL ENGLAND

ROCHESTER : GREAT TOWER.

MILITARY ARCHITECTURE IN MEDIEVAL ENGLAND

BY

A. HAMILTON THOMPSON
M.A., F.S.A.

Illustrated by 200 Photographs, Drawings, and Plans

EP Publishing Limited
Rowman and Littlefield
1975

Republished 1975 by EP Publishing Limited
East Ardsley, Wakefield
West Yorkshire, England
and in the United States of America by
Rowman and Littlefield
Totowa, New Jersey
by kind permission of the copyright holders
Copyright © 1975 Oxford University Press
First published in 1912 by Henry Frowde,
Oxford University Press, under the title,
'Military Architecture in England During
the Middle Ages'

ISBN 0 7158 1074 x
(EP Publishing)

Library of Congress Cataloging in Publication Data

Thompson, Alexander Hamilton, 1873–1952.
Military architecture in medieval England.

Reprint of the 1912 ed. published by H. Frowde, Lon-
don, New York, under title: Military architecture in
England during the Middle Ages.
Bibliography: p.
Includes index.
1. Military architecture—England. 2. Castles—
England. 3. Architecture, Medieval—England. I. Title
[NA497.E53T48   1975b]   725'.18   75-2121
ISBN 0-87471-684-5

Please address all enquiries to EP Publishing Limited
(address as above)

Printed in Great Britain by
REDWOOD BURN LIMITED
Trowbridge and Esher

PREFACE

APART from the late Mr G. T. Clark's *Mediæval Military Architecture*, published in 1884, the greater portion of which is a series of monographs dealing with individual castles, there has been no attempt, until within the last few years, to apply systematic treatment to this branch of science. Recently, however, more than one book has been published upon the general subject of the castles of England. Mr Alfred Harvey has lately given a lucid account of the growth of the castle, with a valuable essay upon English walled towns ; and the present year has seen the appearance of a book in which Mrs Armitage has embodied the result of labours of the utmost importance, extending over many years. In addition to works of a general character, a number of separate monographs, indispensable to students, have been published during the last twenty years, in the transactions of various archæological societies. The contributions of Mr W. H. St John Hope to the study of castle architecture take a foremost place among these, with papers such as those by Mr J. Bilson on Gilling castle and by Mr Harold Sands on Bodiam and the Tower of London ; and the late Mr Cadwallader Bates' unfinished *Border Holds of Northumberland* contains accounts of Warkworth and Bamburgh, as well as of smaller castles and peles, which must take rank among the classics of the subject.

In the present volume an attempt is made to trace the growth of the general principles of medieval fortification, with special reference to castles, in which, within their limited area, the most complete illustration of those principles is given. In order to give greater clearness to the account of their evolution, a prefatory chapter deals generally with earlier types of fortification in Britain, and the critical period of Saxon and Danish warfare is treated in the second chapter with some detail. This leads us to the early Norman castle of earthwork and timber ; and the stone fortifications to which this gave place are introduced by a brief account of the progress of siegecraft and siege-engines. The Norman castle and its keep or great tower are then described. The developments of the later part of the twelfth century and the arrangements of the thirteenth-century

castle, with those of the dwelling-house within its *enceinte*, follow
and prepare the way for the castles of the reign of Edward I.
which represent the highest effort of military planning. In
the last two chapters is related the progress of the transition
from the castle to the fortified manor-house, which followed
the introduction of fire-arms into warfare and preceded the
Renaissance period. It will be seen that the castle is taken as
the unit of military architecture throughout; but illustrations
are constantly drawn from walled towns, which are, in fact, the
castles of communities, and in the eleventh chapter extended
allusion is made to the chief features of their plan and defences.

In speaking of the walled town, however, as the castle of the
community, it must not be forgotten that the castle is, in its
origin, the stronghold of a single owner. That origin is still to
some extent a vexed question; for the well-known theory of
Mr G. T. Clark, that the castle of Norman times was identical
with the *burh* of the Saxon Chronicle, was accepted as a dogma
by the antiquaries of twenty-five to fifty years ago, and a theory
thus established, however precipitately, is not easily shaken.
The patient and thorough work of Mrs Armitage, which deserves
the admiration of every scholar, has done much to disturb the
foundations on which Mr Clark built his hypothesis; and
Mr Neilson, Dr Round, Mr St John Hope, and others, have
contributed their share to the discovery of the real character of
the evidence, and the formulation of a sounder theory. The
present writer has devoted much time to the study of the
original authorities for Saxon and Norman military history, and
it is his conviction that the weight of documentary evidence is
entirely upon the side of the views upheld with so much ability
and originality by these recent investigators. At the same time,
the earthworks of early castles still present several difficult
problems; and the discredit into which Mr Clark's theory has
fallen is a warning against the too confident acceptation of the
conclusions of a more critical age, and against the danger of
forcing exceptions into the service of the rule.

In the earlier part of this book, some allusion is made to
methods of Roman warfare; and the main points of two of the
sieges conducted by Cæsar and his lieutenants are summarily
described. It need hardly be said, in view of what follows, that

the methods of military architecture in the middle ages have, for the most part, their exact prototypes in Roman and Byzantine history. The student of the siege-campaigns of Philip Augustus will be constantly reminded, for example, of the relation by Ammianus of the exploits of Julian the Apostate. Too much emphasis cannot be laid on the importance, first, of the contact of the Northmen who overran England and France with the traditional expedients of Roman siegecraft, as they existed in the eastern empire, and secondly, of the influence of the Crusades upon the development of medieval fortification. The conditions of our military architecture in the middle ages were naturally governed by the methods of attack employed by a besieging force. As these had been brought to a high state of perfection in the east, an advance upon which was hardly possible, the history of English fortification, from the Norman conquest to the general adoption of fire-arms in warfare, is that of a progress towards a system of defence in which western Europe lagged far behind the older centres of civilisation.

It is to be noted that, although the architecture of the castle and the fortifications of towns naturally took its share in the formal progress of Gothic art, the laws under which it was evolved bear no resemblance to the principles of construction, in obedience to which the medieval cathedral assumed its characteristic form. Ribbed vaults, Gothic mouldings, and traceried windows afford a clue to the dates of the various parts of a medieval castle, as they do to those of a church; but they are merely incidental to a type of construction to which the solid and impregnable wall is all-important. The cases are rare in which the builders of castles paid much attention to elaborate detail in the minor parts of their building : their decorative work is used with the economy and simplicity appropriate to the massive construction which their fortresses demanded.

A vast amount of work still remains to be done in the exploration of our military buildings and the reconstruction of their history ; and, until that is accomplished, no thoroughly satisfactory general hand-book can be written. Nevertheless, it is hoped that there is room for books which may serve as general indicators to what has been done, up to the present time, in this direction. The bibliography which will be found

preceding the text of this volume includes a selected list of
monographs or articles upon individual castles, many of which
have appeared in the transactions of various archaeological
societies. These vary considerably in value ; but, taken as a
whole, they serve to enlarge our knowledge of the history and
architecture of the buildings with which they are concerned.

The author desires to express his thanks, first to his wife,
without whose constant help in the preparation of the book and
in the provision of drawings and plans to illustrate its pages, it
could hardly have been written. Mr Francis Bond, the editor
of this series, has aided the author with unfailing kindness,
by reading through the proofs, making suggestions as to the
general form of the book, and arranging for its adequate illustration. To the following, who have kindly allowed the use
of photographs, special thanks should be returned : Mrs Jessie
Lloyd, the Revs. J. Bailey and G. W. Saunders, and Messrs
Harold Baker, F. Bond, J. P. Gibson, F.S.A., G. J. Gillham, G.
Hepworth, P. M. Johnston, F.S.A., R. Keene, W. Maitland, E. A.
and G. R. Reeve, F. R. Taylor, and G. H. Widdows. The
editors of the *Archaeological Journal* have sanctioned the use of.
various plans from the annual programmes of the Archaeological
Institute. Mr A. Hadrian Allcroft and Messrs Macmillan have
given consent to the reproduction of three illustrations from
Mr Allcroft's *Earthwork of England.* Permission to found
the plan of Chepstow castle on one in the official *Guide* to that
building was kindly given by his Grace the Duke of Beaufort,
through Mr Noel H. P. Somerset. MM. Camille Enlart and
Auguste Picard have permitted the insertion of a plan of
Château-Gaillard, founded on that in M. Enlart's *Manuel.* Mr
R. Blair, F.S.A., has authorised a similar use of illustrations
founded on those of Dr Bruce's *Roman Wall.* Thanks are also
due to the editor of the *Yorkshire Archæological Journal* for the
plan of Sandal castle, and to Mr W. G. Watkins, jun., for his
plan of Lincoln castle. Special acknowledgments are due to
Mr Godfrey L. Clark for his liberality in putting at the disposal
of the writer valuable plans and drawings from his father's work.
The author much regrets that questions of space and cost have
prevented him from taking advantage of more than a limited
number of the generous offers of illustration which reached him
during the preparation of the book for the press.

TABLE OF CONTENTS

xi

BIBLIOGRAPHY

1. Chief Original Authorities cited.

ABBO, De Bello Parisiaco libri tres (Migne, *Patrologiae Cursus Completus*, vol. 131 (1853), pp. 722-62).

AMIENS, GUY OF. Carmen de Hastingae proelio (Chroniques Anglo-Normands). Rouen, 1836-40.

ANGLO-SAXON CHRONICLE, ed. C. Plummer. 2 vols. Oxford, 1892-9.

ANNA COMNENA. Alexias, ed. A. Reifferscheid. 2 vols. Leipzig, 1884.

ANNALES BERTINIANI (Annales Francorum, vulgo Bertiniani dicti), ed. Dom. M. Bouquet, *Recueil des historiens des Gaules et de la France*, vols. vi. (1749), 192-204; vii. (1749) 59-124; viii. (1752), 26-37.

ARDRES, LAMBERT OF. Extracts in Bouquet, *Recueil des historiens*, vols. xi. (1767) 295-307; xiii. (1786), 423-53; xviii. (1822), 583-8

BEDE. Historia Ecclesiastica, ed. C. Plummer. Oxford, 1896.

BRETON (LE), GUILLAUME. Philippidos libri xii., ed. Bouquet, *Recueil des historiens*, vol. xvii. (1818) 117-287.

CAESAR. Commentaries, ed. B. Kübler. 3 vols. Leipzig, 1893-6.

COLMIEU, JEAN DE, canon of St Martin, Ypres. Vita beati Joannis Morinorum episcopi (*Acta Sanctorum*, January, vol. iii. 409-17).

DICETO, RALPH DE. Historical Works (Ymagines Historiarum and Abbreviationes Chronicorum), ed. W. Stubbs, 2 vols. (Rolls Series, No. 68).

DOMESDAY BOOK (Record Commission). 4 vols. Lond. 1816.

HENRY VIII., LETTERS AND PAPERS, ed. Brewer and Gairdner, vol. iv.

HOVEDEN, ROGER OF. Chronicle, ed. W. Stubbs. 4 vols. (Rolls Series, No. 51).

JOINVILLE, JEAN, SEIGNEUR DE. Histoire de Saint Louis, ed. N. de Wailly. Paris, 1874 (translation of Chronicle by Sir Frank Marzials, London, 1908).

MONTE, ROBERT DE (Robert de Torigny, abbot of Mont-Saint-Michel). Cronica (continuation of Sigebert of Gemblours), ed. Migne, *Patrologiae Cursus*, vol. clx., 423-546.

ORDERICUS VITALIS. Historia Ecclesiastica, ed. A. le Prévost. 5 vols. Paris, 1838-55.

PATENT ROLLS, CALENDARS OF, 1216-66, 1271-1364, 1377-1485. 47 vols. (in progress).

PETERBOROUGH, BENEDICT OF.   Chronicle, ed. W. Stubbs.   2 vols.
    (Rolls Series, No. 49).
PIPE ROLLS.   Pipe Roll Society Publications.   27 vols. (in progress).
    London, 1884, etc.
RYMER, THOMAS.   Foedera.   20 vols.   London, 1704-35.
STUBBS, WILLIAM, D.D.   Select Charters and other Illustrations of
    English Constitutional History, 8th edit.   Oxford, 1905.
SUGER.   Gesta Ludovici Grossi, ed. A. Molinier.   Paris, 1887.
VEGETIUS.   Epitoma Rei Militaris, ed. C. Lang.   Leipzig, 1885.
VETUSTA MONUMENTA, vol. vi. (Bayeux Tapestry).   London, 1842.
VILLEHARDOUIN, GEOFFROI DE.   De la Conqueste de Constantinople
    par les Barons François associez aux Venitiens, ed. N. de Wailly.
    Paris, 1872-4 (trans. Sir Frank Marzials, London, 1908).
VITRUVIUS.   De Architectura, ed. V. Rose.   Leipzig, 1899.
WENDOVER, ROGER OF.   Chronica sive Flores Historiarum, ed. H.
    G. Hewlett, 3 vols. (Rolls Series, No. 84).

2. General.

ALLCROFT, A. HADRIAN.   Earthwork of England.   London, 1908.
ARMITAGE, ELLA S.   Anglo-Saxon burhs and early Norman castles
    (*Proc. Soc. Antiq. Scotland*, xxxiv. 260-88).
—— The Early Norman Castles of England (*English Historical
    Review*, xix. 209-45 and 417-55).
—— The Early Norman Castles of the British Isles.   London,
    1912.
BRUCE, J. C., LL.D., F.S.A.   Hand-book to the Roman Wall, ed.
    Robert Blair, F.S.A., 5th edition.   London and Newcastle-on-
    Tyne, 1907.
CHRISTISON, DAVID, M.D.   Early Fortification in Scotland : Motes,
    camps, and forts.   Edinburgh and London, 1898.
CLARK, G. T., F.S.A.   Mediæval Military Architecture in England.
    2 vols.   London, 1884.
CLEPHAN, R. COLTMAN, F.S.A.   An Outline of the History of
    Gunpowder and that of the Hand-Gun, from the epoch of the
    earliest records to the end of the fifteenth century (*Archaeol.
    Journal*, lxvi. 145-70).
—— The Military Handgun of the sixteenth century (*Archaeol.
    Journal*, lxvii. 109-50).
—— The Ordnance of the fourteenth and fifteenth centuries (*Archaeol.
    Journal*, lxviii. 49-138).
CODRINGTON, THOMAS.   Roman Roads in Britain.   London, 1903.

D'Auvergne, Edmund B.   The Castles of England.   London, 1907.
—— The English Castles, London, 1908.
Dieulafoy, M.   Le Château-Gaillard et l'architecture militaire au
XIIIme siècle (*Mémoires de l'Académie des Inscriptions*, tom. xxxvi.,
part. 1).   Paris, 1898.
Enlart, Camille.   Manuel d'Archéologie française, vol. ii.   Paris,
1904.
Harvey, Alfred.   The Castles and Walled Towns of England.
London, 1911.
Haverfield, Prof. F. J., LL.D., D.Litt., V.P.S.A.   The Romaniza-
tion of Roman Britain.   London, 1905.
—— Roman Britain (*Cambridge Medieval History*, i.   367-81 : see
ibid. 666-7 for bibliography of various articles by the same writer).
Hochfelden, G. H. Krieg von.   Geschichte der Militar-Archi-
tektur in Deutschland.   Stuttgart, 1859.
Hope, W. H. St John.   English fortresses and castles of the tenth
and eleventh centuries (*Archaeol. Journal*, lx. 72-90).
Mackenzie, Sir J. D.   The Castles of England, their Story and
Structure.   2 vols.   London, 1897.
Neilson, George.   The motes in Norman Scotland (*Scottish Review*
xiv. 209-38).
Oman, Prof. C. W. C., F.S.A.   A History of the Art of War in the
Middle Ages.   London, 1898.
Orpen, G. H.   Motes and Norman castles in Ireland (*Proc. Royal
Soc. Antiq. Ireland*, xxxvii. 123-52).
Parker, J. H., and Turner, T. Hudson.   Some account of domestic
architecture in England.   3 vols. in 4.   Oxford, 1851-9.
Round, J. Horace, LL.D.   The Castles of the Conquest. (*Archaeologia*,
lviii. 313-40).
—— Feudal England, Historical Studies on the XIth and XIIth
Centuries (new edition).   London, 1909.
Saint-Paul, Anthyme.   Histoire Monumentale de la France, 6th
edition.   Paris, 1903.
Turner, T. Hudson ; *see* Parker, J. H.
Van Millingen, A.   Byzantine Constantinople.   London, 1899.
Viollet-le-Duc, E.   Dictionnaire Raisonné de l'Architecture française
du XIe au XVIe Siècle.   10 vols. Paris, 1854, etc.
—— Essai sur l'architecture militaire au moyen âge.   Paris, 1854
(translated by M. Macdermott, Oxford and London, 1860).
—— Histoire d'une forteresse.   Paris, n.d.
Ward, W. H.   French Châteaux and Gardens in the XVIth Century
(drawings reproduced from Androuet-du-Cerceau).   London, 1909.

WESTROPP, T. J. Irish motes and alleged Norman castles (*Proc. Royal Soc. Antiq. Ireland*, xiv. 313-45, and xv. 402-6).

3. Special Monographs, etc.

ACTON BURNELL. Hartshorne, C. H., F.S.A. (*Archaeol. Journal*, ii. 325-38).

ALNWICK. Clark, *Mediæval Mil. Architecture*, i. 175-85.

—— Knowles, W. H., F.S.A., F.R.I.B.A. The Gatehouse and Barbican of Alnwick Castle (*Archaeologia Æliana*, 3rd ser., v. 286-303).

AMBERLEY. Clarkson, G. A. (*Sussex Arch. Coll.*, xvii. 185-339).

ARUNDEL. Clark, i. 195-203.

AUCKLAND. Rev. J. F. Hodgson (*Archaeologia Æliana*, xix. 89-92).

AYDON. Knowles, W. H. (*Archaeologia*, lvi. 78-88). *See* also Bates, *Border Holds*.

BAMBURGH. Bates, *Border Holds*; Clark, G. T. (*Archaeol. Journal*, xlvi. 93-113).

BARNARD CASTLE. Clark, i. 204-13.

BEAUMARIS. Clark, i. 213-17.

BELSAY. Bates, *Border Holds*.

—— Middleton, Sir Arthur E., Bart. An account of Belsay castle (privately printed). Newcastle-on-Tyne, 1910.

BERKELEY. Clark, i. 228-39.

BERKHAMPSTEAD. Clark, i. 223-38.

BERWICK-ON-TWEED. Norman, F. M. (Commander R.N.): Official Guide to the Fortifications. Berwick, 1907.

BODIAM. Clark, i. 239-47.

—— Sands, Harold, F.S.A., in *Sussex Archaeol. Collections*, xlvi. 114-33.

BOTHAL. Bates, *Border Holds*.

BOWES. Clark, i. 259-64.

BRIDGNORTH. Clark, i. 273-81.

BRISTOL. Harvey, Alfred, M.B. Bristol, a historical and topographical account of the city. London, 1906.

—— (castle). Pritchard, J. E., F.S.A. (*Proceedings of Clifton Antiquarian Club*, iv. 17-19).

BRONLLYS. Clark, i. 283-6; *Archaeologia Cambrensis*, 3rd ser., viii. 81-92.

BROUGHTON. Lord Saye and Sele (*Berks, Bucks, and Oxon. Archaeol. Journal*, new ser., vii. 23-5).

BUILTH. Clark, i. 304-8.

CAERPHILLY. Clark, i. 315-35.

CALDICOT. Bellows, J. (*Cotteswold Field Club*, vi. 263-7).

CALDICOT. Cobb, J. R. (*Clifton Antiq. Club*, iii. 35-40).

CAMBRIDGE. Hope, W. H. St John (*Camb. Antiq. Soc.*, xi. 324-46).

—— Hughes, Prof. T. M'Kenny, F.S.A. (*ibid.*, ix. 348).

CARCASSONNE. Viollet-le-Duc, E. La Cité de Carcassonne. Paris, 1858.

CARDIFF. Clark, i. 336-50; Ward, J., F.S.A. Cardiff castle, its Roman origin (*Archaeologia*, lvii. 335-52).

CAREW. Cobb, J. R. (*Archaeologia Cambrensis*, 5th ser., iii. 27-41).

CARISBROOKE. Beattie, W. (*Journal Archaeol. Assoc.*, xi. 193-205).

—— Stone, P. G., F.S.A. (*Proc. Soc. Antiq.*, 2nd ser., xvi. 409-11).

CARLISLE. Clark, i. 350-8

CARNARVON. Clark, i. 309-15.

—— Hartshorne, C. H. (*Archaeol. Journal*, vii. 237-65 ; *Archaeologia Cambrensis*, 3rd ser., i. 242-6).

CHÂTEAU-GAILLARD. Clark, i. 378-85; Dieulafoy, M., *see* General Bibliography.

CHEPSTOW. Clark, G. T. (*Bristol and Glouc. Archaeol. Soc.*, vi. 51-74).

—— Wood, J. G., F.S.A. The Lordship, Castle, and Town of Chepstow. Newport, 1910.

CHESTER. Cox, E. W. (*Archit., etc., Soc. Chester and North Wales*, v. 239-76).

CHILLINGHAM. Bates, *Border Holds*.

CHIPCHASE. Bates, *Border Holds*.

—— Knowles, W. H. (*Archaeologia Æliana*, 3rd ser., i. 32-4).

CHRISTCHURCH. Clark, i. 385-92.

CILURNUM. An Account of the Roman Antiquities preserved in the Museum at Chesters, 1903.

CLUN. Clark, i. 402-9.

COLCHESTER. Clark, i. 418-31.

—— The History and Antiquities of Colchester castle. Colchester, 1882. *See also Archaeol. Journal*, lxiv. 188-191.

CONISBROUGH. Clark, i. 431-53.

CONWAY. Clark, i. 453-60.

—— Hartshorne, C. H. (*Archaeologia Cambrensis*, new ser., v. 1-12).

CORFE. Blashill, T. (*Journal Archaeol. Assoc.*, xxviii. 258-71).

—— Bond, T. History and Description of Corfe Castle. London and Bournemouth, 1883.

—— Clark, i. 461-75.

COUCY. Clark, i. 476-87.

—— Lefèvre-Pontalis, E. Le Château de Coucy (with special bibliography). Paris, n.d.

—— Viollet-de-Duc, E. Description du Château de Coucy. Paris, n.d.

DENBIGH. Ayrton, W. (*Chester Archit., etc., Soc.*, ii. 49-60).

DOLWYDDELAN. Barnwell, E. L. (*Archaeologia Cambrensis*, 4th ser., xiv. 174-5).

DOMFRONT. Blanchetière, L. Le Donjon ou Château féodal de Domfront (Orne). Domfront, 1893.

DOVER. Blashill, T. (*Journal Archaeol. Assoc.*, xl. 373-8).

—— Clark, ii. 4-24.

DUFFIELD. Cox, J. C., LL.D., F.S.A. (*Derbyshire Archaeol. Soc.*, ix. 118-78).

DUNSTANBURGH. Bates, *Border Holds.*

—— Compton, C. H. (*Journal British Archaeol. Assoc*, new ser., ix. 111-16).

DURHAM. Clark, ii. 32-5, and *Archaeol. Journal*, xxxix. 1-22.

—— Gee, H., D.D., F.S.A. (*Proc. Soc. Antiq.*, 2nd ser., xx. 17-18, and *Trans. Durham and Northumb. Archaeol. Soc.*).

EXETER. Clark, ii. 44-7.

FALAISE. Ruprich-Robert, V. Paris, 1864.

GILLING. Bilson, J. (*Yorks Archæol. Journal*, xix. 105-92).

GUILDFORD. Clark, ii. 53-71.

—— Malden, H. E. (*Surrey Archaeol. Soc.*, xvi. 28-34).

HADDON. Cheetham, F. H. Haddon Hall. London and Manchester, 1904.

HALLATON. Dibbin, H. A. (*Proc. Soc. Antiq.*, 2nd ser., vii. 316-21).

HARLECH. Chapman, F. G. W. (*Journal British Archaeol. Assoc.* xxxiv. 159-67).

—— Clark, ii. 72-81.

HASTINGS. Clark, ii. 82-88.

—— Dawson, C., F.S.A. History of Hastings Castle. 2 vols. London, 1909.

HAWARDEN. Clark, ii. 88-99.

HELMSLEY. Clark, ii. 100-8.

KENILWORTH. Clark, ii. 130-53.

—— Knowles, E. H. The Castle of Kenilworth. Warwick, 1872.

KENTISH CASTLES. Sands, Harold. Some Kentish Castles (*Memorials of Old Kent*, 1907).

KIDWELLY. Clark, ii. 153-62.

KNARESBOROUGH. Clark, ii. 168-76.

LANCASHIRE CASTLES. Fishwick, H. Lancashire castles (*Lancs. and Chesh. Antiq. Soc.*, xix. 45-76).

LANCASTER. Cox, E. W. (*Hist. Soc. Lancs. and Cheshire*, new ser., xii. 95-122).

LANGLEY. Bates, C. J. (*Archaeologia Æliana*, x. 38-56).

LEEDS. Clark, ii. 176-8.

—— James, F. V. (*Archaeologia Cantiana*, xxv. pp. xlix-liii).

LEICESTER. Clark, ii. 182-8.

—— Thompson, James. Leicester Castle. Leicester, 1859.

LEWES. Clark (*Sussex Archaeol. Collections*, xxxiv. 57-70).

LINCOLN. Clark, ii. 189-201.

—— Sympson, E. Mansel, M.D. Lincoln, a historical and topographical account of the city. London, 1906.

LLANSTEPHAN. Williams, Sir John (*Archaeologia Cambrensis*, 6th ser., vii. 108-18).

LONDON, TOWER OF. Clark, ii. 203-72.

—— Sands, H., F.S.A. (*Memorials of Old London*, London, 1908, vol. i. 27-65).

LUDLOW. Clark, ii. 273-90.

—— Hope, W. H. St John (*Archæologia*, lxi. 258-328).

LUMLEY. Dodd, J. (*Journal British Archaeol. Assoc.*, xxii. 45, 46).

MANORBIER. Duckett, Sir J. (*Archaeologia Cambrensis*, 4th ser., xi. 134-145, 286-91, xiii. 166-73).

MIDDLEHAM. Clark, ii. 293-300.

MITFORD. Clark, ii. 300-3.

MONTGOMERY. Clark, ii. 303-12.

MONT-ST-MICHEL. Corroyer, E. Description de l'abbaye du Mont-Saint-Michel et de ses abords. Paris, 1877.

—— Massé, H. J. L. J. A short history and description . . . of Mont S. Michel. London, 1902.

NEWARK-ON-TRENT. Blagg, T. M., F.S.A. A Guide to Newark, 2nd ed., 1911.

NEWCASTLE-ON-TYNE. Bates, C. J. (*Archaeologia Æliana*, ix. 120-9).

—— Heslop, R. O., F.S.A. (*ibid.*, xxv. 91-105; *Journal of British Archaeol. Assoc.*, new ser., xii. 137-8, 214-5).

—— The Castle of Newcastle, a short descriptive guide. Newcastle, 1906 (4th ed.).

NORHAM. Bates, C. J. *Archaeologia Æliana*, v. 52-5).

—— Clark, ii. 322-35.

—— Jerningham, Sir H. E. H. Norham Castle. Edinburgh, 1883.

NORTHAMPTON. Hartshorne, C. H. (*Archaeol. Journal*, iii. 309-32).

NORTHUMBRIAN CASTLES Bates, Cadwallader J. The Border Holds of Northumberland (*Archaeologia Æliana* [Newcastle-on-Tyne], xv. 1-465),

—— Hartshorne, C. H. Feudal and military antiquities of Northumberland and the Scottish Borders (*Memoirs of Brit. Archaeol. Inst.*, Newcastle, vol. 2, 1858).

NORWICH. Hartshorne, A., F.S.A. (*Archaeol. Journal*, xlvi. 260-8).

—— The Walls of Norwich (report of corporation). Norwich, 1910.

NOTTINGHAM. Green, Emanuel, F.S.A. (*Archaeol. Journal*, lviii. 365-97).

OAKHAM. Hartshorne, C. H. (*Archaeol. Journal*, v. 124-42).

—— Thompson, A. Hamilton, F.S.A. (*Rutland Magazine*, v. 80-88).

ODIHAM. Clark, ii. 336-45.

OLD SARUM. Clark, ii. 447-458.

—— Hope, W. H. St John, and Hawley, Lt.-Col. W., in *Proc. Soc. Antiq.*, 2nd ser., xxiii. 190-200 and 501-17.

ORFORD. Hartshorne, C. H. (*Archaeologia*, xxix. 60-9).

—— Redstone, V. B. (*Trans. Suffolk Archaeol. Inst.*, x. 205-30).

OXFORD. Hartshorne, C. H. (*Archaeol. Journal*), viii. 354-65).

—— Hope, W. H. St John (*ibid.*, lxvii. 363-6).

—— Lynam, Charles. The Crypts of the Churches of St Peter in the East, and of St George within the Castle, Oxford (*ibid.*, lxviii. 203-17).

PEAK CASTLE. Hartshorne, C. H. (*Archaeol. Journ.*, v. 207-16).

—— Hope, W. H. St John (*Derbyshire Archaeol. Soc.*, xi. 120-6).

—— Kirke, Henry (*Derbyshire Archaeol. and Nat. Hist. Soc.*, xxviii. 134-46).

PEMBROKE. Clark (*Archaeologia Cambrensis*, 3rd series, v. 1-13, etc.; vi. 1-11, etc.; vii. 185-204).

—— Cobb, J. R. (*ibid.*, 4th series, xiv. 196-220, 264-73).

PEVENSEY. Clark, ii. 359-67.

—— Salzmann, L. F. (*Sussex Archaeol. Collections*, xlix. 1-30, etc.).

PICKERING. Clark, ii. 368-75.

PONTEFRACT. Clark, ii. 375-88.

—— Hartshorne, C. H., *Journal British Archaeol. Assoc.*, xx. 136-55).

PORCHESTER. Clark, ii. 388-400.

PRUDHOE. Bates, *Border Holds*.

RABY. Scott, O. S., Raby, its Castle and its Lords. Barnard Castle, 1908.

RAGLAN. Beattie, W. (*Jour. Archaeol. Assoc.*, ix. 215-30).

—— Bradney, J. A. (*Bristol and Glouc. Archaeol. Soc.*, xx. 76-87).

RICHMOND. Clark (*Yorkshire Archæol. Journal*, ix. 33-54).

—— Curwen, J. F., *Cumberland and Westmorland Antiq. and Archaeol. Soc.*, vi. 326-32).

—— *Yorks Archæol. Journal*, xx. 132-3.

RISING. Beloe, E. M., F.S.A. (*Norfolk Archaeology*, xii. 164-89).

—— Clark, i. 364-77.

ROCHESTER. Beattie, W. (*Journal Archaeol. Assoc.*, ix. 215-30).

—— Clark, ii. 405-23.

ROCHESTER. Hartshorne, C. H. (*Archaeol. Journal*, xx. 205-23).

—— Payne, G. (*Archaeologia Cantiana*, xxvii. 177-92).

ROCKINGHAM. Bigge, H. J. (*Assoc. Archit. Soc. Reports*, xi. 109-18).

—— Clark, ii. 423-46.

—— Hartshorne, C. H. (*Archaeol. Journal*, i. 356-78) ; and privately printed, Oxford, 1852.

—— Wise, C. Rockingham Castle and the Watsons. London, 1891.

SANDAL. Walker, J. W., F.S.A. (*Yorks Archæol. Journal*, xiii. 154-88).

SCARBOROUGH. Clark, ii. 458-67.

—— Stevenson, W. H. (*East Riding Antiq. Soc.*, xiv. 13-17).

SKENFRITH. Bagnall-Oakeley, E. (*Bristol and Glouc. Archaeol. Soc.*, xx. 93-6).

—— Clark, ii. 467-72.

SOUTHAMPTON (town walls). Clark, ii. 472-81.

—— Hope, W. H. St John (*Proc. Soc. Antiq.*, 2nd series, xvii. 221-4).

STOKESAY. De la Touche, G. (*Journal British Archaeol. Assoc.*, xxiv. 238-40).

—— J. G. D. (*Archaeologia Cambrensis*, xvi. 299-304).

SUFFOLK CASTLES. Redstone, V. B. Suffolk Castles (*Suffolk Archaeol. Inst.*, xi. 301-19).

SUSSEX CASTLES. Blaauw, W. H. Royal licences to fortify towns and houses in Sussex (*Sussex Archaeol. Collections*, xiii. 104-17).

SWANSEA. Capper, C. (*Archaeologia Cambrensis*, 5th series, iii. 302-7).

TAMWORTH. Clark, ii. 481-8.

TATTERSHALL. Sympson, E. Mansel (*Memorials of Old Lincolnshire*, 1911, pp. 179-97).

TICKHILL. Clark, ii. 494-9.

TRETOWER. Clark, ii. 499-503.

TUTBURY. Clark, ii. 505-8.

WARK. Bates, *Border Holds*.

WARKWORTH. Bates, *Border Holds*.

WELLS (bishop's palace). Davis, C. E. (*Journal British Archaeol. Assoc.*, xiii. 177-86).

WINGFIELD. Cox, J. C. (*Derbyshire Archaeol. Soc.*, viii. 65-78).

—— Edmunds, W. H. Guide to Wingfield Manor.

YORK. Clark, ii. 534-48 (The Defences of York).

—— Cooper, T. P. York, The Story of its Walls and Castles. London, 1904.

—— —— The Castle of York. London, 1912.

YORKSHIRE CASTLES. Thompson, A. Hamilton. The Castles of Yorkshire (*Memorials of Old Yorkshire*, 1909, pp. 236-64).

MILITARY ARCHITECTURE IN ENGLAND DURING THE MIDDLE AGES

————✳————

CHAPTER I

EARLY EARTHWORKS AND ROMAN STATIONS

THE history of military fortification in England begins with those strongholds which, at vast expense of labour, the early inhabitants of Britain hewed out of the soil, surrounding defensible positions with ramparts of earth, divided by deep fosses. The approximate date of these earthworks can be determined only by excavation, and a vast amount of work remains to be done in this direction. The number, however, of those which can be proved to be earlier than the Roman occupation is very large ; and, of this number, a considerable portion, including some of the most stupendous examples of fortified hill-camps, may have been the work of neolithic man some two thousand years before the Christian era. Relative dates in this connection concern us less than principles of fortification. The hill-camps of pre-Roman Britain may be divided roughly into two classes. In the first place, there are those which occupy the summit of a promontory of high land, which slopes so steeply on all sides but one that artificial defence is necessary on that side alone. The second class is that of the so-called "contour forts," in which the summit of a hill is utilised for the camp, and encircled by trenches following the contour of the ground.

In each case the defences provided by the inhabitants consist of earthen banks, the materials of which have been dug from the fosses or ditches which surround their outer face. An earthen bank and fosse, thrown across the neck of land between

the promontory and the plateau beyond, convert the extremity
of the promontory into a fortified enclosure. Well-known
examples of such fortresses are the three camps, one on the
east and two on the west side of the river, which guarded the
valley of the Avon at Clifton. The labour necessary for the
construction of these was naturally far less than that which
went to the making of the great contour fortresses, of which so
many splendid examples remain in Somerset, Wiltshire, Dorset,
and in the chalk districts generally. In these cases, the whole
area, or at any rate the greater part of it, stood in need of
entrenchment. There are points at which the slope is so precipitous that the bank and ditch were dispensed with, or, as in
part of Cissbury camp near Worthing, only a single bank or
ditch was necessary.[1] Also, the steeper the ground, the less
was the labour required in constructing the entrenchments.

Maiden Castle

But these positions often took the form of enclosures surrounded by double or triple lines of defence, often of stupendous size. For the greater part of its extent, the *vallum* or
bank of the oval camp of Cissbury is double, and along the
outer edge of the encircling fosse is a formidable counterscarp
or parapet. Poundbury, which lies on the high ground west
of Dorchester, has a single bank and ditch on its east and
south sides. On the west side the bank is doubled; but the
north side, where the hill falls almost perpendicularly to the
Frome, was left without artificial defence. The superb fortress
of Maiden Castle (2), which crowns an isolated hill, 432 feet high,
south of Dorchester, shows a bewildering complication of plan.

[1] Plan in Allcroft, *Earthwork of England*, 1908, p. 647. The same
feature is well seen in the fine camp of Bury Ditches (6) in Shropshire, between Clun and Bishops Castle.

The oval central space is ringed by a number of banks and ditches, which varies from three on the north side to as many as eight about the western entrance.

These early camps form merely the preface to our subject, and attention need be called only to some general features. Their character, like that of the medieval town or castle, was strictly defensive. They were the strongholds of races whose weapons were of a very primitive description, and could carry to no great range. What their inhabitants needed was an impregnable fortress, within which they and their herds could be well sheltered from attack. They belong to a day before siege operations were possible. To carry them, a determined onset and a hand-to-hand fight were necessary. Their strength

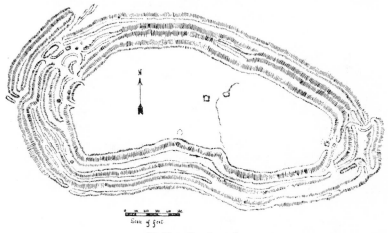

Maiden Castle ; plan

therefore depended on the complexity of their defences. No enemy could hope to scale the flanking banks of Maiden Castle, one by one. The entrances to the camp, at its eastern and western ends (3), were so elaborately concealed by the over-lapping ramparts, that even on a ground-plan they are far from obvious ; and it was almost inevitable that an attacking force, without a guide acquainted with the ground, would be decoyed into a *cul-de-sac* and overwhelmed by the missiles of the defenders on the ramparts.

The steepness of the bank itself constituted a formidable means of defence. At Maiden Castle the great northern banks rise to a height of 60 feet or more. The top of the outer bank of Old Sarum (4) is 106 feet above the level of the ditch

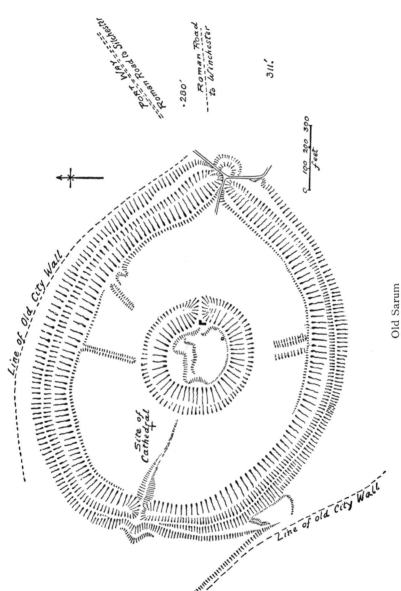

PORT WAY Roman Road to Silchester

280'

Roman Road to Winchester

311'

0 100 200 300 feet

Line of Old City Wall

Site of Cathedral

Line of old City Wall

Old Sarum

(From Mr Hadrian Allcroft's *Earthwork of England* by kind permission of Messrs Macmillan & Co.)

below.[1] In many cases, and probably in all, the inner bank was crowned by a stockade, consisting of a series of upright stakes, between and round which was twined an impenetrable hedge of thorns. The plateau or berm which was sometimes left behind the parapet of the bank, where there was more than a single bank and ditch, was a valuable asset to the defenders of prehistoric strongholds, forming an advance post from which they were able to wield their missiles freely; while sometimes the summit of one or more of the outer banks was made for the same purpose into a broad platform, which allowed greater freedom of movement. The parapet or counterscarp of the outer ditch was probably defended by a stockade, and it is known that in some cases sharpened stakes or stones were fixed firmly in the bottom of the ditches.

The impregnable character of the *enceinte* was thus ensured. But further skill was necessary to defend the entrances of the camp. Of these there was usually more than one, and these were necessarily formed by cuttings through the banks. As in the case of Maiden Castle, the path of entry could be converted into a labyrinth by multiplying the banks and ditches. Every inch of this circuitous path is guarded by tall ramparts: there are seven or eight points in its course at which fatal error was possible, and one at any rate where an attacking army could hardly fail to rush securely upon destruction. The eastern entrance is so guarded by transverse banks that the path is almost equally difficult to find. It was seldom, however, that entrances were so elaborately protected. At Old Sarum the western entrance is covered by a semicircular outwork, on the flanks of which are the two inlets to the passage through the outer *vallum*. On the east side the entrance is through a narrow passage which runs for some distance between the parapet of the outer ditch and an outwork, and is at right angles to the actual passage through the bank. The most common method of defending the entrance was to make a diagonal path, usually from right to left, through the banks. Each bank would thus overlap the next: the summits above the path would be broadened out into platforms, capable of occupation by bodies of defenders; and the right flank of the enemy, unprotected by shields, would be exposed to their missiles. The entrance, however, might be substantially protected by giving an inward curve to the inner bank on each side of the path; and this is a plan

---

[1] The defences of Old Sarum are now in process of excavation, and the plan of the medieval castle, in the centre of the early camp, has been recovered. See *Proceedings Soc. Antiquaries*, 2nd series, vol. xxiii., pp. 190-200 and 501-18.

very frequently employed.[1]   Where outworks were specially constructed, their form differs considerably : we have seen them employed in two ways at Old Sarum—as a kind of horn-work thrown out in front of a passage, and as a spur projecting at right angles in front of an entrance.   In both cases an absolutely straight approach is precluded.   Occasionally, where an approximately direct approach was permitted, it is guarded on one side by a spur thrown out at right angles to the bank.   At Blackbury castle, an early earthwork in south Devon, the main entrance has a straight approach guarded on either side by a triangular outwork, which is formed by a most ingenious arrangement of banks

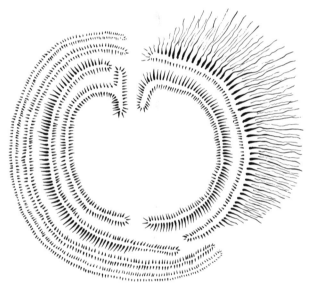

Bury Ditches

and by prolongations of the main ditch (7).   At the actual entrance the main bank is curved outwards, with broad platforms at the top.   The hollow interiors of the outworks might serve as guard-houses, or the attacking force could be driven into them from the gateway of the fort, and penned in a position from which escape was impossible.   Sometimes hollows were made in the bank or in a projecting outwork near the gateway to serve as guard-houses.   On either side of the main entrance, the bank

[1] It is well seen at Bury ditches (6), where the diagonal entrance is also a feature of the south-west side of the camp, and on the west side of Caer Caradoc, between Clun and Knighton.

was often slightly raised. At least one instance is known in which the main gate was concealed by making a break in another part of the rampart, and raising the bank on either side. The enemy, making for this point, would miss the real entrance, and run the risk of losing his life in a *cul-de-sac* purposely constructed within the rampart.

In these fortresses, the defences of which were due to instinctive skill in the face of constant danger, it is impossible not to

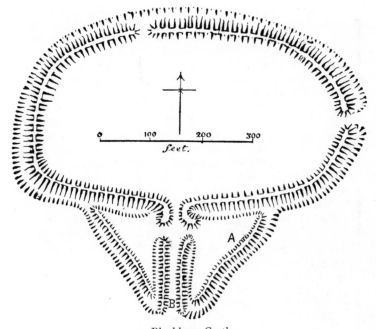

Blackbury Castle

(From Mr Hadrian Allcroft's *Earthwork of England*) by kind permission of Messrs Macmillan & Co.)

recognise how many of the most scientific features of medieval fortification were anticipated. The concentric plan of Caerphilly castle (270), with its easy provisions of egress, and its difficulty of access; the spurs which guard the approaches to Beaumaris (277) and Conway castles; the barbicans which form so prominent a defence of Alnwick castle (243), and the gateways of York have prototypes, of which their engineers were probably unconscious, in the huge earthworks of prehistoric Britain. Through a long interval, in which military art pursued a very gradual evolution, the wheel came full circle. The devices of the earthwork builders were translated into stone with far greater economy of labour.

Although the most conspicuous examples of early earthwork are found in hill fortresses, camps were not confined to hilly sites, nor were their defences always composed of earthwork. There are districts where the hard nature of the soil forbade the construction of earthen banks and fosses; and consequently there are many camps which are surrounded by walls of rough uncemented stone, originally kept in place by facings and bondings of larger and smoother stones.[1] These camps are usually not large. They occur very commonly in the north of England: a good example is that known as the Castles, in the valley of the Bedburn, seven or eight miles west of Bishop Auckland. The enclosure, situated on a boggy slope, is surrounded by shapeless masses of *débris*, the ruins of the dry-built ring wall, which has lost its facing and so has fallen to pieces. Stone was also used in the ramparts of some of the camps on the rocky hills of Somerset, as in the camps on either side of the Avon at Clifton. The great fortress of Worlebury, above Weston-super-Mare, was surrounded by an immense wall of uncemented stone, brought to great thickness by building several walls, each with its own set of facing stones, up against each other. On its eastern front, separated from the main rampart by a deep ditch, cut in the solid rock, was another wall of stone; and this again was protected by a series of outer earthworks (9). Dolebury, at the western extremity of the Mendips, is surrounded by a double wall of loose limestone.[2] In these cases, as in the Welsh strongholds of Penmaenmawr and Tre'r Ceiri, geological conditions made the earthen bank an impossibility, and the stone of the neighbourhood took its place.

It has often been argued that these prehistoric fortresses were merely places of refuge, to which, in time of war, the dwellers in the levels below betook themselves and their flocks. But it is much more probable that they were the permanent habitations of communities, not merely camps, but fixed settlements, chosen for habitation on account of their strong position, and gradually fortified by labour which may have been the work, in the more elaborate examples, of many generations. The need of permanent protection for themselves and their flocks and herds seems to have been felt by the early inhabitants of Britain to such an extent that their regular settlements naturally took the

---

[1] The effect of similar conditions on the construction of early Norman castles will be noticed in a later chapter.

[2] Plan in Allcroft, *op. cit.*, p. 686; the camp is described fully pp. 682-97.

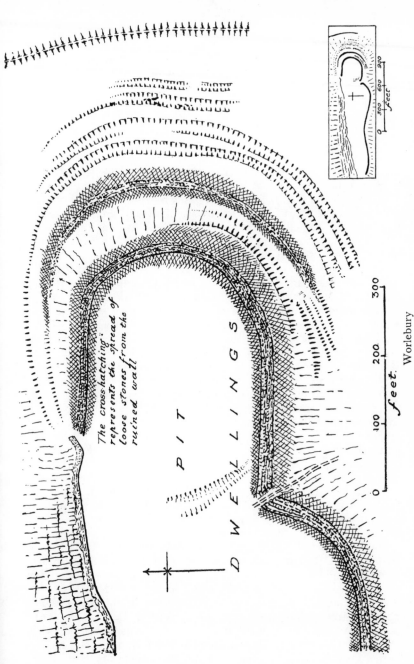

The crosshatching represents the spread of loose stones from the ruined wall

PIT

DWELLINGS

Feet.

0   100   200   300

Worlebury

(From Mr Hadrian Allcroft's *Earthwork of England*, by kind permission of Messrs Macmillan & Co.)

0   300   600   900

Feet

2

semblance of fortified camps.   This is very evident in the case
of those camps which are found in positions where the natural
advantages are very small—positions which might be chosen
by people in search of an abode, but would hardly be chosen
merely as a refuge.   Camps in these positions are never so
imposing as those which crown hill-tops : the labour of exca-
vating the ditches and heaping up the banks was not aided by
the natural slope of a hill, and the earthworks, being slighter
and nearer the more recent haunts of men, are more liable to
destruction.   But the defensive nature of such settlements is
unmistakable.

The Roman invaders brought to England new methods of
military construction and the tradition of an architecture of
dressed and cemented stone.   Their whole system of warfare
was far in advance of that pursued by the British tribes.   They
had developed the art of siege to a high pitch.   Their operations
in open field were orderly and scientific.   Their walled strongholds were constructed with a view which took into account, not
only the mere strength of the ramparts, but also the capacity
of the defenders to man them.   Men, not fortresses, were the
main asset of Roman warfare ; and consequently their earthwork was far less imposing than that of the Britons of the prehistoric age.   Their camps and permanent stations were usually
surrounded by a single fosse of no great depth : the rare cases
in which traces remain of more than a single fosse are camps
upon the exposed northern frontier of Roman Britain, where
the onrush of the barbarian enemy was stayed by a series of
trenches, either covered with brushwood or filled with sharp
stones or stakes.   Camps were hastily constructed of earthwork ;
bank, ditch, and parapet playing their part.   But where a
camp became a permanent station a stone wall took the place of
the earthen bank.   The most important relic of the Roman
occupation in Britain, the great frontier wall from the Tyne to
the Solway, was preceded by a *vallum* of turf, a temporary
defence which was superseded by permanent masonry.

No system of connected operations can be traced between
prehistoric forts.   Each of these was probably an isolated
stronghold.   Roman stations, on the other hand, were military
posts manned by detachments of one army, and connected by
strategic roads.   This is seen very clearly in the case of the
great wall already mentioned.   The wall can be traced for about
73 miles, from Wallsend (Segedunum) on the Tyne to Bowness
on the Solway.   It is built in the usual Roman method, with
a core of cemented rubble between ashlar facings.   Its breadth
varies between 7 and 9½ feet : the height appears to have been

originally from 16 to 18 feet.[1]   Its northern face is defended
by a ditch, marked *a* in the section below ; but, as it follows the
highest ground in its course, and runs for some distance along
the edge of basaltic cliffs which dip northward, the ditch at
these points becomes unnecessary and is dispensed with.   There
were twenty-three stations in its length, each garrisoned by
a cohort of infantry or squadron of cavalry, chosen from the
Roman auxiliary troops of Gauls, Spaniards, Moors, &c.[2]   These
were connected by a paved military road (*c*) along the south side of
the wall.   At distances of a Roman mile from one another were
placed rectangular forts, now known as mile-castles, built against
the wall upon its south side ; and the interval between each of
these was strengthened further by turrets, apparently two in
number, which also projected southward, but encroached slightly
upon the thickness of the wall.   The south side of the military
road was defended by an earthen *vallum*, marked *d*,[3] the course of
which is not directly parallel to the wall, but is in places as much
as half a mile distant, keeping to lower ground where the wall

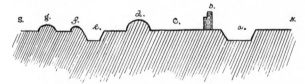

Section of Roman Wall and *Vallum*.

prefers the summit of the basalt ridge.   This bank has a ditch (*e*)
on its southern side, divided from it by a level space or berm : the
ditch has a southern parapet (*f*), and another bank beyond (*g*).
In certain places the ditch has also a northern parapet ; but
the general arrangement of the earthen ramparts is as described.
Of the controversy as to the relative date of the wall and its
flanking earthworks nothing need be said here.   Its military
purpose is abundantly clear.   It provided not only a strong
means of defence against the attacks of the northern tribes,
but a base of operations for offensive warfare.   Each of the
stations and mile-castles has a northern gateway in addition
to its other entrances ; and two of the Roman roads which met
the wall at intervals from the south passed through it on their
way to the Scottish border.

[1] See Bruce, *Hand-Book to the Roman Wall*, 5th ed., 1907 (ed. R. Blair),
pp. 19-21.
[2] The list from the *Notitia Dignitatum* is given, *ibid.*, pp. 11, 12.
[3] The bank is, strictly speaking, the *agger*, the *vallum* being the
rampart on the top of the bank.

The object of the great system of Roman roads was purely military.[1]   Along these broad paved "streets" the troops from the various stations could be mobilised with great quickness. They kept as a rule to high ground, choosing a convenient ridge, like that which runs from end to end of Lincolnshire, and preserving as straight a line as possible.   The most important stations were placed at the crossing of rivers or at the junction of roads.   In the early days of the Roman occupation, the operations of the army were directed entirely against the native tribes.   No system of coast defence was adopted.   The necessity for this came later when Britain, under Roman dominion, was attacked by bodies of Saxon pirates.   A chain of fortresses was then constructed along what was known as the Saxon shore, from Branodunum (Brancaster) in north Norfolk to Portus Adurni in Sussex or Hampshire.   The remains of the walls of Gariannonum (Burgh Castle in Suffolk), Rutupiae (Richborough in Kent), Anderida (Pevensey in Sussex), and Portus Magnus (Porchester in Hampshire), are, next to the great wall, perhaps the most interesting relics of the Roman epoch which we possess.   The forts of the Saxon shore were placed, for the most part, at the mouths of estuaries, for which the foreign pirates would naturally make.

In several cases a Roman station was founded on the site of a British settlement.   It was, however, more compact in plan, and occupied only a portion of the site.   The earthworks defending the west side of the settlement which preceded Camulodunum (Colchester) are two to three miles beyond the Roman wall of the city, which occupied merely the north-east angle of a very large and straggling enclosure.   The original Roman station at Lincoln may be taken as a typical example of a walled town of this epoch.[2]   It was a rectangular enclosure, with its longer axis from east to west, occupying the south-west angle of the high ridge above the valley of the Witham.   In each of the four walls was a gateway.   The inner arch and the postern, with part of the side walls, of the northern gateway still remain, and of the southern gateway there are still substantial fragments ; the line of the street which led from one to the other is still fairly, though not accurately, preserved.   The positions of the east and west gateways are known : the line of the street from the east gate to the centre of the city was deflected in the

---

[1] The large villas of Romano-British landowners, as at Bignor (Sussex), Chedworth (Gloucestershire), Horkstow (Lincolnshire), were within easy reach of the military roads, but were not directly upon them.

[2] The topography of Roman Lincoln is described by Dr E. M. Sympson, *Lincoln* (Ancient Cities), 1906, chapter I.

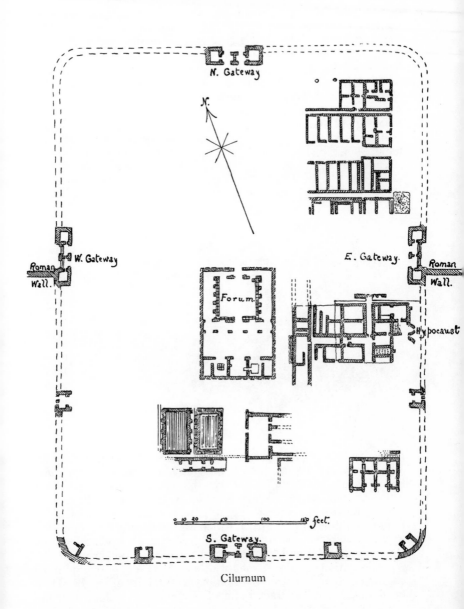

Cilurnum

middle ages, but its continuation to the west gate is represented by the course of a street, much widened in modern times. Close to the meeting of the four streets was the market-place or *forum*. This, in the early days of Roman Lincoln, was the *praetorium*, or military headquarters of the camp. But the legion quartered at Lincoln was removed to York, as it seems, in the time of Vespasian, and the city settled down to a civil and commercial existence. Round the *forum* were clustered the chief public buildings of the city, and the foundations of a large colonnaded building are still to be seen below the present ground level. At Gloucester, Chichester, and Chester, the course of the four main streets has been little, if at all, disturbed, and their present

Borcovicus

meeting-place nearly represents the centre of the Roman city. The arrangements of the *forum* of a Romano-British town have been made out very clearly by the excavations at Calleva Atrebatum (Silchester) in Hampshire.[1] It was a closed rectangle, entered by a gateway and surrounded by public buildings, in front of which were colonnades; one side at Silchester was occupied by a great basilica, which served the purposes of a hall of justice and mercantile exchange.

The stations on the Roman wall were of a more purely military character than the towns which have been mentioned. They have the general characteristic of a rectangular plan, with the angles rounded off, and with a gateway, flanked by guard-houses,

[1] See *Archæologia*, vol. liii., pp. 539-73.

in each of the four sides.   In the two largest stations, however,
Amboglanna (Birdoswald) and Cilurnum (Chesters), there were,
in addition to the main gateways, two smaller gateways in the
east and west walls respectively.[1]   The walls of the stations are
generally 5 feet thick, and are built, like the wall itself, of a core
of cemented rubble, with facings of dressed stone.   The main
gateways have a double passage, divided by a longitudinal wall,
which is pierced by a narrow passage in the centre.   Their inner
and outer openings were spanned by arches, and closed by gates
which were hung on iron pivots fixed in the jamb of each opening next the wall.   At Borcovicus (Housesteads) there was no
dividing wall through the passage between the outer and inner
openings of the gateway ; but each of these openings is composed of two arches, divided by a square pier (15).[2]   Each
gateway had a stone sill, raised above the level of the stone pave-
ment.   The interior passage was flanked by rectangular guard-
houses.   The gateways of Borcovicus show interesting signs
of reconstruction, which point to the fact that, not long after
its construction, the station was seized by an enemy.   At a
subsequent time, its
Roman occupants re-
duced the width of the
gateways by walling
up one half of the
double openings.

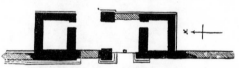

Borcovicus ; West Gateway

This was done ap-
parently at different times, the east gateway bearing signs of
being treated in this way at an earlier period than the others.
The west gateway was walled up with great ingenuity.   Of its
outer entrances, the northern, and of its inner entrances, the
southern, were blocked ; so that a foe, choosing this face of the
station for attack, had to press his way through an elbow-
shaped, instead of a straight passage.
    The wall of a Roman station, between the gateways, was
often flanked by a series of towers, each projecting from the wall
in the form of a semicircle or rather more than a semicircle.
This was the case in some of the large Gallo-Roman cities,
like Autun.[3]   While the rounded form of these towers made

----

[1] See below as to the blocking of the main gateways at Cilurnum after
the building of the great wall.   The small single gateways at Cilurnum are
on the south side of the wall.   At Amboglanna both gateways were south of
the wall.

[2] Borcovicus is described by Bruce, *u.s.*, pp. 140-60.

[3] Plan in Besnier, *Autun Pittoresque*, 1888.   The north-west and north-
east gateways of the Roman city remain, but the centre of the city was
shifted in the middle ages.

them difficult to undermine or batter down, their summits served
as standing-ground for the large *ballistae* or catapults, from which
javelins or stones could be hurled upon the attacking force. Their
projection at regular intervals made it possible for the defenders
to command the whole line of wall between each pair of towers ;
so that the besiegers' attack would necessarily be concentrated
upon the towers themselves. At Pevensey (16), where the
enclosure of the station is almost oval, and not, as usual,
rectangular, in shape, there are remains of twelve solid round
towers, including those which flank the south-western gateway. At Burgh Castle there are four towers in the east
wall, two of which are angle-towers.[1] Owing to the scarcity
of good building stone in the district, the walls at Burgh Castle
are unfaced, and are built of flint with bonding courses of tiles ;

Pevensey

only the upper portions of the towers were bonded into the
walls. A bed of concrete, with a platform of oak planks above,
formed the foundation of the towers.[2] The angles of the wall
of Roman York were strengthened by large polygonal towers.
A large portion of one of these, a magnificent example of
Roman masonry, remains ; it formed the north-western angle
of the city, and was hollow, with an internal as well as an
external projection (17). No outward projections appear to occur

[1] Plan in Allcroft, *u.s.*, p. 322. As Burgh Castle had the sea on its west
side, it possibly had no west wall. Another tower, on the east side of the
north gateway, has fallen away from the wall.
[2] At Pevensey the foundation of the wall is of chalk and flint, covered in
one part by an upper layer of concrete, composed of flints bedded in mortar.
Below the foundation is a layer of puddled clay, in which oak stakes were
fixed vertically at intervals. See L. F. Salzmann, F.S.A., *Excavations at
Pevensey*, 1906-7, in *Sussex Archæol. Collections*, vol. li.

upon the Roman wall or in the walls of its stations. The
"mile-castles," as already noted, are built against the inner
side of the wall. At Cilurnum (13) and Borcovicus there are
foundations of square towers against and inside the containing
walls, while the angles of the stations are simply rounded off.
The western part of the north wall of Borcovicus has also been
doubled in thickness, apparently to give a safe foundation for a
large catapult planted on the top of the wall. The thickening
was accomplished, at a date later than the original building,
by constructing an inner wall, and filling up the space between

York ; Multangular Tower

this and the outer rampart with clay. At Cilurnum, which
appears to have been in existence before the great frontier wall
was made, the original east and west gateways were left on the
north side of the wall, which intersects the station. As they were
thus insufficiently protected, they were filled up solid with masses
of rubble, and were probably used as platforms for catapults,[1]
smaller gateways being made on the south side of the wall.

[1] Cilurnum is described by Bruce, *u.s.*, pp. 86-119, with plan. See also
the description and plan in *An Account of the Roman Antiquities Preserved
in the Museum at Chesters*, 1903, pp. 87-120.

3

In the interior of the station, as at Lincoln, York, and
Borcovicus, the main street, or *via principalis*, led directly from
the north to the south gate.[1]   The centre of the station, west of
of the *via principalis*, was occupied by the *praetorium*, the headquarters of the commander of the legion, answering to the space
where, in a temporary camp, the tents of the general and his
staff were pitched.   As we have seen, the place of the *praetorium*
was taken in commercial towns by the *forum*.   The *praetorium*
at Borcovicus consisted of two rectangular courts, open to the
sky in the centre.   The outer court, with its main entrance facing

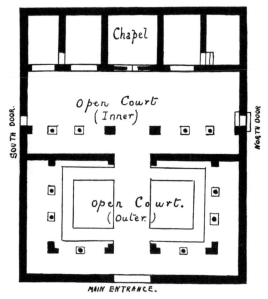

Borcovicus ; Praetorium

the eastern street or *via praetoria*, was surrounded on three sides by
a colonnade.   A doorway, immediately opposite the main entrance,
opened into the eastern colonnade of the inner court.   This had
no northern or southern colonnades, but had doorways to north
and south : its western side was occupied by a line of five
rectangular chambers, the central one of which was the chapel
where the standards, with the other sacred treasures belonging to
the cohort,[2] were kept.   The *praetorium* faced the eastern street of

---

[1] This was not invariable. At Cilurnum the main street was from east to
west, and this was also the case at Corstopitum (Corbridge-on-Tyne).

[2] In this case, the first cohort of the Tungri.

the station, which led to the east gate or *porta praetoria*. The gate at the end of the western street was called *porta decumana*.[1] The remaining buildings of the station consisted of straight blocks, intersected by lanes: the majority of these buildings would be used as barracks. It should be noted that, in the planning of a Roman station or walled town, the *praetorium* or *forum* was taken as the central point: the *via principalis*, in order to run clear from gate to gate, was thus on one side of an axis of the rectangle, and the north and south gates [2] were not in the centre of their respective walls.

It is clear that, as time went on and the power of Rome in Britain grew weaker, the defensive character of the great wall and that of the stations which it connected were emphasised at the expense of their character as bases of active warfare. But it must be repeated that Roman stations in Britain were not planned to form impregnable shelters for communities mainly pastoral. They were centres for bodies of fighting men, linked to each other by a splendid system of roads. The Roman station at Dorchester, the lines of which are so well preserved to-day, was founded, not within the ramparts of Maiden Castle or Poundbury, but on the lower slopes near the passage of the Frome. The single rampart and single ditch of a Roman town were almost invariable. Free egress as well as entrance, provisions for attack as well as defence, were necessary ; and, with these objects in view, immense earthen defences, such as those of Maiden Castle, would be cumbersome. Bodies of Roman troops, as at Lincoln or Colchester, occasionally occupied part of the *enceinte* of a British settlement ; but it is very rarely that, as in the case of Old Sarum, we find a British hill fort which also probably served as a Roman station. In this instance, the occupation of the fort was due, doubtless, to its neighbourhood to the military road : the road would not have been brought out of its way to include the fort in its course. Roman stations, although they differed in size, were small and compact, when contrasted with the large and straggling areas occupied by the British settlers. Suburbs naturally grew up outside their walls, and sometimes, although not very often, the walled enclosure was extended to include a growing outer district. This is supposed by many antiquaries to have happened at Lincoln, where the original Roman station occupied the summit of the hill

---

[1] The tenth cohort of the legion had its quarters here : hence the name.

[2] Or the east and west gateways, as already noted, at Cilurnum. The *forum* occupied the centre of Cilurnum, the *praetorium* forming a block of buildings east of the centre. The first wing or squadron of the Astures was stationed at Cilurnum.

north of the great bend of the Witham, which here turns from its northerly course due eastward. After the city of Lincoln had settled down to civil life, practically the whole slope of the hill south of the first *enceinte* was included within the city and encircled by a wall. Part of the east wall of this later enclosure is still visible: the Stonebow, the medieval south gate of the city, about a hundred yards from the river and the bridge, appears to be on the site of the later south gateway of Roman Lincoln.[1]

[1] Prof. Haverfield holds the view that this southern extension is post-Roman. See *Archæol. Journal*, lxvi. 350.

CHAPTER II

THE SAXON AND DANISH PERIOD

THE Saxon invasions were a rude disturbance to the progress of English civilisation. The Romanised Britons lay more and more at the mercy of the invaders, as the soldiery were called away to take part in the last struggles of the western Empire in Italy. Barbarians from the country north of the wall, Saxon and Jutish pirates from across the sea, saw in the monuments of the Roman occupation fair ground for pillage. It is difficult to estimate the destruction caused by the invaders. But, apart from the havoc wrought by the Teutonic immigrants and the northern tribes, it is certain that the walled city of Roman times did not commend itself as a habitation to the new settlers. The fact that their settlements flank Roman roads, like Ermine street or the Fosseway, at distances of a mile or so from the main thoroughfare, proves little in itself; for the villas of the Roman period, which probably included, like the *latifundia* of Italy, a considerable population of labourers on each estate, lay at some distance from the main roads. The frequent villages—hams, tuns, and worths—were, however, a new feature ; and the life of each village, for which a clearing was made in the wooded country-side, was pastoral, not military. This fact is of importance with regard to the scanty traces of defensive fortifications constructed during the Saxon occupation. Here and there natural opportunities prompted the Saxon invaders to found settlements on sites of Roman cities. The geographical position of London or Exeter, at the head of a broad estuary, made such places natural centres of traffic, of high importance to trade routes. On the other hand, while some of the larger provincial capitals preserved their life in part, other *urbes* and the smaller *oppida*, or walled towns, were left desolate. Pons Aelii, near the east end of the Roman wall, was abandoned until in the tenth century a small monastery was founded on the site, and the cluster of houses which gathered round it received the name of Muncanceaster (Monkchester). The place, however, did not recover its importance or become a permanent settlement until the Conqueror founded there his New Castle on the Tyne, which became the nucleus of the city of the middle ages and modern times. The military stations of the Saxon shore were ruined and abandoned. We know of the sack of Anderida in 492 A.D.: the walls of the station were left standing, but the later settlement of Pevensey grew up in the open country outside the walls. Richborough, Othona at the mouth of the Blackwater, Burgh Castle, sheltered no new settlements: the new villages or towns, Sandwich, Bradwell, Burgh, were all at a distance from the Roman walls or outside their area. Othona (Ythanceaster) was deserted when Cedd made it a missionary centre in the seventh century; and the little church, which exists to-day and may have been Cedd's own church, was built across the site of the east gate of the station. In Leicester, which became an important Danish centre, the topography of the Roman station was much disturbed, and the church of St Nicholas, the nave of which is probably a little earlier than the Norman conquest, was built within the walls directly in front of the blocked west gate of the city. Towns like Chester, Gloucester, or Chichester, which have preserved the line of their Roman streets with little alteration, are rare; and the continuity of plan does not necessarily prove that there was a similar continuity in the life of the places. On the contrary, the present lay-out of either town shows four streets meeting at an open space or Carfax in the centre of the city: no trace remains above ground of the closed *forum*, which at Silchester and Corstopitum formed the centre of the plan and directed the course of the streets. Silchester, laid waste by Saxon invaders, has shared the fate of Anderida, Othona, and many other once prosperous Romano-British towns.

In French history there was no such interruption as the Saxon invasion caused in our own. The consequence is that the chief provincial capitals of to-day, the centres of local government and religion, are and always have been cities of Roman origin, which, although their Latin name has not always been kept, preserve the names of the Gallic tribes amid which they were founded. Reims, Paris, Amiens, Beauvais, Bourges, Le Mans, Tours, Rouen, Sens, Troyes, Chartres, cities which have taken a most prominent place in French history, and contain the most noble monuments of French religious architecture, have an unbroken history from Roman times and even earlier. The cathedrals of Christianised Gaul rose in the centre of the cities: outside the walls, as time went on, rose abbeys like those of Saint-Ouen at Rouen, Saint-Taurin at Evreux, La Couture and Le Pré at Le Mans. The fortresses of

the eleventh and twelfth centuries, like the older castle of
Rouen, were founded in a corner of the city, possibly on the site
of the Roman *arx* or citadel, of which we have substantial remains in the abandoned Roman station of Jublains (Naeodunum
Diablintum). In time the city grew, extending into suburbs far
outside the original walls : a suburb sprang up round the
neighbouring monastery. The circuit of the walls was extended
beyond their old limit. The eastern Roman wall might be
broken down, as at Le Mans, where the cathedral was in a
corner of the city, to make way for the thirteenth-century quire
of the principal church :[1] the defences of the city were here
transferred to a new outer ring of wall, the line of which can
be seen on the bank of the Sarthe. Within the present extent
of such cities the plan of the Roman station can frequently be
traced : whatever the vicissitudes of the place may have been,
no year has passed in which the chatter of the Vieux-Marché
has been silent, or the Grande-Rue has been untrodden daily by
busy footsteps. But in English towns of corresponding importance the case is different. If the cities were preserved from
pillage, traces of Christianity and civilisation were obliterated.
If York kept its position as an inhabited town, its population
must have been small and poor : the Anglian sovereigns of
Northumbria dwelt, not in the old Roman capital, but at country
settlements like Goodmanham. The history of York begins
again with the mission of Paulinus and the foundation of the
first Saxon cathedral there. We also hear of Lincoln in connection with Paulinus, who consecrated a church there ; and
this city, like York, was large and important at the time of the
Conquest. But, in both these cases, the Anglian invasion first,
and the Danish invasion later, caused a serious disturbance to
civic and religious life. Although there is evidence that the
Saxon bishops who ruled at Dorchester (Oxon.) in the tenth
and eleventh centuries looked upon Lincoln as the real seat
of their authority, it did not recover its position as an ecclesiastical capital until a Norman bishop raised his cathedral in the
south-eastern corner of the hill city. Even then the cathedral
stood, not with its front to the *via principalis*, as at Le Mans,
nor with its face to the *forum*, as at Coutances, but in an
enclosure of its own, apart from the main life of the city. When
we think of the great ecclesiastical centres of England, there are
some names which recall the Roman occupation ; but of these
Chichester, Exeter, Lincoln, did not become sees of bishops
until the time of the Norman conquest ; Chester, although

---

[1] The same thing happened at Lincoln, where the eastern wall of the city
followed a line now covered by the eastern transept of the cathedral.

regarded as one seat of their authority by the medieval bishops of Lichfield, was never the real capital of their diocese. Bath and Old Sarum were given episcopal rank by Norman prelates. The true Saxon cathedral towns were villages of post-Roman origin—Lichfield, Wells, Sherborne, Durham, Ripon, Elmham, Thetford. The fact is significant; for, upon the continent of Europe, the ecclesiastical importance of a city was the result of its prominent position as the civil metropolis of a district. The choice of these obscure villages for the sees of Saxon prelates is a testimony to the practical abandonment of Roman cities by the invaders.

As a matter of fact, the Saxons trusted little to walls: their strength, after they had settled in the country, lay neither in earthwork, nor in stonework, but in the boundary of wood or marsh that extended round their settlements. Consequently, during the six centuries and a half between the final departure of the Roman legions and the Norman conquest, the history of military construction in England is very obscure. Work in stone, which can be distinguished as Saxon, is practically confined to churches. Such fortifications of this long period as can be identified are entirely in earthwork. In only a few cases we hear of a stone wall of *enceinte* being built, or an old Roman town wall being repaired. Further, it may safely be said that these fortifications, at any rate until the end of the period, whether their builders were Saxons or Danes, were intended to protect, not private individuals, but a community. Of the private citadel or castle we hear nothing until the period immediately before the Conquest, and then it is heard of only as a foreign importation.

The most formidable earthworks of the Saxon period are the great dykes known as Wansdyke and Offa's dyke, with the subsidiary works of the Bokerley dyke and Wat's dyke. Offa's dyke, which ran from the Dee in the north to the Wye in the south, with a ditch along its western side, and the parallel line of Wat's dyke,[1] are generally acknowledged to have formed the boundary line between the Mercian kingdom of Offa (757-96) and the territory of the conquered Britons. The object and date of Wansdyke and the Bokerley dyke is not so clear. The Wansdyke ran from the Bristol Channel near Portishead, across north Somerset and along the downs south and south-west of Bath, passed through Wiltshire, north of Devizes and south of Marlborough, and, leaving Wiltshire east of Savernake park, turned southwards in the direction of Andover. The Bokerley

---

[1] Wat's dyke, of which remains can be traced south of Wrexham and near Oswestry, was to the east of Offa's dyke.

dyke, in its present state, is only some four miles long, and forms the boundary between Wilts and Dorset, on the road from Salisbury to Cranborne. In both cases the ditch is upon the north or north-east side of the bank or dyke, which is clear proof that the defence was provided against attack from that quarter. The Wansdyke is obviously a late Roman or post-Roman work, for it encroaches in places upon the adjacent Roman road. The system on which it is planned resembles that of the Roman wall, in that its course includes a series of forts, presumably of earlier date. The conclusion which seems irresistible is that propounded by the late General Pitt-Rivers, that the Wansdyke was raised by the Roman Britons, to defend their last refuge in the south-west against the invading Saxons. If this is really the case, one can only wonder at the energy of despair which constructed this huge rampart, and at the uselessness of its builders' attempt to ward off an invasion from the inland country alone. Ceawlin's victory at Dyrham in 577 brought Gloucester, Cirencester, and Bath into the hands of the Saxons, and cut off the communication between the Britons of the south-west and those of Wales. Whatever part the Wansdyke, on the hills north of which the battle was fought, may have played during the century before the fight at Dyrham, its history must have closed with Ceawlin's conquest.

The first work of fortification by the Teutonic invaders, of which we have any account, is the royal city of Bebbanburh or Bamburgh in Northumberland, which Ida (547-59), king of Northumbria, called after his wife Bebba. This, says the Anglo-Saxon Chronicle,[1] was first girt by a hedge, and afterwards—probably long after the days of Ida—by a wall. One of the most noble of English castles stands upon the basaltic rock of Bamburgh, and its walls embrace the site of Ida's capital. But the later stronghold must not be confounded with the earlier. The *burh* of Ida, which Penda sought to burn in 651,[2] was not the private castle which William Rufus afterwards besieged. The name of Bebbanburh is significant. *Burh* or *burg* was a term applied by Saxons to fortified places. Cissbury in Sussex, Badbury and Poundbury in Dorset, Battlesbury and Scratchbury in Wilts, Cadbury, Dolebury, and Worlebury in Somerset, are early camps to which Saxons gave the name of *burh*. Searobyrig, the later Salisbury, was the name given by them to the great fortress of Old Sarum. Peterborough and Bury St Edmunds bear names derived from *burh* and its dative *byrig*,

---

[1] *A.-S. Chron.*, anno 547.
[2] Bede, *Hist. Ecc.*, iii. 16.

and were towns enclosed by a rampart.[1] And, although, by a not very satisfactory method of argument, the Saxon *burh* has been taken very generally as the prototype of the castle, the very cases on which this argument chiefly rests show that the *burh* was a fortified town, and not the fortress of an individual lord. It is true that, at any rate until the time of Alfred the Great, the word *burh* implies a fortified house as well as a fortified collection of dwellings; but the *burhs* of which we read in connection with the Danish wars were towns and villages. The term is equivalent to the Roman *oppidum* the French *bourg*, or the German *burg*. The first of the Saxon emperors, Henry the Fowler, made the founding of *burhs* a leading part of his policy:[2] Merseburg, Brandenburg, Würzburg, all bear the familiar suffix. And, had not a later age chosen perversely to call the greatest of our prehistoric camps Maiden Castle, we should have had a Maidenbury of our own to show, far more ancient than the German Magdeburg.[3]

Some uncertainty attaches to the rare remains of fortifications of *burhs* "wrought" by Saxons and Danes. It would seem that they cannot have been very strong. The defences consisted of the usual earthen bank with a stockade on the top and an outer ditch; but one may safely assume that the strength of the defence lay mainly in the actual stockade, and that the bank and ditch never reached formidable proportions. Thelwall, near Warrington, takes its name from the wooden stockade, the wall of thills or upright palisades with which Edward the Elder surrounded the village in 923.[4] There are exceptional cases in which we hear of a stone wall; but in these instances the *burh* was a Roman city or station, and the wall was a Roman wall. This may be fairly assumed with regard to the wall of Edward the Elder's *burh* at Towcester (921). It was certainly the case at Colchester, where the Danish defenders were worsted in the same year by the *fyrd* of Kent and Essex. When Alfred the Great "repaired Lundenburh" in 886,[5] he undoubtedly made

---

[1] It may be noted that not all names in "borough" and "bury" are derived from *burh* and *byrig*. Some are merely derived from *beorh* or *beorg* = a hill (dative *beorge*).

[2] See Oman, *Art of War*, p. 120.

[3] In Germany the word *burg* is also applied to the citadel of a town or to a castle. In England and France more careful discrimination was made between the two types of stronghold.

[4] References to *burhs* wrought by Edward and his sister Æthelflæd will be found in *A.-S. Chron.* under the dates mentioned in the text. There is some variety of opinion with regard to the exact accuracy of these dates.

[5] *A.-S. Chron.*, sub anno.

good the weak places in the stone wall which the Romans had made round their city of London.

The *burh*, the fortified stronghold of a Saxon community, comes into prominence as the result of the Danish invasions of the ninth century. The method of the invaders was in almost every case the same. Seamen before everything else, they sought in their long ships the estuaries of rivers, and proceeded to penetrate inland as far as the stream would take them. From a base of operations, preferably an island in the river, where they could harbour their boats safely, they rode into the surrounding country, burning and pillaging. In 835, allied with the Britons of Cornwall, they came up the Tamar, and fought a battle with Egbert at Hingston down, west of Tavistock, in which they suffered defeat.[1] In 843, they effected their first permanent settlement in France, on the island of Noirmoutier, south of the estuary of the Loire : they invaded the banks of the river, sacking Nantes and killing the bishop, and, after their summer campaign was over, settled down to build houses for winter quarters on their island.[2] Each of the great French rivers was infested during the next few years by bands of northern pirates. Northmen in 845 sailed up the Garonne to Toulouse, and up the Seine to Paris, where destruction was avoided only by buying them off. Towns which lay near the rivers or sea coast were invariably sacked. Sometimes the pirates, growing bolder, left their ships and rode for some distance inland. In 851, starting from Rouen, they pillaged Beauvais. In 855, after burning Angers, they took to the land and sacked Poitiers. In both cases, however, their return journey was successfully cut off by a French army. In 856 the Danes of the Seine made their winter quarters at Jeufosse, on the bend of the river between Vernon and Mantes, and within no great distance of Paris. Within the next few years, they established themselves in strong posts at Oissel, above Rouen, and at Melun, above Paris. The greater part of the last sixteen years of Charles the Bald (*d.* 877) was occupied in defending Paris against their annual forays, repairing the bridges they had destroyed, and so cutting off their return from expeditions up the Marne and Oise. But, although they were constantly checked, they always returned. They abandoned the siege of Paris in 885-6, but only after Charles the Fat had paid them off. The last great invasion of France by the Northmen was in 911, when,

---

[1] *A.-S. Chron.*, sub anno. The true date seems to be 837 or 838.

[2] The chief authority for the early invasions of the Northmen in France is the *Annales Bertinenses*, of which the portion from 836 to 861 is attributed to Prudentius, bishop of Troyes.

by the treaty of Saint-Clair-sur-Epte, Charles the Simple ceded the duchy of Normandy to Rollo.

The actual settlement of the Northmen in England began in 851, eight years after the occupation of Noirmoutier. They wintered in Thanet, and sailed thence up the Stour and Thames, taking Canterbury and London. As in France, their landward excursions from their boats were less successful, and they were seriously beaten by Æthelwulf at Ockley in Surrey. But failure did not hinder them from returning. As in France, the system of buying off their attacks was adopted—a ready inducement to repeated plunder. In 887 they were in the Humber, and dealt a final blow to the decaying power of Northumbria at York. Next year they invaded Mercia up the Trent, and established themselves at Nottingham. The years 870 and 871 were remarkable for their land operations. The defeat of the East Anglian king Edmund in Suffolk laid Mercia and Lindsey open to their ravages, and so established their power in what was to become the Danelaw; while in 871, within reach of the Danish camp on the Thames at Reading, occurred the great series of battles in Berkshire and Wiltshire, in which Alfred's bravery was proved. The details of Alfred's defence of Wessex against the Northmen are well known: the compromise effected at Wedmore in 878 preserved the south of England to Englishmen, but established the Danes north of a line which may roughly be represented by the course of the Welland, Soar, upper Trent, and Mersey.

England, however, had to endure a long intestine warfare for years after the death of Alfred. The strenuous efforts of his children, Edward the Elder and Æthelflæd, prevented the men of the Danelaw from extending their power southwards. But the Northmen used persevering tactics, and not merely the enemy within, but fresh invasions from without, disturbed the peace of the monarchs of Wessex during the later part of the tenth century. After the disastrous reign of Ethelred the Redeless came a period of Danish rule over the whole of England ; while the reigns of the last Saxon kings formed the prelude to the final invasion of the Northmen, the Norman conquest.

The most interesting feature, from a military point of view, of the contest between Wessex and the Danelaw, is the systematic defence of the Midland rivers by *burhs* during the reign of Edward the Elder, either by himself or his sister Æthelflæd. Æthelflæd, who fixed her chief residence at Tamworth, on the edge of Staffordshire and Warwickshire, ruled over Mercia, and fortified her frontier between 909 and her death in 921. Her brother died in 925 : his activity in con-

structing *burhs* began about 913.   Of the construction of these
fortresses two phrases are used : their builders either " wrought "
or " timbered " them.   Both words probably mean the same
thing : the town or village to be fortified was enclosed within the
usual wooden stockade.[1]   The identity of a few of the *burhs* is
uncertain ; but the remainder may be classified as follows : (1)
Burhs wrought by Æthelflæd on the river banks of her frontier :
these include Runcorn and possibly Warburton on the Mersey,
Bridgnorth and possibly Shrewsbury on the Severn, Tamworth
and Stafford on tributaries of the Trent, and Warwick on the
Avon.   (2) Frontier *burhs* taken by Æthelflæd from the Danes
were Derby and Leicester, both on tributaries of the Trent.   (3)
Eddisbury in Cheshire, an early hill fortress, was the site of one
of Æthelflæd's *burhs :* here the inference is that the existing hill
fort was palisaded by her orders, and garrisoned as a camp of
refuge.   Of Edward's *burhs*, Witham and Maldon on the Essex
Blackwater, of which some probable traces remain, belong to
class (1), as also does Thelwall, his fortified post on the Mersey.
To class (2) belong Colchester, Huntingdon, and Tempsford,
the first on the Colne, the two latter on the Great Ouse.   None
of Edward's works bear any analogy to class (3), unless his last
burh, Bakewell in Derbyshire, may be taken into account.   But
(4) Bakewell represents a push northward along a hostile border,
and may be claimed, with Towcester, as belonging to a fourth
class of *burh*, unconnected with a navigable river, but providing
a constant menace to the enemy.   (5) Towcester may, however,
also be classed with Colchester as a Roman *burh* with stone
walls.   A sixth class of *burh* was riverine, like class (1), but with
this difference, that it was double.   There was one *burh* on one
side, the other on the opposite side of the river.   The cases are
Hertford on the Lea, Buckingham and Bedford on the Ouse,
Stamford on the Welland, and Nottingham on the Trent.   At
Hertford and Buckingham both *burhs* were the work of Edward.
At Bedford, Stamford, and Nottingham, the northern *burh* was
in the hands of the enemy, and Edward took it by converting
the southern suburb into a fortified and garrisoned post.   His
proceedings were exactly analogous to those of Charles the Bald
in 862.   He gained control of the navigable rivers by placing
garrisons on both their banks ; the natural places which he chose
were the existing towns on the river, and the garrison, as at
Nottingham, was formed out of the inhabitants.

Some of these *burhs*, as we have seen, were in the occupation
of the Northmen ; and at a later date, when the frontier of the

[1] *Timbrian* is the ordinary Anglo-Saxon word for " to build," but it indicates the prevalent material used for building.

west Saxon kingdom had been pushed back, and English kings were again placed on the defensive, Lincoln, Nottingham, Derby, Stamford, and Leicester became known as the five *burhs*, the centre of Danish power in the Midlands. There is no reason to suppose that there was any essential difference between the *burhs* of Danes and Saxons—that the *burh* which Æthelflæd took at Derby was in any way different from her own *burh* at Tamworth. When the Danes first landed on a river bank or island and beached their ships, they constructed what is called in the Chronicle a *geweorc*, *i.e.*, a thing wrought. This probably consisted of a slight bank and ditch enclosing the landward side of their position. Where they raised permanent dwellings within the *enceinte*, the *burh* grew out of the *geweorc*, just as a Roman station developed out of a mere camp. However, it is unsafe to push the phraseology of the Chronicle too far, or to fasten a too technical meaning upon its words ; and the fact remains that the term *geweorc* may be very well applied to a wrought *burh*. The Danish *burhs* at Huntingdon and Tempsford, the landmarks of their progress up the Ouse to recover Bedford in 921, are called indiscriminately *burh* and *geweorc*.

Many of the *burhs* wrought or taken during the Danish war became, after the Norman conquest, sites of castles ; and the presence of a Norman castle at such places has led to the still popular inference that the castle simply usurped the earthworks of the earlier stronghold, and that therefore the *burh* was equivalent to the later castle.[1] It is not surprising that all the five places where we hear of a *burh* on either side of the river should have been chosen for the foundation of later castles. But the castle earthworks of Hertford and Bedford, the castles of which there is record at Buckingham and Stamford, were private strongholds which formed part of the defences of one of the *burhs*, but were not identical with either. The Conqueror's castle of Nottingham, greatly transformed in its present state, looked down from its sandstone cliff upon the northern *burh* where Edward welded together Englishman and Dane in one common work of defence and bond of citizenship.[2] But even were it not self-evident that the *burh* is identical with the *burgus* or *burgum* of Domesday and the "borough" whose organisation plays so large a part in English history, there is one fact which makes its

---

[1] This is the main contention of the theory so attractively enunciated by the late G. T. Clark, and endorsed by the authority of Professor Freeman.

[2] Nottingham castle is, in fact, considerably to the west of the probable site of the Saxon *burh*, which was more or less identical with the "English borough" of the middle ages, the western part of Nottingham being known as the "French borough."

Map of Saxon and Danish Burhs

[The line from the Mersey to the Wash roughly
indicates the Danish frontier.]

identification with the castle impossible. At Hertford, Buckingham, Bedford, Stamford, Nottingham, there were two *burhs*, but
there never has been more than one castle. When the Conqueror
wrought a castle on either side of the river at York, he did not
repeat Edward the Elder's tactics literally : he applied them to a
form of fortification of which Edward knew nothing. If the test
by which the Norman castle is identified with the Saxon *burh*
fails in these instances, we are obviously forbidden to make the
identification in the cases of single *burhs* like Warwick or
Tamworth. The great earthen mount and curtain wall which
stand in the south-west corner of Tamworth, beside the Tame,
are not the remains
of Æthelflæd's *burh*,
although it is not im-
probable that they
were raised on the
site of her dwelling-
house. Her *burh* is
the town of Tam-
worth itself; and al-
though her wall of
palisades is gone,
there are still traces
of the ditch with
which, in the eighth
century, Offa had
ringed the *burh* about.

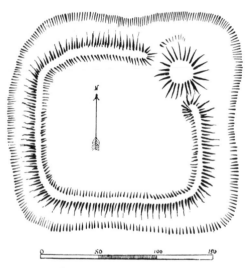

Earthwork at Tempsford.

There is no trace
of any *arx* or citadel
within these enclos-
ures. Their defenders
were the citizens. In
France, for reasons
sufficiently indicated, the art of fortification was more advanced.
Roman traditions survived there without that abrupt break which
the historical continuity of England had suffered. No fortress
of stone and wood, such as that which Charles the Bald, in 869,
built within the *enceinte* of the abbey of St Denis, is heard of
in Saxon England. The state of society in which, as early as
864, Charles found it necessary, by the edict of Pistes, to forbid
his vassals to raise private fortresses without royal authority, did
not exist in England, and was only beginning to exist there two
centuries later. In both centuries we have to deal with the same
invaders, but with defenders whose state of social development
was quite different.

Although the private fortress or castle was introduced into England by the Normans, and although the type of earthwork associated with it was developed to its highest extent by Northmen, not only in Normandy and England, but also in Denmark, it is nevertheless probable that the earliest development of that form of earthwork took place on Frankish soil. The Danish *geweorc* or *burh*, where it can be traced with any certainty—and this is in very few cases—supplied accommodation for the force, and probably a harbour for its vessels, but no private stronghold belonging to a prominent leader. The earthwork called Gannock's castle (32), close to the Ouse near Tempsford, is sometimes supposed to be the *geweorc* wrought by the Danes in 921. In plan, it very closely resembles a rather small mount-and-bailey castle of the usual early Norman type, and could have accommodated only a very small body of defenders. But the point in which it differs from the ordinary mount-and-bailey plan—the smallness of the mount, which is a mere thickening of the earthen bank, and the absence of a moat round its base—may show that here the Danes anticipated their Norman successors with a plan with which some of them may have gained acquaintance during marauding expeditions in France. This, however, is mere conjecture, and the utility of such a fortress for the immediate purposes of the Danes may well be questioned.[1] Of the private dwellings of the Danish leaders, and how far they may have approximated to the later type of the castle, we know nothing. St Mary's abbey at York is on the site of Galmanho, the residence of the Danish earls outside the western wall of the Roman city, but nothing of its earthworks remain. If they were at all considerable, like those of a mount-and-bailey castle of Norman times, it seems strange that no trace of them should be left.

The details of the doings of the Danish army, during the reign of Ethelred the Redeless (979-1016), are recorded at great length in the Chronicle. They show the old tactics, familiar for two hundred years : the long ships are brought to the nearest point convenient for a campaign of pillage ; there the "army is a-horsed," and they ride at their will inland, lighting their "war-beacons," the blazing villages of the country-side, as they go. Year after year records its tale of disaster, until the partition of England in 1016 between Cnut and Edmund Ironside. The whole story of river and land warfare, of plundering and burning, of the paying of Danegeld as a temporary sop to the army, is

---

[1] The Danes were again at Tempsford in 1010, and, if the earthwork is of pre-Conquest date, it is more likely to have been thrown up during the earlier than during the later visit.

5

in no way different from the record of the Danish operations in France during the ninth century.   In France the Danish conquest was quicker, because the invaders had to deal from the beginning with a worn-out civilisation : the partition of France, owing to the superiority of the Danes to their opponents, was effected within seventy years of their first settlement.   The power of Normandy, however, was checked by the rise of the Capetian dynasty in the later part of the tenth century : the Northmen were kept strictly to their Danelaw, and their subsequent expansion took place, not in France, but in England.   On the other hand, in England, the Danish invaders of the ninth century had to contend with the rising power of Wessex and a race younger and more vigorous than the contemporary Gauls of Neustria. Their inroads were therefore checked and their conquest was delayed until the house of Wessex had run its natural course, and Englishmen and Danes had had time to be practically amalgamated into one nation.   The glory of Wessex ceases with Edmund Ironside, the glory of the Danes with Cnut. Before Cnut died, the child William already had succeeded to his father's duchy of Normandy, and thirty-one years after the death of Cnut, William was king of England, and, for all practical purposes, the inroads of the Northmen from Scandinavia were over.

CHAPTER III

THE ENGLISH CASTLE AFTER THE CONQUEST

A CASTLE is a private fortress, built by an individual lord as a military stronghold, and also as an occasional residence. In England at the time of the Norman conquest, this type of military work was known as *castel*, a word which is obviously the same as the Latin *castellum*. *Castrum, munitio*, and *municipium* are names which are frequently given to it by chroniclers of the eleventh and twelfth centuries. Its existence was the direct result of the consolidation of the feudal system. The lord separated his dwelling from those of his vassals : he defended it against the attacks of other individual lords who naturally would seek to aggrandise themselves at his expense : he also needed a stronghold which might be impregnable on occasion against those vassals themselves, and might be a perpetual reminder to them of their subject position. The castle rose within or as an addition to the *burh*, the independent stronghold of one person within the walled or stockaded town of the many. Thus, at one and the same time, it protected and overawed the *burh*. Or it rose by itself, like the Peak castle in Derbyshire, on a spot where no *burh* existed, and so in many cases drew a small community to seek its protection.

An unlimited number of castles implies an unlimited number of independent magnates, uncontrolled by a supreme authority, and each ready to fly at the other's throat. The feudal lord, however, was the king's man, and his castle was therefore theoretically the king's. We have already noticed the edict of Pistes (864), which ordered the destruction of all castles built without royal licence ; and, save in periods of total anarchy, legislation of this type, safeguarding feudal order, was in operation during the middle ages wherever the feudal system was at the base of the constitution. The king was *de jure*, if not *de facto*, the owner of the castles of his realm.

The castle or private fortress was a feature in French social life and warfare from at any rate the middle of the ninth century. But in England it was certainly an unfamiliar and almost as certainly an unknown feature, until the middle of the eleventh century. Danish pirates who up to this time had visited England, had come from the north and east, and passed on to France. There, in contact with the feudal system as it existed under the later Carolingian monarchs, they may have learned the use of the private fortress. At any rate when the North-men came back upon England from their continental duchy, they brought with them the fully organised social system of the Continent, and its most powerful symbol, the castle.

We have seen that, throughout the Saxon and Danish period, the *burh*, the home of the community, formed the unit, if the expression may be used, of military defence by fortification. The English or Danish nobleman lived, it may safely be

Harold's *aula*, from Bayeux Tapestry

assumed, in houses like the two-storied house in the Bayeux tapestry, where Harold and his friends are feasting on the upper floor, while the ground floor apparently forms a cellar or store-room (36).[1] It is possible that such a house, the prototype of the larger medieval dwelling-house, may sometimes have been protected by its encircling thorn hedge or palisade; but it was not a castle. In the eleventh and twelfth centuries, a castle meant to an Englishman a special type of fortress, of a construction and plan of a character more or less fixed. The loose phraseology which, in later times, applied the title of castle

[1] The story (*A.S. Chron.*, sub an. 755) of the murder of Cynewulf and its consequences, mentions the *burh* or *burg* of Merton with its gate : the house in which the king was murdered within the *burh* is called *bur* (*i.e.*, bower, private chamber).

indiscriminately to prehistoric camps and medieval manor-houses, was not yet customary.

The first castles on English soil appear to have been raised by Norman favourites of Edward the Confessor before the Conquest, and to have excited alarm among the English population. In 1048 some foreigners or " Welshmen," as the English called them, encroached on the territory of Sweyn Godwinsson in Herefordshire, constructed a *castel*—the first mention of such a thing in the Chronicle—and wrought harm to all the country round. That they were Frenchmen appears from the events of 1052 : one of Godwin's demands to the king at Gloucester was that " the Frenchmen of the castle " should be given up, and in the same year " the Frenchmen of the castle " helped to defend the borders against a Welsh inroad. The very fact that the Frenchmen's stronghold was known as " *the* castle " proves that it was at any rate an unfamiliar type of fortress. But, if it was the first, others were soon constructed. When Godwin returned from his outlawry in 1052, and forced himself back into Edward's good graces, the Frenchmen in London left the city. The archbishop of Canterbury, Robert of Jumièges, made his way to the east coast : some fled westward to Pentecost's castle, which is probably identical with the Herefordshire fortress, others northward to Robert's castle, which is now identified with Clavering in Essex. The Herefordshire castle is supposed to have been at Ewias Harold, some twelve miles south of Hereford, where there is still the great mount of a Norman stronghold on the north-west side of the village.[1]

These two may not have been the only castles in England before the Conquest. The reference to Arundel in Domesday Book, for example, seems to imply an origin almost as early for the castle there.[2] Ordericus Vitalis speaks of Dover as though there were already a castle there, when William the Conqueror stormed the town after Hastings.[3] But Ordericus is our authority for the important and explicit statement that, in 1068, " the fortresses, which the Gauls call *castella*, had been

[1] Dr J. H. Round, *Feudal Englana*, 1909, p. 324, points to the phrase *hoc castellum refirmaverat* in the Domesday notice of Ewias, as indicative of the existence of the castle before the Conquest, and gives other reasons for the identification.

[2] Domesday, i., f. 23 ; " Castrum Harundel Tempore Regis Edwardi reddebat de quodam molino xl solidos," etc. " Castrum Harundel," however, applies to the town, not the castle; and it does not follow that the name was given to the town before the Conquest.

[3] Ord. Vit., *Hist. Eccl.*, iii. 14 ; " id castellum situm est in acutissima rupe mari contigua." The phrase may be used generally to describe a site which, in Ordericus' own day, had become famous for its castle.

very few in the provinces of England ; and on this account the English, although warlike and daring, had nevertheless shown themselves too feeble to withstand their enemies."[1] A statement of this kind at once disposes of the theory that the *burhs* of the Danish wars were castles ; it could hardly be argued that such *burhs* were very few, or that the English had not taken advantage of them. As a matter of fact, when William came to England, his military policy consisted in the founding of castles, and many of these in places which had been and were *burhs*, where, if the *burh* and castle were one and the same thing, the foundation of a castle was quite unnecessary. *Arcem condidit, castellum construxit, munitionem firmavit*, are terms used over and over again to describe the making of these new strongholds. To William, the strength of a monarch lay in the castles

Hastings Castle : from Bayeux Tapestry

which he controlled ; in warfare the castle formed his natural base of operations. His first work on landing at Hastings was to throw up a castle (38). Harold, on the other hand, although, as the Bayeux tapestry shows us, he had seen something of castles and siege warfare in William's company, trusted for his defence to the shield-wall of his men, and the protection of the banks and ditches of an old earthwork in advance of his position. In 1067, after his coronation, William stayed at Barking, close to the walls of London, while the city, the Lundenburh whose walls Alfred had restored, was being overawed by the construction of certain *firmamenta*—one of them, no doubt, the White Tower, the other probably Baynard's castle, near the present

[1] Ord. Vit., *Hist. Eccl.* iv. 4.

Blackfriars.[1]   Again, we find him at Winchester, building a strong fortress within the walls of the city—a castle within a *burh*.

William's operations in 1068 and 1069 were of great military importance.   In 1068 he quelled the resistance of Exeter.   The city was still surrounded by its Roman walls, to which the inhabitants now added new battlements and towers.   They manned the rampart walks and the projections of the wall,[2] which for eighteen days William endeavoured to undermine. When at last the keys of the city were surrendered to him, his first work was to choose within the walls a place where a castle might be raised ; and, on departing, he left, as at Winchester, a constable in charge of the castle, the king's lieutenant charged with the task of keeping the *burh* under.   From Exeter a rebellion in the north called William to York.   The insurgents, an irregular band of freebooters, had thrown up defences in remote places in woods and by the mouths of rivers ; some were harboured in the larger towns, which they kept in a state of fortification.   As William travelled northwards, he founded castles at Warwick and Nottingham.   He constructed a fortress in the city of York, and on his way home founded castles at Lincoln, Huntingdon, and Cambridge.   No sooner had he left York than the rebels again began to stir ; a movement was made on behalf of the ætheling Edgar, and Danish aid was called in.   William Malet, the governor of York castle, was hard pressed by the enemy.   The Conqueror came to his relief, and, as a result of this visit, founded a second castle in York.   Both castles, however, were of little use when the Danes came.   The garrison of one or both rashly advanced to fight the invaders within the city itself, and were massacred.   It is a significant fact that the castles were left open and deserted ; neither the men of York nor the Danes had any use for them.   When William came north again on his campaign of vengeance he repaired both the castles.   Shortly after, on his expedition to Wales, he founded castles at Chester and Shrewsbury.[3]

What do we find to-day at these places where William founded his first English castles ?   At Hastings, on the cliff which divides the old town from the modern watering-place, there are important remains of a later stone castle within lines

---

[1] The Tower of London was outside the east wall of the medieval city. Baynard's castle was at the point where the west wall approached the Thames.

[2] Ord. Vit., *op. cit.*, iv. 4; "pinnas ac turres . . . in munimentis adde-bant vel restaurabant . . . Portæ offirmatæ erant, densæque turbæ in pro-pugnaculis et per totum muri ambitum prostabant."

[3] The foundation of these castles is noted by Ord. Vit., iv. 4, 5.

of earthwork which are, no doubt, William's. The mount remains at the north-east corner of the enclosure: the later curtain wall has been carried up its side and over it. The present remains of the castle of Winchester are later than William's day. At Exeter the gatehouse and much of the adjacent masonry of the castle are unquestionably of a very early " Norman " date. In London we have the White tower, probably much extended from William's early plan, and not completed till his son's reign. But the stone fortresses of London

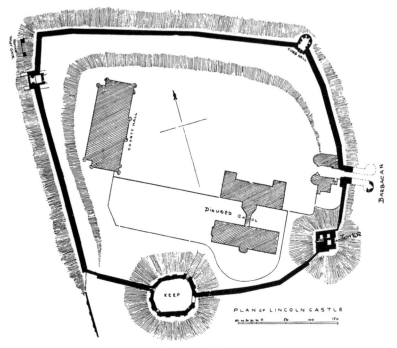

Lincoln ; Plan

and Exeter were exceptional. When we come to his northern castles, we find that at Warwick, York, Lincoln, Huntingdon, Cambridge, and Shrewsbury, the plan of the castle consists of a bailey or enclosed space,[1] with a tall mount on the line of its outer defences, and on a side or at an angle of the *enceinte* remote

---

[1] The word "bailey" (*ballium*) literally means a palisaded enclosure. The synonym "ward," applied to the various enclosed divisions of a medieval castle, means a guarded enclosure. The term "base-court" (*basse-cour*) is also applied to the bailey.

from the main entrance. At Nottingham the plan of the early castle is not so easy to make out. But, in the other cases, although, at various dates during the middle ages, additions were made in stone, the nucleus of the plan is a collection of earthworks, which takes this form—a *motte* or mount with a bailey attached. At Lincoln there are two mounts. At York there are two castles, one on either side of the river, but each with its mount. On the mount of the castle north-east of the river is a later stone keep ; the mount of the south-western castle has never carried stone-work, and its bailey is now almost filled up with modern houses.

The presence of the double castle at York has been a great temptation to those who would identify the castle with the *burh*. The fortification of both banks of the river is, on the face of it, so like the system adopted by Edward the Elder, that the York castles have been often quoted as *burhs* of Edward the Elder's date, and it has been concluded that similar earthworks must have existed at Nottingham, Stamford, and so on. This idea is quite untenable. Had William followed the example of Edward and Æthelflæd, he would simply have repaired or renewed the defences of the two divisions of the *burh* at York.[1] But what he had to provide against was the spirit of rebellion in the *burh* itself, as well as the possible use of the water-way by Danish pirates. Which castle he first founded at York we do not know. On the tongue of land which runs out between the Ouse and Foss, outside the *burh*, and between it and the river approach to the city, one castle rose. The other, a fortress known in later times as the Old Baile, was possibly from the beginning partly within the ramparts of the southern *burh*. Later, at any rate, the city wall was built across the foot of the outer side of its mount, and enclosed the bailey on two sides. Elsewhere, the distinction between William's castles and the *burhs* within which they rose is very noticeable. At Lincoln the castle filled up an angle of the Roman city. At Cambridge, the mount rises on the highest point of a large enclosure—the original *burh*—surrounded by earthworks of early date. Further, if any documentary proof is needed of anything so self-evident as the distinct nature of the castle and the *burh*, Domesday is clear upon the point. Apart from the evidence which it gives us with respect to the borough or *burh*, it speaks in one place of the *burgum circa castellum*—the *burh* about the castle. The case in point is the castle of Tutbury in Staffordshire, a fine example of the mount-

---

[1] It should be noted that at York there were not two distinct *burhs* or fortified towns, such as are found in the earlier cases. The river passed through and bisected the *burh*, which was surrounded by an earthen bank, save at the point where the Foss formed the boundary of the city.

and-bailey stronghold.[1]   One important feature here is that the castle, very large in area, and with a ditch of great depth on two sides, was apparently raised on the site of an early hill-fort or *burh*, and that the actual *burh* about the castle, the modern village of Tutbury, has grown up under its protection on the slope towards the Dove.

The castle, then, was a Norman importation into England. It was a stronghold with a definite plan, so that the word *castel* had no vague meaning to English ears.   It is found in many cases in close proximity to a *burh*, or fortified dwelling of a community ; but it was a royal stronghold, in charge of an individual, and its intention was at once to protect and to keep the *burh* in subjection.   Or, again, it may occupy, as at Tutbury or Conisbrough, the whole site of an early *burh ;* but in such cases the character of the *burh* is entirely changed by the presence of the castle, and the dwelling-place of the community is shifted to the outskirts of the enclosure. At York, Lincoln, and other places where a castle was constructed within part of a *burh*, Domesday tells us that the site was *vastata in castellis—i.e.*, that houses were taken down to make room for the new earthworks.

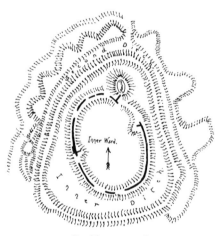

Berkhampstead

A figure of eight, with the lower portion elongated and widened to form the bailey, may be taken as the normal form of the castle plan.   Often, as at Berkhampstead (42), where the mount and bailey were surrounded by a broad wet ditch and outer earthworks, the bailey is much the larger portion of the figure on plan ; and it was only in small and unimportant strongholds that the bailey formed, as at Mexborough, a mere forecourt to the mount. At Alnwick (115) the mount stood as part of the outer defences of the enclosure, on the slope to the river ; but it was so placed that it divided a western or outer from an eastern or inner ward or bailey, and almost filled up the space between them.   The arrangement at Berkeley (186) is somewhat

[1] Domesday, i. 248 *b*.

similar.   If the larger mount at Lincoln (40) were removed to
the centre of the present enclosure, and the lines of the curtain-
wall returned inwards to meet it, the plan of Alnwick would be
obtained.   Possibly, however, both at Alnwick and Berkeley, the
outer ward may form an extension of the earlier plan, or may
have been merely a covering platform, like the outer earthworks
at Hastings.   The later stone defences have obscured the original
designs in both cases.

Although the plan followed fixed and familiar lines, there
were no fixed dimensions to the castle.   The mount was intended
to bear the strong tower or donjon : within the bailey were the
ordinary lodgings
of the garrison, and
such   domestic
buildings as might
be needed.   The
bailey, which in-
clined,   on   the
whole, to be oval
in form, was sur-
rounded by a low
earthen bank, out-
side which was a
dry ditch of more
or less depth, with
a parapet or coun-
terscarp   on   the
further side.   The
mount   was   sur-
rounded by its own
ditch, which was
joined at two points
by the main ditch

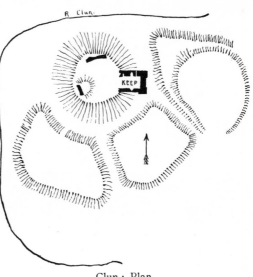

Clun ; Plan

on the side next the bailey.   The entrance to the castle was at the
end of the bailey, opposite the mount.   These dispositions might
vary: the mount might be within the enclosure, even, as at Pickering, in its centre, and the position of the entrance might be different, if the site required it.   There might be more than one
bailey, and these might be set side by side, divided by an intermediate ditch, as on the fairly level site at Clun (43), or end on
end, as on the ridge at Montgomery, or a small bailey might project as a kind of outwork common to mount and bailey alike.[1]

---

[1] An example of this is the fine earthwork at Lilbourne, in Northamptonshire.   There are many other instances, and the lesser bailey at Clun
partakes of this character.

The usual arrangement, however, was as described. The mount might be of any height, of enormous proportions, as at Thetford, or of more modest size, as at Brecon or Trecastle. It was usually entirely artificial ; but positions were sometimes chosen in which the ground afforded natural help. The mount, for example, at Hedingham in Essex, on the levelled top of which the later square donjon was built, appears to be partly natural ; while the great mount at Mount Bures, not many miles away, is wholly artificial. The bailey, again, might vary much in size. It might have a very large area, as at Lincoln and Tutbury, a moderate area, as at Warkworth (49) or Durham (199); or it might be small and compact, as at Trecastle (44). There are many cases, as at

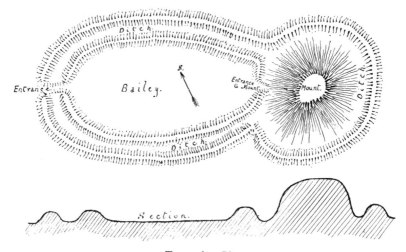

Trecastle ; Plan

Clifford's hill, near Northampton, where the mount is found by itself : in such instances, the bailey may have disappeared as the result of local cultivation, and only the more important part of the earthworks may have been left. But it is also probable that here and there the fortified mount with the tower on its summit would be all that was needed, and that the absence of a large garrison would render a bailey unnecessary. The size of the bailey, in any case, would depend upon the importance of the position and the size of the garrison required.

The mount, at any rate, was the essential feature of this type of fortress. The Bayeux tapestry gives us pictures of some of these mounts, the fidelity of which is demonstrated by the remains which we possess of such castles, and by some pieces of documentary evidence (38).   Two points are noticeable: (1) The mounts portrayed are all either in Normandy and Brittany, or, like the *castellum* at "Hestengaceaster," are the work of Norman hands.   (2) The fortifications shown in connection with these mounts are of timber, not stone.   The accuracy of the tapestry is not absolutely photographic, but the workers knew well the type of structure which they wanted to represent.   Their work, in fact, whether the castle represented be Dol or Dinan or Bayeux or Hastings, gives us a repeated picture of the recognised type of castle mount.   And the two points just noted lead us to the conclusions, (1) that the castle was foreign to England and Englishmen, and (2) that the time-honoured notion that the Englishman raised the earthworks,[1] and

Castle of Rennes : from Bayeux Tapestry

the Norman built stone castles upon them is open to objection, the fact being that the stone castle was an exception in Normandy itself.   The picture of the Breton castle of Dinan (46) shows, as in a section, a large pudding-shaped mount surrounded by a ditch, with a low bank of earth on the side towards the bailey. On the top of the mount is a tower, clearly of timber.   Round the edge of the mount, encircling the tower, is a stockade formed of uprights with stout hurdles between—a work to which Cæsar's

---

[1] There are cases, of course, which give rise to perplexity.   Thus at Earls Barton, in Northamptonshire, the famous pre-Conquest church tower stands on a site which appears to be within the original limit of the ditch of the adjacent castle mount.   It is doubtful, however, whether the mount was ever ditched on this side ; and the church does not encroach upon the mount.

description of his breastworks at Alesia might well be applied.[1]
Access to the mount is gained by a steep ladder, probably
formed of planks with projecting pieces of wood nailed to them
for foot-holds, which spans the ditch, and has its foot within
the bailey. The mount itself—and this may be proved by many
surviving examples—is too steep to be scaled with any ease;
and the ladder, although affording the defenders an excellent
communication with the bailey, is hardly to be climbed with
impunity by the opposing force. The ladder ends in a wooden
platform at the edge of the mount, which serves as a *propugna-
culum* for the garrison, in front of the stockade. In the picture
of the construction of the castle at Hastings, a timber tower and
stockade are in course of erection. The pioneers are busy

Castle of Dinan : from Bayeux Tapestry

digging earth from the fosse for their nearly completed mount,
and compacting the surface with blows from the flat of their
spades (38).

In France the mount was usually known as the *motte* from
the turf of which it was composed, and the occurrence of the
word Lamotte as part of a place-name is as tell-tale as a name
like Mount Bures in England. But a common name for the
motte, employed by medieval writers, was the Latin *dunio* or
domgio, a debased form of the word *dominio*. This became in
French *donjon*, and in English *dungeon*. The *motte* at Canterbury
is still known by the corrupted name of the Dane John. The

[1] Cæsar, *De Bell. Gall.*, vii. 73; "huic [vallo] loricam pinnasque adiecit,
grandibus cervis eminentibus ad commissuras pluteorum atque aggeris, qui
ascensum hostium tardarent." See p. 60 below.

mount, the symbol of the dominion of the feudal lord, and the centre of his *dominium* or demesne, bore his strong tower ; and to this tower the name of the mount was transferred. When the tower on the mount was superseded by the heavy and lofty rectangular or cylindrical tower of later times, the new tower kept the old name. By a strange transference of meaning, our English *dungeon*, frequently applied to the chief tower of a castle until the seventeenth century, became connected with the vaults or store-rooms in the basement of such a tower, and now reminds us less of the dominion of the castle builders than of the cruelty with which they are supposed to have exercised that dominion.

It may safely be assumed that the very large majority of castles

Colchester Castle : great tower or keep.

of the eleventh and early twelfth century were constructed on this plan. There were exceptions, and certainly several English castles have stonework of the period of the Conquest. London and Colchester (47) had rectangular donjons from the first. At Richmond (93) the stonework of part of the curtain and of the lower part of the rectangular tower-keep is unquestionably of the eleventh century, when the castle was constructed by Alan of Brittany. In several other places, in the curtain at Tamworth (48) and in part of the curtain at Lincoln, there is eleventh century stonework. But more will be said of these cases later. It is enough to say here that, in most cases, stonework forms a late Norman or Plantagenet addition to early Norman earthwork. At Newcastle part of the early mount remained, side by side with the late twelfth century tower-keep, until within the last hundred years. Warkworth, most instructive of English castles, preserves the base of its mount and the area of its original bailey: the mount bears a strong tower-house of the early fifteenth century; on the line of the bank of the bailey is a stone curtain of about the year 1200; within the area is a series of elaborate and beautiful buildings of two or three dates (49). Warkworth is the epitome of the

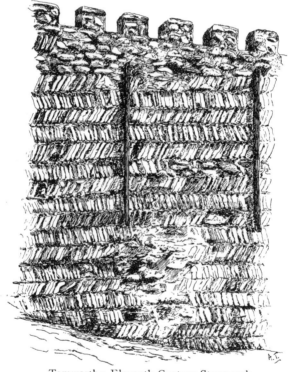

Tamworth; Eleventh Century Stonework

history of the castle, from its Norman origin to its practical identification, in the later middle ages, with the large manor house; and to Warkworth we shall return more than once.

There are exceptional cases in which two mounts occur. At Lincoln (40), the smaller mount is at the south-east corner of the enclosure, and probably may have carried the original donjon. The larger mount, of formidable height and steepness, is west of the centre of the south side. Both mounts, as is usual, are half within and half without the line of the rampart. The stone curtain-wall has been brought up their sides, and the larger mount is crowned by a stone " shell " keep of the late twelfth century. The provision of this second mount was possibly due to the exposed position of the castle, which formed the outer defence of the city on the west and south-west, and needed its greatest strength on that side. At Pontefract and Lewes, again, there were two mounts, one at each end of the enclosure. At both places, the later stone keep was built in connection with the western mount, at the end nearest the town and the slope of the ridge on which it was built. The sites are rather similar, and, in either case, the eastern mount overlooked the river-valley defended by the castle. It is not certain that two mounts ever formed part of an original plan. The natural tendency would be to throw up the mount at first on the side

nearer the valley, where the slope was steeper, and the labour required in construction would be less. An attack, however, on the town and castle would come most naturally from the higher ground to the west, which commanded the castle and its de-fences. A new mount would, in process of time, be constructed on this side, and the old

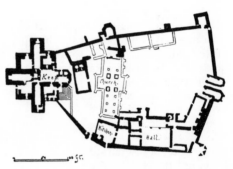

Warkworth ; Plan

mount would become of secondary importance. At Lewes (50), where the slope of the hill is abrupt, the western mount rises from a higher level, and commands a much wider stretch of country than the mount at the north-east angle of the en-closure. At Lincoln, where an enemy's force had no advantage of higher ground, the larger mount simply occupies the most advantageous position, protecting the most exposed side of the enclosure, and commanding one of the most extensive views in England. The foot of one mount is little more than two hundred feet distant from the foot of the other ; while, at Lewes and Pontefract, the length of the whole bailey lay between the mounts. Thus, while it is possible that, at Lewes and Pontefract, both mounts may be original, with the idea of strengthening the enclosure at either end with a donjon, two original mounts at Lincoln would not have this excuse ; and

7

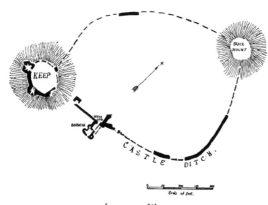

Lewes ; Plan

we may infer that, at some date later than the foundation of Lincoln castle, the Norman lords of the fortress threw up a new mount at a point from which the slope of the hill and the approaches from the valley of the Trent could be commanded more thoroughly.

The provision of more than one bailey, as at Clun (43), where two small baileys, separated by ditches, cover the south and west sides of the mount, was due, partly to the irregular nature of the site, and partly to the need for the multiplication of defences. Such an arrangement, inconvenient in time of peace, would be a considerable advantage in case of siege, when each bailey would provide a separate difficulty to the assailants, and a separate rallying point to the defenders. At Builth (50), where the whole area of the castle earthworks is small, and the ditches of mount and bailey are of considerable strength, the main bailey is a narrow segmental platform covering the south side of the mount. On the west side of the mount is a smaller and narrower platform, between which and the main bailey is a broad ditch, forming a cross-cut or traverse be-

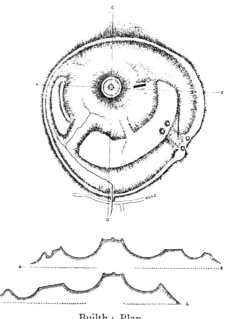

Builth ; Plan

tween the ditches of the mount and bailey. As the enclosure is very nearly circular, with the mount north-west of the centre, this second platform is somewhat squeezed into the space, and the ditch between it and the counterscarp which runs continuously round both mount and bailey is very narrow. In the more usual instances, where the mount and its ditch form a regular circle, which intersects with the bailey and its ditch, a secondary platform, as has been noted, occurs outside the line of both ditches, and is surrounded by a ditch of its own, communicating with both. This is the case with the very symmetrical example of a mount-and-bailey castle at Mexborough, at Lilbourne in Northants, Hallaton in Leicestershire (51), and other cases. Here the secondary platform is an excres-

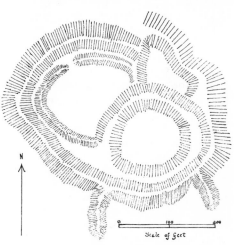

cence on one side of the meeting of the two circles. Such platforms were mere outworks where additional defence was necessary ; it is possible that on them stone-throwing engines might be planted by the defenders, as the narrowness of the ditch would at these points bring the assailants more nearly within range than at any other point within the enclosure. Such engines would encumber

N

Scale of feet

Hallaton ; Plan

the larger bailey, which would necessarily be kept as clear as possible for the operations of the main body of the garrison.

The mount-and-bailey castle has been derived by some from a Teutonic origin,[1] but it is difficult to trace it with any certainty at an early period outside France and Normandy. There are many remains of these castles in Normandy itself. The famous castle of Domfront (Orne), founded originally by Guillaume Talvas (*d.* 1030), ancestor of the house of Bellême, possibly took this form : as at Newcastle, a rectangular tower of stone took the place, in the twelfth century, of the tower on the mount.[2] The

[1] See Enlart, ii. 494.
[2] Domfront, however, on its rocky site, may, like Richmond, have been surrounded by a stone wall from the first.

writer of a monograph on the castle of Domfront enumerates
five such mounts which exist or are known to have existed
within the local *arrondissement*.[1] Two, at Sept-Forges and
Lucé, remain intact, covered by plantations of trees. At Sept-
Forges the church and castle were side by side, as may still be
seen at Earls Barton in Northamptonshire.[2] At Lucé there are
traces of a bailey. On the other hand, at La Baroche, a large
mount seems to have borne the whole castle : one may compare
with this the great mount of Restormel in Cornwall, which is
the natural summit of a hill, artificially scarped and surrounded
by a fosse, like a contour fort of early times. It is important
to notice that on these artificial mounts of southern Normandy,
there appears "no ruin, no trace of construction in masonry."
The inference is obvious. The buildings which they carried were
of wood, and have yielded to the action of fire or the weather.
On no other hypothesis can the speed with which castles were
constructed in England after the Conquest, or the ease with which
they were destroyed, be explained. William's subjects in Normandy threw up fortifications against him with a speed which
positively forbids us to imagine that they procured masons to
work in stone. In 1061, Robert, son of Giroie, one of the powerful nobles of the Alençonnais, joined forces with the Angevins
against William, and fortified his castles of La-Roche-sur-Igé and
Saint-Cénéri. His cousin, Arnold, son of Robert, driven from
the castle of Échauffour, returned secretly and burned it.[3] The
quickness with which the two castles at York were constructed,
destroyed, and repaired, allowed no time for dressing stone.

The points which our evidence leads us to accept may be recapitulated as follows :—(1) The castle was a foreign importation
into England, of the period of the Norman conquest. (2) It
consisted, in its simplest form, of a moated mount or *motte*, with
a bailey or base-court attached. (3) Its earliest fortifications
were entirely of timber, save in rare instances.

We may now examine the evidence which, in default of
actual remains, survives with regard to the timber constructions
of these castles and their use. The tower on the mount first
demands our attention. Apart from the pictures of the Bayeux
tapestry, certain early twelfth century chronicles of northern
France have preserved for us accounts of the main features of
this structure and its *enceinte*.[4] Jean de Colmieu describes the

---

[1] L. Blanchetière, *Le Donjon ou Château féodal de Domfront (Orne)*,
1893, pp. 29, 30.
[2] See note above, p. 45.
[3] Ord. Vit., iii. 5.
[4] The essential portions of these texts are quoted by Enlart, ii. 497-9.

castle of Merchem, close by the church, as *munitio quedam quam castrum vel municipium dicere possumus.* " It is the custom," he says, " with the rich men and nobles of this district, because they spend their time in enmity and slaughter, and in order that they may thereby be safer from their enemies, and by their superior power either conquer their equals or oppress their inferiors, to heap up a mount of earth as high as they can, and to dig round it a ditch of some breadth and great depth, and, instead of a wall, to fortify the topmost edge of the mount round about with a rampart (*vallo*) very strongly compacted of planks of timber, and having towers, as far as possible, arranged along its circuit. Within the rampart they build in the midst a house or a citadel (*arx*) commanding the whole site. The gate of entry to the place "—the word used is *villa*, implying a place of habitation rather than a stronghold—" can be approached only by a bridge, which, rising at first from the outer lip of the ditch, is gradually raised higher. Supported by uprights in pairs, or in sets of three, which are fixed beneath it at convenient intervals, it rises by a graduated slope across the breadth of the ditch, so that it reaches the mount on a level with its summit and at its outer edge, and touches the threshold of the enclosure." It will be noticed that the moated mount described here had no bailey. It was also obviously not merely a fortified stronghold, a place of refuge in time of war, but a definite residence of the local lord. The turrets round the timber rampart of the mount are mentioned as occasional, not invariable features of the design. The habitation within the rampart may be a strong tower or a mere house. The sense of the passage shows clearly that there was a doorway in the rampart, by which the house was approached from the bridge. Finally, the description is not applicable merely to a single castle, but is a generic description of strongholds in a particular neighbourhood.

The domestic, apart from the military, character of the building, is emphasised in the story which follows the description. John of Warneton, the sainted bishop of Thérouanne (*d.* 1130), was entertained here, when he came to hold a confirmation in Merchem church. After the confirmation was over, he went back to the castle to change his vestments before proceeding to bless the churchyard. As he returned across the sloping bridge, which at its middle point was about 35 feet above the ditch, the press of the people who crowded to see the holy man was so great, and the old enemy, says the chronicler, so alive to the opportunity, that the bridge broke, and the bishop and his admirers, amid a terrible noise of falling joists, boards, and spars, were thrown to the bottom of the ditch.

The castle was, in fact, the private residence of a man who, if he could indulge in the peaceful pleasure of entertaining his bishop, could not afford to live in an unfortified house. Private warfare with his neighbours was the business of his life, and he had to make himself as comfortable as he could within his palisade. Jean de Colmieu does not tell us whether the castle stronghold at Merchem took the shape of a tower or not ; but Lambert of Ardres has left a description of the great wooden tower of three stories which the carpenter Louis de Bourbourg constructed about 1099 for Arnould, lord of Ardres. The elaborateness · of its design and plan is remarkable, and the *motte* which bore it must have been of considerable size. The ground-floor contained cellars, store-rooms, and granaries. The first floor contained the chief living-rooms—the common hall, the pantry and buttery, the great chamber where Arnould and his wife slept, with two other rooms, one the sleeping-place of the body-servants. Out of the great chamber opened a room or recess with a fire-place, where the folk of the castle were bled, the servants warmed themselves, or the children were taken in cold weather to be warmed. One may assume that the great chamber was at the end of the hall opposite to the pantry and buttery. The kitchen was probably reached, as in the larger dwelling-houses of later days, by a passage between these offices : it was on the same floor as the hall, but occupied a two-storied extension of the donjon on one side.[1] Below the kitchen were the pig-sty, fowl-house, and other like offices. The third stage of the donjon contained the bed-chambers of the daughters of the house: the sons also could sleep on this floor, if they chose, and here slept the guard of the castle, who relieved one another at intervals in the work of keeping watch. On the eastern side of the first floor was a projecting building, called the *logium* or parlour, and above this on the top floor was the chapel of the house, "made like in carving and painting to the tabernacle (*sic*) of Solomon." Lambert speaks of the stairways and passages of the donjon, but his description of the projecting parlour and chapel is not sufficiently explicit, and his admiration may have magnified the proportions of the building. His description, however, is of great service when applied to the tower donjon of stone, the arrangements of which it serves to explain. Here, again, the fortress was clearly designed as a dwelling house : the supply of rooms, if it is not exaggerated, was quite remarkable for the age. The *motte* or donjon—Lambert gives it these alternative names—rose in the middle of a marsh, which Arnould converted

[1] The "lesser donjon" at Falaise, which contained the great chamber, is a rectangular projection of two stories from the great donjon.

into a lake or moat by forming sluices: his mill was near the first sluice.

No definite description is left of the defences of the bailey in a castle of this date. There is no doubt, however, that the scarp, or encircling bank of earth, was protected, like the summit of the mount, by a hedge or palisade of the traditional type. Such hedges were the normal defence of any kind of stronghold: the edict of Pistes ordered the destruction of all unlicensed *castella*, *firmitates, et haias*—castles, strong dwellings, and hedges. In 1225 Henry III. ordered the forester of Galtres to supply the sheriff of Yorkshire with timber for repairing and making good the breaches of the palisade (*palicii*) of York castle. The "houses" and "bridge" of the same castle—that is, the buildings within the bailey, and the drawbridge by which the bailey was entered across the ditch, were also of timber. As late as 1324 the stockade on the mount was still of wood, surrounding the stone donjon of the thirteenth century.[1] This is an interesting example of the survival, until a late date, of primitive fortification in a strong and important castle. There is abundant evidence, in fact, that the Norman engineer put his trust, not in stone, but in his earthen rampart and its palisades. When, about 1090, the freebooter Ascelin Goël got possession of the castle of Ivry, he enclosed it "with ditches and thick hedges."[2] In 1093, Philip I. of France and Robert of Normandy took the part of William of Breteuil, the dispossessed lord of Ivry, and laid siege to the fortified town and castle of Bréval (Seine-et-Oise). With the aid of a siege engine, constructed by Robert of Bellême, they were able to destroy the rampart and encircling hedges.[3] Bréval was in a wooded and remote district, where stone would have been hard to obtain in any case. The grand necessity, in places which were in danger of constant attack, was to provide them with adequate defences which could be constructed in the shortest time possible.

Of the nature of the houses within the bailey, little can be said. They doubtless included shelters for the garrison of the castle, stables for their horses, and various sheds or store-houses. The hall, or building, which was the centre of the domestic life of the castle, was, from the earliest times, the chief building within the circumference of the bailey. We read of the

---

[1] Mrs Armitage in *Eng. Hist. Review*, xix. 443-7.
[2] Ord. Vit., viii. 12 ; "fossis et densis sepibus."
[3] *Ibid.*, viii. 24 ; "Hic machinas construxit, contra munimentum hostile super rotulas egit, ingentia saxa in oppidum et oppidanos projecit, bellatores assultus dare docuit, quibus vallum et sepes circumcingentes diruit, et culmina domorum super inhabitantes dejecit."

destruction of the *principalis aula* of the castle of Brionne in 1090, by the red-hot darts which were hurled upon its shingled roof;[1] and stone halls, as at Chepstow and Richmond, were built before the beginning of the twelfth century. But it is certain, on the other hand, that the donjon was, now and later, adapted to domestic as well as purely military uses ; and it seems likely that the owner of the castle, in certain cases, was content with his dwelling upon the mount, until, at a later date, the strengthening of the whole enclosure with a stone curtain made it possible for him to raise a more convenient dwelling house within the more ample space of the bailey. In the larger castles, however, where there was a strong permanent garrison, a hall was a necessity for their entertainment.

Where mount-and-bailey castles are found without a trace of stonework, it does not follow that they are necessarily of a date immediately subsequent to the Conquest. Many of these castles, founded by the Conqueror and his followers, became permanent strongholds, and in due course of time were fortified with stone walls and towers. Others were probably founded as an immediate consequence of the Conquest, and were abandoned in favour of other sites. Thus it has been thought that the earthworks at Barwick-in-Elmet, near Leeds, were abandoned by Ilbert de Lacy, when he fixed upon Pontefract as the head of his honour.[2] Trecastle may have been deserted by Bernard of Newmarch for Brecon, or it may have been held by a small garrison as the western outpost of his barony. But it is well known that, for a long time after the Conquest, in the period of constant strife between the Norman kings and their barons, a large number of castles came into existence in defiance of royal edicts. We know that, during the reign of Stephen, when every man did what was right in his own eyes, an almost incredible number of unlicensed or "adulterine"[3] castles were constructed. As a result of the agreement between Stephen and Henry II., many of these were destroyed, and the number of English castles was materially lessened. Later on, when the revolt of the Mowbrays against Henry II. took place, the victory of the king's party was followed by the destruction of the Mowbray castles at Thirsk, Kirkby Malzeard, and Kinnard's Ferry in the isle of Axholme, and of Bishop Pudsey's castle at Northallerton.

---

[1] Ord. Vit., viii. 13 ; "Callidi enim obsessores in fabrili fornace, quæ in promptu structa fuerat, ferrum missilium callefaciebant, subitoque super tectum principalis aulæ in munimentis jaciebant, et sic ferrum candens sagittarum atque pilorum in arida veterum lanugine imbricum totis nisibus figebant."

[2] See J. H Round, *Castles of the Conquest* (*Archæologia*, lviii. 333).

[3] *Adulterinus* = spurious, counterfeit.

Of these four castles earthworks or traces of earthworks, but no stonework, remain. It is reasonable to suppose that the material of their fortifications was timber. Haste in the construction of castles, speed in their destruction, during the century following the Conquest, are easily explained if their works were merely of earth and wood. And it is thus possible that, when we meet with a mount-and-bailey fortress, unnamed in history and untouched by medieval stonemasons, it may be neither on a site chosen and then abandoned by an early Norman lord, nor a mere outpost of some greater castle, but a stronghold hastily entrenched and heaped up in time of rebellion, by some noble of the time of Stephen or Henry II., and dismantled when peace was restored, and the authority of the sovereign recognised.

CHAPTER IV

THE PROGRESS OF ATTACK AND DEFENCE

THE earthwork fortifications, the progress of which we have traced up to the Norman conquest, were of a very simple kind. It is obvious that, in the history of military architecture, any improvement in defence is the consequence of improved methods of attack. The stone-walled town of the middle ages, the castle or private citadel, with its curtain wall and the subdivision of its enclosure into more than one bailey, succeeded the palisaded earthwork as a natural result of the development of the art of siege. Against an enemy whose artillery was comparatively feeble the stockaded enclosure was effective enough : slingers and bowmen, working at close quarters, might do damage to the defenders, but the palisade on the bank, divided from the besiegers by a formidable ditch, was proof against missiles launched against it by individuals, and could be carried only by a determined rush, or if it were not sufficiently protected against fire. Modern warfare against uncivilised tribes has shown that a stronghold defended by a thick hedge is a serious problem to a besieging force. If, under modern conditions, the stockade is a barrier to troops equipped with powerful firearms, the difficulty which it afforded to the early medieval warrior is obvious.

The age of firearms, however, which brought the death-blow to medieval siegecraft, was long in coming ; and meanwhile the progress of the science of attack depended upon the improvement in methods which could be employed only in close proximity to the besieged stronghold, or within a very limited range. Engines for hurling stones or javelins increased in size and strength. Devices were brought into play for scaling or undermining the defences of the town or castle. The attack was directed against the defences rather than against the defenders. A casual stone might do injury to the medieval soldier, or an arrow might pierce between the joints of his harness ; but his armour, which became more heavy and more carefully protected as the chance of risk from such missiles increased, made loss of life in the course of a siege a misfortune rather than an inevitable contingency. His first anxiety, therefore, was to make the defensive works which sheltered him impregnable. As the enemy multiplied his designs against the palisaded enclosure, the palisade gave place to the stone wall ; as the enemy's means for prosecuting his attempts increased in power, the wall increased in height and strength ; and at last, during the transitional epoch in which firearms gradually superseded the older and more primitive weapons of attack, the wall presented to the besieger a thoroughly guarded front which rendered his medieval siege tactics obsolete, and called for new developments in his craft.

The progress of fortification under these conditions will be the subject of the remaining chapters of this book, with special reference to the castle, in the defences of which the military engineers of the middle ages displayed the epitome of their science. Before we proceed, however, to the growth of the stone-walled castle, some description is necessary of the improvement in siege-engines and methods of attack by which its development was governed. It must be kept in mind that the siege-craft of the middle ages advanced upon lines that were by no means new. Its engines, its devices for breaking down or scaling walls and towers, were not new inventions, but relics of Roman military science. With the decay of the Roman power in western Europe, these materials of warfare, unknown to the Teutonic conquerors of Britain, had fallen into disuse. Preserved in the east by the Byzantine empire, the inheritor of Roman civilisation, they became familiar to the barbarians who overran Europe in the dark ages ; and their revival in the parts of Europe most remote from the historic centres of Roman influence was due in no small measure to the adoption of traditional siegecraft by the invading tribes which had come into conflict with Byzantine strategy. So far as England is concerned, the first advance in the art of attack was the direct result of the Norman conquest ; while subsequent improvement in western Europe generally was primarily due to the knowledge of eastern warfare gained during the Crusades. A slight retrospect, under these conditions, is desirable, which will give us some insight into the methods of siegecraft during the period of whose strongholds and art of fortification we already have seen something.

Many classical texts, from the time of Cæsar to the latest days of the western Empire, supply us with authority for Roman military methods. No passage throws fuller light on their siege practice than Cæsar's description of his siege of Alesia in Burgundy, the hill fortress occupied by Vercinge-

torix.[1] The lines which were first drawn round the stronghold
by Cæsar were eleven miles in circuit, and communicated with
three camps, on hills of a height equal to that of the hill of Alesia.
Along the lines there were twenty-three *castella*, small forts to
hold pickets, and temporary examples of the type of which the
"mile-castles" of the Roman wall were permanent instances.
The stubborn resistance of Vercingetorix and the prospect of
the arrival of a relieving army, however, gave Cæsar occasion to
elaborate his lines, the character of which is very minutely
described. They consisted of an earthen bank with a ditch
20 feet broad, 400 feet in front of it on the side towards the
besieged stronghold. The ditch was dug with perpendicular
sides: its distance from the bank was a precaution against
sudden attacks of the enemy, and placed the bank out of the
range of casual missiles. The space between the bank and
ditch was not a level "berm," but was furrowed by two ditches,
15 feet in breadth and depth, of which the inner was wet, the
water of the neighbouring streams being diverted into it.
Behind the inner ditch rose the earthen *agger* or bank, to the
height of 12 feet. The *vallum*, the rampart on the top of the
agger, was of a type common in early warfare and for many
centuries later, consisting of a breastwork of interlaced twigs
stiffened by a row of palisades. The hurdles of the breastwork
were finished off with battlement-like projections: at intervals
there were tall uprights with forked tops, which were called *cervi*
or "stags," and acted as *chevaux-de-frise* along the whole
rampart. There were also towers, obviously temporary constructions of timber, at distances of 80 feet from one another.
This, however, was not enough. Cæsar aimed at holding his
lines with as few men as possible, so as to allow the rest to do
the necessary foraging at a distance. He therefore proceeded
to sow the approach to the lines with pitfalls. Five ditches,
5 feet deep, were dug out and filled with upright stakes sharpened
to a point and fastened together at the bottom by continuous
cross pieces. In front of these were three rows of pits, 3 feet
deep, arranged in a series of *quincunces* or saltires: in these
were placed smooth sharpened stakes, so that little more than
their points stuck out of the ground, and the pits were then
covered over with twigs and brushwood. The eight rows formed
by these obstructions were each 3 feet apart. The whole
arrangement, producing the effect of a row of fleurs-de-lys, was
called *lilium :* to the stakes the soldiers gave the name of *cippi*

---

[1] Cæsar, *Bell. Gall.*, vii. 68 *seq*. Alesia, near the modern village of
Alise-la-Reine, is in the Côte d'Or department, some 36 miles N.W. of
Dijon.

or "grave-stones." On the opposite side of the *vallum*, where an attack from a relieving army was expected, a similar arrangement was made. Also, in front of the *lilium*, wooden cubes with hooks fastened into them were hidden in the ground, bearing the appropriate name of *stimuli*.

Cæsar's method of besieging Alesia was dictated by the probability that, with an enemy on both sides, he would have to stand a siege himself. After a doubtful battle, the Gallic army of relief made a night attack on the lines, in which they found to their cost the effectiveness of Cæsar's death-traps. They brought with them hurdles, with which to help themselves across the ditches, and scaling ladders and grappling hooks, with the help of which they might climb or pull down the rampart. Their weapons were slings, arrows, and stones, to which the Romans replied with extemporised slings and spears. They suffered two repulses, and then turned their attention to the weakest of Cæsar's camps, while Vercingetorix left Alesia to attack the rampart. His force brought hurdles with long balks of timber to form a footway across them, mantlets, or coverings under which an attacking party, sheltered from Roman missiles, could undermine or make a breach in Cæsar's earthwork by the use of a bore, and hooks with which to cut down the rampart on the top of the earthen bank. The attack was long and determined. The Gallic pioneers filled up Cæsar's fosses, so far as they could, with earth, and themselves raised a mound from which his devices of defence were easily seen. Where his lines were on level ground, they were too formidable to attack: on the steep slopes of the hills, on the tops of which his camps were pitched, there was more chance for an enemy. Here the fiercest fighting took place: the towers of the *vallum* were assailed with javelins, the ditch was filled, and an attempt was made to tear down the palisade and breastwork. Labienus, unable to hold the lines, sent a message to Cæsar, whose intervention with his cavalry turned the day and brought about the total defeat of the Gallic army and the surrender of Vercingetorix.

The account of the siege of Marseilles by Gaius Trebonius in B.C. 49 gives us many of the methods employed by the Romans, and by Byzantine and medieval engineers after them, in the siege of a walled town.[1] Marseilles was no mere hill stronghold like Alesia: it was a strongly fortified seaport town, well equipped for war with engines which hurled pointed stakes 12 feet long against the besiegers, as they threw up their earthen bank round the landward side of the city. Trebonius

---

[1] Cæsar, *De Bell. Civ.*, ii. 1 *seq.*

had to make the line of penthouses (*vineæ*), by which his pioneers were protected, of more than ordinary thickness to withstand these missiles. In advance of the bank, a body of men, sheltered by a large penthouse (*testudo*) levelled the soil. While this leaguer was established on the landward side, Brutus gained a naval victory over the Massiliotes, who nevertheless continued to hold out against the besiegers. The right wing of the Roman army was especially open to attack from the city ; and on this side the besiegers built a tower of brick, to serve as a base of operations and a refuge from attack. This tower, which was raised to a height of six stories, was built by workmen who were sheltered by hanging mantlets of rope. A roof was made of timber, covered with a layer of bricks and puddled clay, to protect it against fire, and with raw hides, to make it proof against darts and stones. As the tower grew, this roof, from which the rope mantlets depended, was raised by levers and screwed down as a covering to each story in succession. When it was nearly completed, a wooden penthouse known as the mouse (*musculus*) was constructed, consisting of a gallery 60 feet long, with a gabled roof, which was covered, like that of the tower, with bricks, clay, and hide. This was moved forward on rollers to the nearest point in the city-wall. It withstood the huge stones which were cast upon it ; lighted barrels of pitch and resin, hurled from the wall, rolled off its sloping roof and were pushed to a safe distance by the men inside, armed with poles and pitchforks. Covered by their friends' fire from the brick tower, the soldiers in the mouse were able to sap with their levers and wedges the foundations of the tower on the wall, and managed to effect a breach. The defenders submitted, and asked for a truce until Cæsar arrived ; but, taking advantage of the interval, they made a treacherous sally from the city, and, aided by a favourable wind, burned down the besiegers' constructions, including the mouse and the brick tower, and destroyed their machines. Trebonius, however, lost no time in constructing, instead of his earthen bank, a strong wall of countervallation, composed of two parallel walls of brick, each 6 feet thick, with a timber floor above. This quickly brought the defenders to their senses, and they reverted to their old conditions of peace. In this account the devices which play the chief part are met again in numberless medieval sieges. The lines of countervallation, the successful sapping operation, appear, for example, in the tactics of Philip Augustus : the besiegers' brick tower is met again in William Rufus' timber castle at Bamburgh : the engines of war and the protected penthouses are commonplaces of medieval warfare.

The bare record of the Anglo-Saxon Chronicle throws little light to speak of upon the strategy or military skill of the Danes. Nor does the lyric form of the songs which celebrate the fight at Brunanburh and the battle of Maldon allow of that definiteness of detail which the student requires. More definite, although not unencumbered by rhetoric, is the account which Abbo, the monk of Saint-Germain-des-Prés, gives of the siege of Paris by the Northmen in 885-6.[1] The city of those days was confined to the isle still known as La Cité, and was united to its suburbs on the mainland by two bridges, where now are the Pont-au-Change and the Petit-Pont. The approach to each bridge was guarded, on the mainland, by a tower or *tête-du-pont*. The attack of the Normans was directed against the northern tower, the construction of which had not been finished. It is curious to notice how they concentrated themselves on single points in the defence, neglecting the prime necessity of closing all lines of communication to the defenders. They came up to the tower with their ships, which were seven hundred in number, not counting sailless boats, battered it with their engines, and hurled darts at its defenders. The tower was shaken, but its foundations stood firm : where the walls threatened to give, they were repaired with planks of timber, and the tower was raised by these wooden additions during a night to one and a half times its former height. At daybreak the Northmen again began the attack. The air, says Abbo, was full of arrows and stones flung from slings and from the *ballistae* or hurling machines. During the day the heightened tower showed signs of succumbing to the enemy's fire and their mining efforts. Eudes, the brave defender of the town, poured down a mixture of burning oil, wax, and pitch, which quenched the enthusiasm of the besiegers, and cost them three hundred men. On the third day, the Northmen established their land camp on the northern bank of the river, near the church of Saint-Germain-l'Auxerrois. The camp was probably a *geweorc* such as they wrought by the Thames or the Ouse, but it was girt, not with an earthen rampart, but with walls of clay mingled with stone. From this centre they cruelly ravaged the surrounding country during the remainder of the siege. Having thus established their base of operations, they returned to the attack of the tower. Their devices were the common devices of Roman warfare, which naturally would recommend themselves to the assailants of the dying Roman civilisation. We hear of the three great battering rams which they prepared, and moved up against the walls

[1] A detailed account of this siege is given by Oman, *Art of War*, pp. 140-7.

under the shelter of wooden penthouses on wheels, of the
bores brought up to undermine the tower by men moving under
wicker mantlets covered with raw hides, of the *mangana* or
stone-throwing machines used by the defenders, and of the forked
beams let down from the tower to catch the heads of the battering-rams and render them powerless.   Some of the Northmen
worked at filling up the ditches with whatever came to hand,
earth, leaves, straw, meadow grass, cattle, even the bodies of
captives.   Still the city held out, and Eudes managed to slip
through the enemy's lines and reach Charles the Fat with a
request for relief.   On his return the Northmen tried to intercept
him : he got back safely into Paris, while a relieving force
attacked the enemy and drove them back on their ships.   When
Charles the Fat arrived he established his camp on the southern
slopes of Montmartre ; but he was content, after a general attack
upon the city had failed, to let the Northmen go, taking with
them an indemnity of seven hundred pounds, and promising to
leave the kingdom in March.   They, however, made an attempt
to reach the upper Seine in boats, as the larger vessels could
not clear the bridges, and so proceed to pillage Burgundy.
Their purpose was discovered : the defenders of Paris launched
arrows at them from the walls, and a chance dart killed their
pilot.   For a time their onward course was checked, but a series
of such assaults could not be sustained by the French.   Eudes,
elected king, neglected the conflict, and gave words for deeds.
"Their barks," says Abbo, "were in crowds on all the rivers of
Gaul."   He ends his poem with a call to France to give proof
once more of those forces which she had used in the past to
conquer kingdoms more powerful than herself.   "Three vices,"
he cries, "are causes of thy ruin : pride, the shameful love of
pleasures, the vain lust of gorgeous apparel."   The same words
might have been said to the English a hundred and twenty-five
years later, when Swegen and Thurkill were gripping London
between their two armies.

A short passage in the Anglo-Saxon Chronicle affords some
help to the question of Danish strategy.   London bridge, like the
two bridges of Paris, was an obstacle to the long Danish ships
with their sails.   In 1016, however, the Danes managed to drag
their ships round the south side of the bridge, apparently by
making a ditch on that side of the river.   They then proceeded
to make entrenchments about the city, their headquarters being
thus removed above bridge.   There is no reason to doubt that
the London which they thus beset was a stone-walled city, the
Roman Londinium which Alfred had repaired.   So was Paris,
and so were a large number of the towns of France, whose walls

had been set in repair by their bishops or lay lords. We read of Saint Didier, bishop of Cahors 630-55, that he "enlarged, built, and made strong Cahors with abundant labour, and a notable work of defence, fortifying gates and towers with a girdle of walls compacted of squared stones." In the next century the Saracen invaders of southern France restored the Roman walls of Narbonne, and checked the advance of Charles Martel into Spain.[1] But for the many instances in which the fortifications of Roman cities in France played a part in the warfare of this troubled epoch, there are few in England. The *burhs* of the Danish wars were, with the exception of London, Towcester, Colchester, and a few more, not stone-walled cities of Roman foundation, such as those which in France were the natural prey of the Norman marauders, but villages or small towns which had grown into existence for the most part since the Saxon conquest, and owed their strength to walls of timber. In France military art, as regards both fortification and siege-craft, was altogether on a higher plane. The break of continuity caused by the extinction of Roman civilisation in England produced a stage in the development of attack and defence to which contemporary French history affords no parallel. It is not till a later period that the finished methods employed by both sides in the siege of Paris were used in English warfare.

The cases hitherto quoted refer to sieges of towns ; and, as we have seen, the castle or private fortress which plays so prominent a part in medieval strategy was the result of the growth of the feudal system, and takes its place in history at a comparatively late period. A fortified town of Roman origin possessed its *arx* or citadel : this was, as it were, the keep of the walled enclosure, to which the defenders could retire if the outer defences of the town were taken. A castle, however, was a distinct enclosure, which frequently occupied a portion of the area of a walled town, but had its own outer lines of defence before the keep could be reached. The Norman conquerors of England, regarding the castle as the main seat of defence and object of attack, directed their attention to its fortification ; and thus the defence of the town or village in or near which the castle stood became of secondary interest. We usually find that, where a castle forms part of the defences of an English walled town, the castle has been surrounded with a wall and provided with its necessary defences before a wall has been built round the town in place of the earlier palisade. In spite, however, of this change in the nature of the besieged stronghold,

---

[1] Enlart, ii. 413, 414.

the object of attack was still a fortified enclosure. The methods of siege developed along the old lines ; and the defences applied to the castle were those which, on a more extended scale, were applicable to the town.

The warfare of the eleventh and twelfth centuries was to a great extent a succession of sieges of castles, by direct attack or by blockade. In 1083 William the Conqueror, besieging Hubert of Maine in the castle of Ste-Suzanne, did not venture to attack the wooded precipice on which the castle stood, but entrenched his army within earthworks in a neighbouring valley. The blockade lasted three years, and the advantage lay much on the side of Hubert, so that eventually the Norman army, after a desperate attack had failed, withdrew.[1] The chief feature of the blockade was the construction of an opposition castle,[2] a method employed upon more than one occasion by William II., who, in 1088, compelled Odo to surrender Rochester castle by making two *castella* upon his lines of communication.[3] In 1095 William II. besieged Robert Mowbray in Bamburgh castle. The great rock, with its girdle of sea and marsh, did not lend itself to direct attack, and William compelled its surrender by building a "new fortress," which took the form of a timber castle, probably of the ordinary mount-and-bailey type, and was nicknamed Malvoisin, the "ill neighbour."[4] From this particular instance, the name of *malvoisin* has been applied generally, without sufficient reason, to the wooden towers which were sometimes constructed to shelter a besieging force. As a matter of fact, Malvoisin was merely one of many nicknames which were given, in individual cases, to such besiegers' castles,[5] and was no more a generic term than is Château-Gaillard.

Until the end of the eleventh century, when the first Crusade taught western warriors the use of more advanced siege-engines, the methods of attack upon a castle seem to have been of a very simple description. Earthworks defended by timber could be gained by a rush and hand-to-hand fighting; while fire would always be fatal to a wooden stronghold ill provided against it. The Bayeux tapestry shows us none of those siege-machines which were employed more and more frequently against stone

---

[1] Ord. Vit., vii. 10.

[2] *Ibid.* "Rex itaque quoddam municipium in valle Beugici construxit ibique magnam militum copiam ad arcendum hostem constituit."

[3] *Ibid.*, viii. 2.

[4] *Ibid.*, viii. 23 ; Roger of Wendover.

[5] Thus Henry I., in his wars with Louis VI., conducted one blockade by building two castles, which the enemy called derisively Malassis and Gête-aux-Lièvres (Ord. Vit., xii. 1). So also (*ibid.*, xii. 22) his castle of Mâte-Putain near Rouen. Many other instances might be named.

castles during the next century ; and, although the Conqueror's army seem to have employed an elementary form of stone-throwing machine, handled, like the later cross-bow, by individual soldiers, and other devices more familiar in later times,[1] such machines can hardly have been common.   It was, no doubt, their growing frequency at the beginning of the twelfth century which made stone walls imperative for the protection of a castle. We have seen *ballistae* and other siege-engines of Roman origin used by the Northmen at the great siege of Paris in 885 ; but such engines were certainly not in common use in western Europe before the period of direct contact with Byzantine civilisation.   Ordericus Vitalis mentions the construction of such machines, a " belfry " on wheels and devices for hurling large stones, by Robert of Bellême's engineer at Bréval in 1093, as though they were a novelty, and says of the engineer himself that his sagacious ingenuity had been of profit to the Christians at the siege of Jerusalem.[2]

Suger's detailed account of the attack made by Louis VI. upon the castle of Le Puiset in 1111 may be taken as a fair description of the methods employed by the besiegers and defenders of an ordinary castle of earthwork and timber.   The king brought numerous *ballistae* to the attack, but we have no indication as to their precise nature : the main weapons employed were the bow, sword, and shield.   The besieged came out of the castle to meet the king ; but, amid a hail of arrows from both sides, were driven back through the main gateway, which was possibly, as at Tickhill,[3] the only stone defence of the enclosure. From the rampart of their stronghold, they hurled down wooden planks and stakes upon the king's knights.   The besiegers, throwing away their broken shields, made use of the missiles to protect themselves and force the gateway.   Carts laden with dry wood smeared with fat were brought up to the doors, and a struggle took place, the royalists trying to set the wood on fire, the defenders · trying to put the fire out.   Meanwhile Theobald of Chartres made an attack on the castle from another quarter, attempting to climb the steep scarp of the bailey.   His followers, however, were too hasty : many fell back into the ditch, while others were surprised and killed by horsemen of

---

[1] Oman, *Art of War*, pp. 135, 139 : his authority is Guy of Amiens, whose poetical rhetoric, however, may not be altogether accurate in description.

[2] Ord. Vit., viii. 24.   *Cf.* viii. 16, where Robert of Normandy, another great Crusader, besieging Courcy-sur-Dives in 1091, caused a great wooden tower or belfry (*berfredum*) to be built, which was burned by the defenders. Robert of Bellême was also present at this siege.

[3] See below, p. 99.

the enemy, who galloped round the defences of the castle to keep out intruders. The royalists had almost given up hope, when a priest, bare-headed and holding before him a piece of wood as an extemporised mantlet, reached the palisade, and began to tear away the planks which covered the spaces between the uprights. He was soon joined by others, who cut away the palisade with axes and iron tools. The royal army poured into the castle, and the defenders, taken between the entering force and Theobald's men, retired into the timber tower on the mount, but surrendered in fear. The king burned the castle, but spared the donjon.[1]

The assault upon a stone castle or walled town was conducted by direct attempts upon the walls themselves, for which movable machines were necessary, and by throwing stones or inflammable materials into the besieged enclosure from stationary machines. The chief engine used directly against the walls was the battering-ram, an enormous pole, furnished with an iron head. Hung by chains within a wooden framework placed on wheels, it was brought up to the wall, and driven against it again and again. The men who worked the ram were protected by a pent-house with a rounded or gabled top, called the "tortoise" (*testudo*), which covered the machine and its framework. The roof of the "tortoise" was made very solidly, to resist missiles thrown from the ramparts, and the whole was covered with raw hides or some other incombustible material, as a precaution against fire thrown by the defenders (69).[2]

While the ram delivered its blows upon the face of the wall, sappers and miners, sheltered by a smaller pent-house, known as the "mouse," "cat," or "sow," made their attack upon the foundations with the bore (*terebra*), a heavy pole with a sharp iron head, which slowly broke up the stonework and hollowed out a cavity at the foundation of the walls (70). This work was assisted by sappers, who, advancing to the wall beneath the shelter of inclined frames of timber or wicker-work, known as mantlets, which they wheeled in front of them, hacked away the stonework with picks. When a sufficient hollow had been made, the miners underpinned the wall with logs, set fire to them, and retired. This device was constantly used throughout the middle ages to effect a breach, and was successful at Château-Gaillard

---

[1] Suger, *Gesta Ludovici Grossi* (ed. Molinier, pp. 63-66).
[2] Pent-houses were sometimes elaborately defended. Thus Joinville describes the large "cats" made by St Louis' engineers to protect the soldiers who were making a causeway across an arm of the Nile near Mansurah (1249-50). These had towers at either end, with covered guard-houses behind the towers, and were called *chats-châteaux*.

Battering-ram protected by pent-house and mantlets

in 1204,[1] and on other occasions; but it obviously must have taken much time, and must often have failed of its purpose.

Before, however, the movable engines could be brought to play upon the stonework, it was necessary to fill up the ditch in front of the walls. This work was done by soldiers, who, under the protection of mantlets, flung into the ditch all the loose material on which they could lay hands. When the Danes used their battering-rams against the northern *tête-du-pont* at Paris, the first thing which they attempted to do was to fill the ditch, using even the dead bodies of their captives when other material failed.[2] At Jerusalem in 1099, before Raymond of Toulouse could bring up his "timber castle"[3] to the walls, a deep natural hollow had to be filled. The work took three days and nights: every man who put three stones into the hollow was promised a penny.[4] Philip Augustus in February 1203-4 began

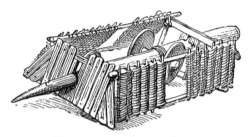

his operations upon Château-Gaillard by filling the ditch between the outer ward and his lines, while his catapults played upon the masonry from a distance and protected the workers between them and the wall.[5]

Bore protected by mantlets

While the battering-ram, the bore, and the mine threatened the stability of the walls, parties of the besiegers attempted to force an entry into the stronghold. The simple method of bringing up fuel to the main gateway, and burning down the door, was frustrated, in process of time, by greater attention to the defences of the gateway, and the reinforcement of its doors by herses or portcullises.[6] Scaling-

---

[1] See the account of the sieges of Boves and Château-Gaillard by Guillaume le Breton, *Philippis*, books ii. and vii. At the siege of Zara in the fourth Crusade, after five days of fruitless stone-throwing, the Crusaders began to undermine a tower which led to the surrender of the city (Villehardouin).

[2] Abbo: see the account of the siege of Paris above.

[3] Ord. Vit., ix. 15: "Machinam, quam ligneum possumus vocitare castellum." It was strictly a belfry (see below).

[4] *Ibid.*

[5] *Cf.* the account of the operations at the siege of Marseilles (Cæsar, *De Bell. Civ.*, ii. 11): "Musculus ex turri latericia a nostris telis tormentisque defenditur."

[6] The *porte-coulis* is literally a sliding door. Its outer bars fitted into grooves in the walls on either side. See pp. 227, 229.

ladders were moved up against the walls: the daring spirits who climbed these drew up with them other ladders, by which they could descend into the enclosure. Another method of scaling walls was by the movable "belfry," a tower of several stories, in each of which a number of men could be sheltered. The floor of the uppermost stage of the tower was approximately on a level with the top of the ramparts, and a drawbridge thrown out from it, when it was wheeled close to the wall, formed a passage for the besiegers. The occupants of the lower stages could mount by stairs to the top floor, and thus a considerable body of men could come to close quarters with the defenders (72).[1] These movable towers could be quickly constructed, where wood of sufficient scantling was procurable. Philip's belfries at Château-Gaillard were composed of tree-trunks, untouched by the plane: all that the carpenters had done to smooth them was to cut off the branches with an axe.[2] In early instances of the employment of such towers, they seem to have been chiefly used for bringing the small artillery of the besiegers close to the walls. At Marrah in 1098, the Crusader Raymond of Toulouse had a very lofty wooden "belfry," of a height equal to that of the towers on the town wall, made upon four wheels. Huge stones were hurled and arrows shot from it upon the defenders of the walls, and grappling-irons were thrust out to catch unwary persons with their hooks. The walls were eventually climbed by scaling ladders of the ordinary kind: if there was a drawbridge in connection with the machine, it does not seem to have been used.[3] Antioch, earlier in the same year, was entered by scaling ladders.[4] The belfry used by Henry I. at Pontaudemer in 1123 was a movable tower, but was not used for purposes of scaling. It was actually 24 feet higher than the rampart: bow-men and arbalasters directed their arrows and bolts from it upon the defenders, while others threw stones down from it.[5] Not even at Château-Gaillard is there much reason to suppose that Philip used his belfries to scale the walls. The miners and catapults did the chief work, by opening breaches in the masonry of the outer and inner wards: the middle ward alone was gained by an escalade, and this was effected by a small body of men, who

---

[1] Vitruvius, *De Architectura*, x. 13, § 3, mentions among Roman scaling-machines, an inclined plane, "ascendentem machinam qua ad murum plano pede transitus esse posset."

[2] Guillaume le Breton, *Philippis*, book vii. This poem is an important source of information for the wars of Philip Augustus, and for the siege of Château-Gaillard in particular.

[3] Ord. Vit., ix. 13.

[4] *Ibid.*, ix. 11.

[5] *Ibid.*, xii. 36.

Besiegers scaling walls from movable belfry

climbed through unguarded openings in the substructure of the chapel, and so were able to unbar the gates of the ward to the main body of the army.

The great siege-engines, capable of shooting stones or bolts, which were often heated red-hot in an oven before delivery, from a considerable distance, did their work from the background. The men who looked after them were protected by a palisade, placed in front of the engines; this was the case with Philip's engineers at Château-Gaillard. These machines are often indiscriminately called "stone-throwers" (*petrariae, pierrières*) or catapults; and accounts of them differ very considerably. It is clear that, in Roman and Byzantine warfare, the two main types of engine were the stone-throwing machine, known later as the mangon or mangonel, and the machine for shooting javelins, known as *ballista*.[1] The first consisted of an upright flexible beam between two solid upright posts. Cords were stretched from post to post and wound round the beam. The beam was then drawn back with the aid of winches and a stone placed in a hollow in its head; it was then suddenly let go, so that the twisted cords slackened, and the stone flew towards its mark, describing a high ellipse in its flight. The force by which the *ballista* was worked, depended, not on twisted cords, but on the tension of the cord which joined the two extremities of a great bow, and was attached to the movable grooved piece in which the javelin was placed. The tension released, the javelin was discharged. While the *ballista* could be discharged with a definite aim, the aim of the stone-throwing machine could be only general, and its chief use was to cast stones which, by their elliptic flight, dropped inside the walls of the besieged place.[2]

The *ballista*, which was simply a huge bow, capable of shooting enormous bolts by the tension of a horizontal cord, was developed upon a small scale into the cross-bow or arbalast, which could be carried and managed by one man. The cross-bow was invented, or at any rate re-invented, in northern Europe towards the end

---

[1] This is the usual distinction. But the use of the names varies. In Vitruvius (*op. cit.*, x. 10, 11) the *catapulta* or *scorpio* is a machine for shooting arrows, while the *ballista* is used for throwing stones. The pointed stakes at the siege of Marseilles (Cæsar, *De Bell. Civ.*, ii. 2) were shot from *ballistae*. Vitruvius indicates several methods of working the *ballista* by torsion: "aliae enim vectibus et suculis (levers and winches), nonnullae polyspastis (pulleys), aliae ergatis (windlasses), quaedam etiam tympanorum (wheels) torquentur rationibus."

[2] For the injuries inflicted by stone-throwing machines, see Villehardouin's mention of the wounding of Guillaume de Champlitte at Constantinople, and of Pierre de Bracieux at Adrianople.

Engine for shooting javelins

of the eleventh century; it was employed in the first Crusade, and struck the Byzantines as a novelty.[1] The development of the larger engines seems to have proceeded with a view to stone-throwing, and combinations of the machines mentioned above may have been employed for this purpose.[2] Viollet-le-Duc, in his elaborate reconstructions of siege-machines, shows, for example, a mangon with a central upright post, working on a pivot, in a slot near the top of which is fixed a javelin. This post is strengthened by two diagonal beams fixed to the

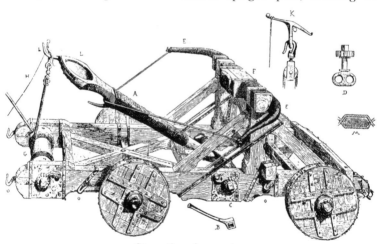

Stone-throwing engine

[1] Oman, *op. cit.*, 139, quotes Anna Comnena to this effect.
[2] Stone-throwing engines and *ballistae* alike were employed by the Saracens at Mansurah (1250), for hurling Greek fire at the towers constructed by St Louis to protect his causeway-makers (Joinville).

back of the framework, which moves on the same pivot, at the foot of the machine. Between these the flexible beam which propels the javelin is fastened by a cord working through a pulley to a winch turned by a man, and a bundle of cords is tightly twisted round the central post and the beam (74). He also shows a large stone-throwing engine on a wheeled

Trébuchet or Slinging machine

carriage, which, in addition to an apparatus of twisted cords held in place by a system of ratchet wheels, and bound round the movable beam, has a cord stretched round the back of the beam, and connected with two huge springs forming a bow. The centre of the bow is a massive upright framework of wood, which acts as a buffer to the beam, when it is allowed to fly

forward and discharge the stone (74). Minute as these reconstructions are, they seem to improve upon the data supplied
by medieval writers and the pictures in MSS. Guillaume le
Breton, the panegyrist of Philip Augustus, describes the stone-
throwing machine used at the siege of Boves in 1185, as a great
sling worked by several men, which threw immense rocks of
great weight. The beam to which the projectile was attached
worked on an axis, and was dragged backwards to the ground
with ropes, and then set free.

This description suggests that the beam, balanced on an
axis, and needing several people to attend to the discharge at
one end, was worked by a counterpoise at the other. This was
the case with the developed slinging machine, known as *trébuchet*.

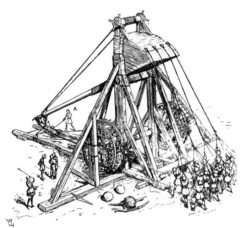

Trébuchet with ropes attached to counterpoise

A pole, working on a
pivot between two
upright stands, was
weighted at one end
with a heavy wooden
chest, filled with earth,
which kept the pole,
when not in use, in a
vertical position. To
the other end was at-
tached a long sling,
capable of containing
large stones. When
the tension of the ropes
which dragged the pole
backwards and lifted
the counterpoise was
released, the counter-
poise fell heavily,
bringing the pole abruptly back into position, and the sling,
describing a circle in the air, let fly the stone when it reached
the summit of the arc (75). Variations of this form of catapult,
which became general in the thirteenth century, are found (76);
the machine known as *cabulus* which Philip Augustus used with
excellent effect against the strong inner wall of Château-Gaillard,
was possibly worked upon the principle of counterpoise.

Against these modes and machines of attack the defenders of
a castle had to contend. The obvious means of defence was to
oppose to the enemy a thickness of wall which would be proof
against the blows of the ram or the slow labour of the pick.
But even the very strong inner wall at Château-Gaillard, which
was constructed with the special object of resisting these engines,

yielded to the miners, reinforced by the great slinging machine. In this instance the castle had undergone a long blockade; its communications had been cut off some months beforehand; and the garrison was greatly reduced in numbers. The lesson of the siege was that against a persistent and well-conducted blockade mere passive strength was of little avail. Here, too, the defenders, driven back from one bailey to another, seem to have renounced the opportunity of final shelter afforded them by the keep, and to have made an attempt to evacuate the castle by a postern before they fell into the hands of the enemy.

Château-Gaillard, however, and the castles of its period will

Aigues-Mortes

be discussed in detail in the sequel. At present, we are concerned with the direct methods employed to meet the attack of siege-engines and attempts at escalade. Against the great catapults the besieged were practically powerless. The use of such machines upon the walls themselves was as dangerous to the stability of the masonry as their use by the enemy, and hastened the chance of a breach: they could not be employed from the interior of the enclosure, without endangering the defenders on the rampart.[1] The summit of the rectangular

---

[1] Thus, in the first siege of Constantinople by the Crusaders (1203), Villehardouin emphasises the number of siege-machines used by the

keep of the twelfth century was never constructed as a platform
for artillery : here, again, engineers probably feared the effect
of the constant vibration upon a flat wooden roof, and were
content to conceal their ridged roofs within high ramparts.   The
main arm of defence which could be employed by the defenders
was the cross-bow.   Their superior position upon the ramparts
enabled them to throw down stones and burning material upon

Carcassonne

the assailants engaged at the foot of the wall, and the wheeled
belfries formed a direct target for their arrows.   The ram could

besiegers upon shipboard and on land, but gives no account of their use
by the defenders.   They were employed, however, by the defence, as we
have seen at Marseilles ; see also Chapter I. above, for possible traces of
their use in the stations of the Roman wall.   A special platform might in
some cases be constructed for them and wheeled to the back of the rampart-
walk.

also be paralysed by letting down grappling-irons or beams with forked heads, which gripped and disabled it ; or sacks of wool or earth could be lowered to meet its strokes.   The assailants, however, worked under their defences of pent-houses and mantlets, the solid tops and sloping surfaces of which were specially devised against the shock of stones and arrows ; while, as we have seen, their coverings were so protected that it was difficult for them to catch fire.

The first improvements in defence, designed to meet an improved attack, consisted in the protection of the ramparts. Behind the outer parapet of the wall was the rampart-walk, a level path along the top of the wall, which was sometimes protected by a parapet in the rear. From an early date in stone fortification, it was customary to break the upper portion of the parapet at intervals by openings called crenellations, through which it was possible for an archer to command a limited part of the field at right angles to the wall.[1] The crenellations, however, were narrow compared with the unbroken parapets between them, and, even in advanced examples of fortification like the ramparts of Aigues-Mortes (77) and Carcassonne (78), these unbroken pieces are still very broad, although they are pierced by arrow-slits. Even

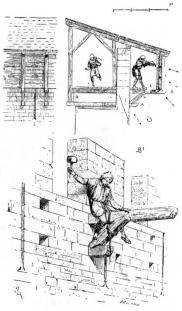

Parapet defended by hoarding, showing elevation, section through *hourd* and *coursière*, and method of construction

allowing for an arrow-slit between each crenellation, the foot of the wall could not be commanded from behind the parapet.   In time of siege, then, it became customary to supply the walls with projecting wooden galleries, known as hoardings or brattices (*hourds, bretèches*), which could be entered through the crenellations.   The joists of the flooring passed through holes at the foot

---

[1] Such crenellations are indicated even in the timber defences at Alesia and Trebonius' second rampart at Marseilles.   They are familiar features of oriental fortification, *e.g.*, of the great wall of China or the walls and gates of Delhi.

of the parapet, and were often common to the outer gallery and an inner gallery (*coursière*) covering the rampart-walk. Both galleries had a common roof.[1]   In the floor of the outer gallery, between the joists, were holes, through which missiles could be directed upon the besiegers at the foot of the wall ; while slits in

Laval

the outer face were still available for straight firing.   The defenders of the ramparts were thus able to work under shelter, with some command both of the field and the foot of the wall.   The

[1] This roof was sometimes gabled, the timbers, as in the donjon at Coucy, following and resting on the slope of the coping of the parapet.

defensive advantages of this scheme are obvious ; but the galleries were also liable, although the usual precautions for their covering were taken, to destruction by fire, whether from arrows tipped with burning tow, or the more formidable red-hot stones flung by catapults. In any case, the catapults were a serious menace to their solidity.

The donjon and the towers of the *enceinte* were also bratticed at the rampart-level.[1] Indications of this practice are common

Coucy ; parapet of donjon

in military architecture abroad. The cylindrical donjon of Laval (80), a work of the twelfth century, is covered with hoarding which is supposed to be contemporary with the tower. The stone corbels which carried the hoarding of the great thirteenth-century tower of Coucy remain ; and a row of plain arches pierced in the tall parapet show how the gallery was entered

[1] Sometimes, as at Constantinople in 1204 (Villehardouin), towers were heightened by the addition of one or more stages of wood. *Cf.* the heightening of the unfinished *tête-du-pont* at Paris in 885-6.

from the roof (81). The somewhat earlier round tower at Rouen was restored by Viollet-le-Duc on the lines of Coucy, with a conical roof and hoarding. The inner wall at Carcassonne and the curtain of Loches, among other examples, keep the holes in which the joists of the hoarding were fixed ; and the walls of Nuremberg are still covered with inner galleries or *coursières*. The practice of supplementing stone walls with timber defences lasted till a late period ; but, even before the end of the twelfth century, corbelled-out parapets with machicolations appeared in isolated instances. In subsequent chapters we shall see how military masons and engineers applied their architectural skill to meet the problems which siege-engines of greater strength and tactics more finished than those of the past forced upon them. We have now to deal with earlier efforts, which we have to some degree anticipated.

CHAPTER V

THE BEGINNING OF THE STONE CASTLE

IN Domesday Book some fifty castles are mentioned by name or implication; and the number was largely increased during the next hundred years. In view, however, of the large number of temporary private strongholds which came into being during the twelfth century, it is difficult to estimate the number of permanent castles until, in the later part of the century, Henry II. regulated and restrained the efforts of private owners to guard their property with fortresses. The castles included in Domesday do not represent the whole number which existed at that period; and of such important castles as Colchester and Exeter, which we know to have been founded before 1086, there is no mention. To estimate the strategic plan which governed the foundation of castles at its full value, we must therefore turn for a moment to the later period at which the defence of England by a connected system of these strongholds had been more thoroughly achieved. Here also, it is not altogether easy, in view of the destruction of older castles by Henry II., and the foundation of new ones at a later epoch, to estimate the exact state of the castles of England at the end of the twelfth century.[1] But, taking one special district, we may at least gain an approximate notion of its lines of defence as they existed about the year 1200. This is the north-eastern district of England, containing the main strategic approach to Scotland, and crossed by the rivers which descend eastwards to the sea. This was the scene of the rebellion of the Mowbrays and the invasion of William the Lion in 1174, in consequence of which four important castles at least, those of Kinnard's Ferry on the lower Trent, Thirsk and Northallerton in the vale of Mowbray, and Kirkby Malzeard, on the highlands above the right bank of the Ure, were demolished.[2]

---

[1] Clark, i. 68-120, gives an elaborate list of castles in England and Wales at this date. A large number, however, of those which he mentions, had been already destroyed; and many were of later foundation.
[2] Accounts of this rebellion are given by Benedict of Peterborough and Roger of Hoveden.

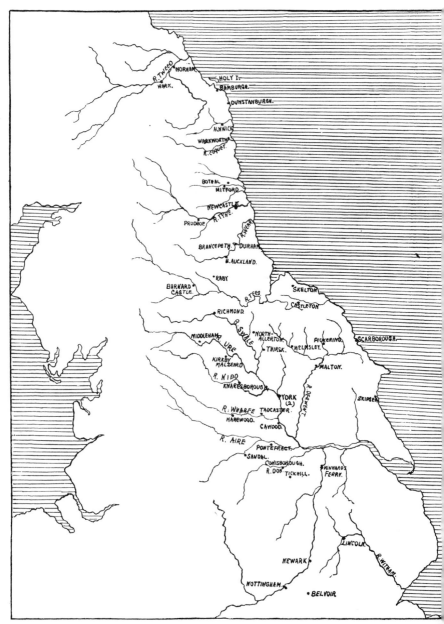

Map of principal castles in north-east England

The chief castles of this district will be found to guard the line of the rivers. On the Trent were Nottingham, on the north bank, and the bishop of Lincoln's castle of Newark,[1] on the south; while the greater part of the lower valley of the river was commanded at some distance by the strongly-placed castles of Belvoir and Lincoln. On the borders of Nottinghamshire and Yorkshire, Tickhill[2] stood in advance of the Don, while the narrow passage of the Don, five miles west of Doncaster, was guarded by Conisbrough. These castles defended the approach from the high land on the west; the marshy country north and east of Doncaster, towards the Humber, although it often proved a refuge for freebooters, needed no permanent garrison. South of the Calder, opposite Wakefield, stood Sandal. To the east, below the junction of the Calder and the Aire, was Pontefract, in a position of great strength and importance.[3] There was no great castle on the Wharfe, although Harewood guarded the south bank of the river between Otley and Tadcaster, and at Tadcaster itself there was a castle, of which little is known; Cawood castle was simply a manor-house of the archbishops of York.[4] On the Ouse, almost in the centre of the shire, were the two castles of York, at the head of the tideway. Knaresborough was west of York, on the north bank of the Nidd. Each of the dales of the North Riding had its strong castle. In Wensleydale was Middleham, south of the Ure. Richmond, from its cliff at the mouth of Swaledale, commanded a vast tract of country, reaching to the Hambleton hills and the forest of Galtres, north of York. Barnard Castle stood in a strong position on the Durham bank of the Tees. The castles of the eastern part of the North Riding were Skelton and Castleton, both in Cleveland, and belonging to the house of Bruce. Helmsley stood at the entrance of Ryedale; Pickering and Malton were on the Derwent, and Scarborough guarded the coast. South of Scarborough, in the East Riding, the one castle of importance at this date was Skipsea, on the low coast-

---

[1] Nottingham was a foundation of the Conqueror: Newark was not founded until after 1123.

[2] Ord. Vit., xi. 2, mentions the capture of the castle of Blyth (Blida castrum) by Henry I. from Robert de Bellême. By this Tickhill is probably meant. It is four miles from Blyth, where was a Benedictine priory founded by Roger de Busli, the first Norman lord of Tickhill, and granted by him to the priory of Ste-Trinité-du-Mont at Rouen. Ordericus, who, as a monk of a Norman abbey, was familiar with the name of Blyth priory, may have supposed the castle of Roger de Busli to have been at Blyth.

[3] See Rymer, *Fœdera* (Rec. Com., 1816), vol. i. pt. i. p. 429: "castrum de Pontefracto, quod est quasi clavis in comitatu Eborum."

[4] The remains are chiefly of the second quarter of the fifteenth century; but it was a residence of the archbishops as early as the twelfth century.

line of Holderness, between Flamborough and Spurn heads. Returning to the border of Durham, and crossing the Tees, we find Brancepeth and Durham on the Wear. On the south bank of the Tyne was Prudhoe in Northumberland: north of the Tyne was the great fortress of Newcastle. Most of the castles and small strongholds of Northumberland were the growth of a later age. The principal castles at this period were Mitford on the Wansbeck, Warkworth on the Coquet, Alnwick on the Alne, Wark and Norham on the Tweed, and Bamburgh and Holy Island, castles on the seaboard. This list might be

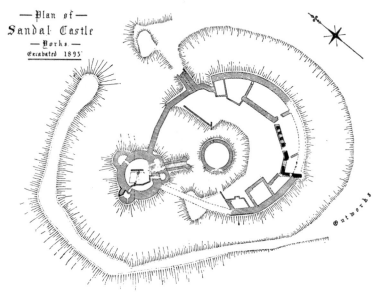

Sandal Castle; Plan

extended, but the most important fortresses east of the Pennine chain are included in it, and from it the strategic geography of this important district can be readily recognised. Of the thirty-four castles in this list, ten, including the gateway-tower at Newark, had rectangular tower-keeps, of which nine remain; Conisbrough and Barnard Castle (87) had cylindrical tower-keeps. Of the rest, in most cases, as at Sandal (86), the mounts remain, and in a few instances, as at Skipsea, there are remains of a shell-keep. The shell-keeps of Lincoln and Pickering are still excellent examples of their type. The masonry at York, Pontefract, and Knaresborough belongs to a later period; and in almost all instances, where masonry remains, it bears trace of substantial later additions.

It will be noticed that castles which guarded passes through hilly districts were generally placed, like Middleham and Richmond, in comparatively open country at the foot of the pass. This was the case with Welsh castles like Brecon and Llandovery, or the tower of Dolbadarn, below the pass of Llanberis. The isolated position at the head of a pass was not easily victualled, nor was it so useful as the situation on more open ground, from which, as at Brecon or Middleham, a larger extent of mountain country could be commanded. Trecastle (44), at the top of the pass between Brecon and

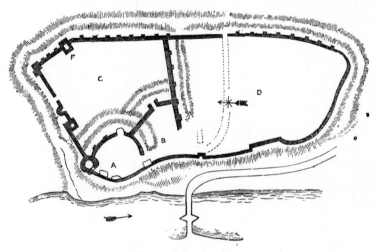

Barnard Castle ; Plan

Llandovery, has already been mentioned as a site which was probably abandoned early : the tract which it commanded is limited compared with that within reach of Brecon, the point towards which all the valleys of the neighbourhood converge.

In places where a castle formed part of the defences of a walled town, it was usually placed upon the line of the wall, so that the wall formed for some distance part of its curtain. This can be well seen at Lincoln, where the castle occupied the south-west angle of the older Roman city. The castle of Ludlow is in the north-west angle of the town, the wall of which joined it on its north face and at its south-west corner. At Carlisle the castle filled up an angle of the town, the town walls meeting its south curtain at either end. In such cases, the castle, while defending the town, was also protected from it by a ditch, across which a passage was furnished by a draw-bridge. The castle of Bristol stood upon the isthmus, east of the town, between the streams of the Avon and Frome, and, in this strong position, was joined by the city wall at either extremity of its west side. In 1313, when the citizens were in rebellion, they cut off the castle from the city by building a new wall on that side.[1] In the case of Bristol, the building of the castle made some alterations in the town wall necessary, as time went on, but, from the beginning, the castle occupied its place in the regular *enceinte*. If, at York, the castles were at first built, as seems to be the case, outside the defences of the town, the circuit was soon extended to include the castle, at any rate, upon the right bank of the river. Although the castle of South-ampton is almost entirely gone, the points of junction of its curtains with the west wall of the town are quite clear. Similarly, the position of castles such as Shrewsbury, Leicester, and Nottingham, or close to the *enceinte* of the town, can be traced, although little is left of the walls. In foreign walled towns like Angers or Laval, the castle formed, as in England, a portion of the outer defences. In later castles like Carnarvon and Conway, the same relation to the plan of the town was preserved. There are exceptions, of which the chief is the Tower of London, within the Roman, but outside the medieval city wall. Chepstow is also outside the town, between which and the castle is a deep ravine: but in this case the town was of a growth subsequent to the foundation of the castle. A distinction must be drawn between castles founded in connection with fortified towns, in which the castle formed part of a general scheme of defence, as at Bristol and Oxford, and castles under the protection of which towns, like Chepstow, grew up, and were subsequently fortified. A good example of this latter class is Newcastle, in which the relations of town and castle are exactly opposite to those at Chepstow. When the castle was founded by the Conqueror, the place, once garrisoned by the Romans, and for a time inhabited by a colony of English monks, was probably an inconsiderable village. The town which grew up on the site took its name from the castle, and was walled in the thirteenth and fourteenth centuries. The walls, however, were brought down to the banks of the Tyne at some distance east and west of the castle, which was thus contained entirely within their circuit. At Norwich, a place of no great importance before the Conquest, the castle is also entirely within the line of the old

[1] A. Harvey, *Bristol* (Ancient Cities), pp. 35, 116.

city wall.   One of the best examples of the connection between a walled town and a castle is at Launceston, where the borough of Dunheved grew up within a narrow area which was virtually the outer ward of the strong hill-fortress.

The establishment of a castle upon a permanent site was followed, sooner or later, by the building of stone fortifications. This work was often very gradual.   We have seen that even a castle so important as that of York retained part of its timber stockade as late as 1324.   This, however, was an exceptional case.   The walls and towers of medieval castles show, as might be expected, a considerable variety of masonry; but the epoch at which their fortification in stone became general may be said to be the third quarter of the twelfth century.   In 1155 Henry II. resumed castles and other royal property into his own hands, and ordered the destruction of the unlicensed castles which had risen during the civil wars of the previous reign.[1]   This step was followed unquestionably by much activity in strengthening the defences of the castles which were left.

At the same time, there are many substantial remains of stone buildings in castles earlier than this era.   Stone donjons or keeps were certainly exceptional in England before the reign of Henry II., although there are a few important examples of an earlier date.   It cannot be disputed, however, that a certain number of castles were provided with a stone curtain-wall[2] and other stone buildings not long after the Conquest.   Curtain-walls thus built would follow the line of the earthen bank surrounding the bailey, and take the place of the timber stockade. They were at first of the simplest form.   An edict of the council of Lillebonne in 1080 laid down the rule, so far as the Norman duchy was concerned, for constructing the defences of private castles; and, although the details refer primarily to the ordinary timber structure, they also have a bearing on the construction of early curtains of stone.   No ditch was to be deeper than the level from which earth could be thrown by the digger, without other help, to the soil above.   The stockade was to follow a course of straight lines, and to be without *propugnacula* and *alatoria—i.e.*, projecting towers and battlements, and rampart-walks or galleries.[3]

---

[1] Rob. de Monte, quoted by Stubbs, *Select Charters*, 8th ed., 1905, p. 128: "Rex Henricus coepit revocare in jus proprium urbes, castella, villas, quae ad coronam regni pertinebant, castella noviter facta destruendo."

[2] The curtain (Lat. *cortina*, Fr. *courtine*) is a general name for the wall enclosing a courtyard, and is thus applied to the wall round the castle enclosure.

[3] Martène, *Thesaurus Anecdotorum*, iv. 47, quoted by Enlart, ii. 418. From *alatorium* is derived the word *allure*, often employed as a technical term for a rampart-walk.

The earliest type of curtain-wall would be strictly in accordance with these rules—a strong wall of stone surrounding the bailey, and climbing the sides of the mount to join the defences of the donjon. We read of the destruction by Louis VI. of France of the stone fortification with which the house of the lord of Maule was surrounded;[1] and the edict already quoted applies to fortifications on level ground, and includes, not merely castles, but strong private houses, which might not necessarily follow the castle plan. The edict, however, proceeds to forbid altogether the construction by private persons of castles on rocks or islands. The reason of this is obvious. Such isolated strongholds might become, in the hands of private owners, a centre of rebellion against the suzerain. In 1083, Hubert of Maine held out successfully against the Conqueror in his rock castle of Ste-Suzanne (Mayenne) on the Erve, "inaccessible by reason of the rocks and the thickness of the surrounding vineyards."[2] William II. in 1095 besieged Robert Mowbray in his castle on the well-nigh impregnable rock of Bamburgh, with considerably better fortune.[3] Such rocks formed, as it were, natural mounts which made the construction of the ordinary mount-and-bailey castle upon them unnecessary. The hardness of the soil, moreover, made the construction of earthworks difficult or impossible. The natural method of defence would be to raise a stone wall which enclosed the stronghold.

Neither at Ste-Suzanne nor at Bamburgh (91) is there existing stonework earlier than the twelfth century. Of the castle of Saint-Céneri-le-Gérei (Orne), which we know to have been fortified with stone walls before the end of the eleventh century,[4] only indistinguishable masses of masonry remain to-day. On the other hand, there are a certain number of castles on rocky and isolated sites, the walls of which may be fairly attributed, in whole or part, to the later half of the eleventh century. The most important example is Richmond castle in Yorkshire (91), on a high promontory of rock above the Swale. The shape of the enclosure is triangular. The most conspicuous feature of the

---

[1] Ord. Vit., v. 19: "Lapideam munitionem, qua prudens Ansoldus domum suam cinxerat, cum ipsa domo dejecit." In this case the wall seems to have been built, not round an open courtyard, but round a house or tower. The French term for a fortified wall, forming the outer defence of a single building, is *chemise*. Thus, in a mount-and-bailey castle, the palisade round the tower on the mount was, strictly speaking, a *chemise*, while that round the bailey was a curtain.

[2] Ord. Vit., vii. 10.

[3] *Ibid.*, viii. 23.

[4] *Ibid.*, viii. 5. Robert, son of Giroie, "castellum Sancti Cerenici . . . muris et vallis speculisque munivit."

BAMBURGH CASTLE: great tower

BAMBURGH CASTLE

castle is the splendid square tower or donjon, which was completed between 1170 and 1180, and stands on the north side of the *enceinte*, at the head of the approach from the town. The curtain, however, west of the donjon, contains "herring-bone" masonry,[1] and is of a rough construction which affords the greatest contrast to the regularly dressed and closely jointed masonry of the great tower. The tower, on three sides, forms an outward projection from the curtain, of great size and strength, and is a structure of one period from the ground upwards. But, on entering the castle, it is at once obvious that the lower part of the south wall of the tower is formed by part of the earlier curtain. In the middle of this section of the work is a wide doorway, with a round-headed arch of two unmoulded orders, which now forms an entrance into the basement of the tower. The capitals of the jamb-shafts of this archway are of an unmistakably eleventh century character, with volutes at the upper angles, and a row of acanthus leaves round the bell. This type of capital is seen in such buildings as the two abbey churches at Caen, the nave of Christchurch

Richmond ; great tower

---

[1] "Herring-bone" masonry consists of courses of rubble bedded diagonally in mortar, alternating with horizontal courses of thin stones, the whole arrangement resembling the disposition of the bones in the back of a fish. The horizontal courses are frequently omitted, and their place is taken by thick layers of mortar.

priory, the west front of Lincoln minster, and other fabrics completed before 1100, and is a sure guide to the date of the work in which it occurs. It would appear, then, that the masonry of this archway and much of the curtain is the work of Alan of Brittany, earl of Richmond, who certainly founded the castle, and died in

Ludlow ; Entrance to inner ward

1088.[1] The castle contains more work of his date, of which something will be said in the sequel.

When the great tower of Richmond was built, an entrance

[1] See *Yorks. Archæol. Journal*, xx. 132, where the evidence quoted points to the conclusion " that the doorway was not erected later than about 1075." Harvey, *Castles and Walled Towns*, p. 85, assumes that the doorway was cut through the south wall of the tower at a later date : the evidence of the masonry is decisively against this idea.

was made on the first floor, from the rampart-walk of the curtain. It is quite clear that, up to this time, the archway just described had been the main entrance of the castle, and had probably been covered on the side next the town by a rectangular building, which formed the lower stage of a gateway-tower or gatehouse, lower than the present donjon. This is borne out by a comparison with the keep at Ludlow, where it is quite clear that an eleventh century gatehouse was converted at a later period into a keep, by walling up the outer entrance (94). A new entrance to the castle, as at Richmond, was made in the adjacent curtain, where it could be easily commanded by the tower. The date of

the lowest stage of the donjon is revealed, as at Richmond, by the details of capitals and shafts, which in this case belong to an arcade in the east wall of the inner portion (95).[1]

Ludlow ; Wall arcade in basement of great tower

The site of Ludlow (96), like that of Richmond, is a rocky peninsula, where a stone curtain, for which material existed on the spot, formed the obvious means of defence. There was no mount and no keep. Exeter, again, is an early example of a stone-walled castle upon a rocky site, where a gateway with a tower above formed the principal entrance. Such sites were protected naturally by the fall of the ground on the steeper sides; the side on which approach was possible was covered by a ditch cut in the rock. The ditch would be crossed by a drawbridge, let down from the inner edge, next the gateway. The gatehouse itself would be a building of two or more stages; at Ludlow the upper stage, as completed, was considerably loftier than the

[1] The architectural history of Ludlow castle has been thoroughly examined by Mr W. H. St John Hope in an invaluable paper in *Archæologia*, lxi. 258-328.

lower.[1]   At Exeter there were probably three stages.   A single
upper stage remains at Tickhill.   At Lewes and Porchester there
is clear evidence of an upper chamber   The gatehouse at Porchester, as at Ludlow, was the entrance to an inner ward, divided
by a ditch from the large outer ward,[2] which, at Porchester, represented the greater part of the *enceinte* of the Roman station,
and contained the priory church and buildings.   In these early
gatehouses, the lower stage was closed at either end by a heavy
wooden door, and was
covered by a flat ceil-
ing of timber.   There
was no arrangement
for a portcullis.   At
Ludlow the lower
stage appears to have
been divided into an
outer porch and inner
hall by a cross wall,
in which there must
have been a door;
but communication
between these parts
was also obtained by a
narrow barrel-vaulted
passage in the thick-
ness of the east wall,
which, opening from
the outer division,
turned at right angles
to itself in the direc-
tion of the length of
the wall, and, with an-

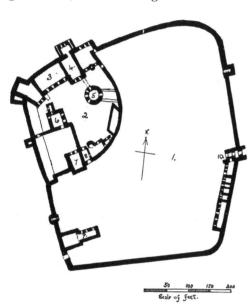

Scale of feet.

Ludlow ; Plan

other right-angled turn, opened into the inner hall (95).   This
passage was guarded by doors, which opened inwards at either end.[3]

---

[1] The original design probably included an upper chamber of moderate
height.   There was, however, a considerable interval between the completion
of the gateway and the building of the upper stage.

[2] The large outer bailey at Ludlow was an addition to the original castle,
late in the twelfth century, and is contemporary with the blocking of the
gatehouse entrance.   Originally the castle consisted merely of the present
inner ward.   The outer bailey or base-court gave enlarged accommodation
for the garrison, and contained stables, barns, and other offices for which
there was no room in the inner ward.

[3] The explanation of this passage through the wall was long a mystery.
Clark, ii. 278, recognised that it led from an outer to an inner "room," but
was puzzled by the bar-holes which showed that the doors had been carefully
defended.

When the outer doorway of the gatehouse was blocked, the lower stage was covered in with a pointed barrel-vault.[1]

As already indicated, the details of these gatehouses are very simple, and it is only where an attempt is made at ornament that their date can be fairly judged. Thus at Porchester, the entrance archway, masked by defensive work of a more advanced period, consists of an unmoulded ring of *voussoirs*, divided from the jambs by plain impost-blocks. The outer bailey or base-court of the castle, which is still surrounded by the Roman walls with their semicircular bastions, has two gatehouses. These occupy the sites of the west and east gates of the Roman *enceinte*, and the east or water-gate is in part Roman. The western gatehouse was rebuilt at a date contemporary with the enclosure of the castle proper within the north-west quarter of the Roman station, and was much altered at a later period. The archways of the Norman building remain, and show no attempt at ornament, the inner one alone having impost-blocks below the arches. The work at Porchester is usually attributed to the early part of the twelfth century, and

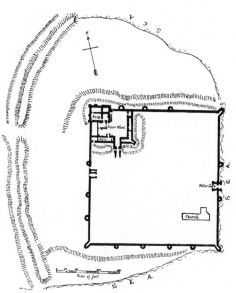

Porchester ; Plan

the ashlar facing of the side walls of the inner gateway appears to be of that date. A similar severity of detail is seen in the parallel case of Lewes, where the original gatehouse was also covered in the fourteenth century by a barbican (98). The great gatehouse of three stages, at Newark castle (99), was the work of Alexander, bishop of Lincoln from 1123 to 1148, whose uncle,

---

[1] Mr Hope thinks that it was originally intended to cover the gateway with a semicircular barrel-vault. The lower stage of the keep at Richmond has a ribbed vault with central column. This, however, with the vice, now blocked, in the south-west corner, was inserted many years after the building of the great tower on the site of the gatehouse.

Roger, bishop of Salisbury (1107-39), appears to have built the gatehouse at Sherborne. The archways of the lower stage at Newark are of great width, and are as simple in detail as those at Porchester. The outer or northern wall of the tower is faced with finely-jointed ashlar, and the archway on this side has a hood-moulding, with billet ornament.[1]

The position of the gatehouse in relation to the curtain varies. At Richmond, Porchester, and Exeter the inner face of the gatehouse was flush with the curtain. At Ludlow, Newark, and Tickhill it was partly outside, but mostly inside

Lewes ; Barbican

the curtain. At Lewes the projection was wholly internal. Its measurements also vary. Porchester was 23 feet in length by 28 feet in breadth : Exeter and Lewes were about 30 feet, Tickhill about 36 feet square : Ludlow was 31 feet broad, but was some feet longer. The area of the gatehouse at Newark is larger than any, and the general proportions and elevation

[1] The string-courses of the upper stages of the tower, and the windows of the southern chamber, which was of the full height of the two upper stories, and probably formed the chapel of the castle, have further enrichment ; but the detail is nowhere elaborate. See T. M. Blagg, F.S.A., *A Guide to Newark, &c.*, 2nd ed., pp. 19-22.

were those of a rectangular donjon rather than a mere gateway-tower.[1]

Stress has been laid on the occurrence of early stone forti-fications on rocky and precipitous sites, where the ordinary earthworks were at once impracticable and unnecessary. It will be noted, however, that the gatehouses which have been described are not found wholly in such positions. Tickhill and Lewes were mount-and-bailey castles with strong earthworks. Porchester is on level ground, open to Portsmouth harbour on two sides, and defended by a ditch on the sides towards the land : the site was already walled, but the rectangular keep appears to stand upon the base of an earlier mount, which may have been thrown up so as to enclose the Roman tower at the north-west angle of the station. Newark (157) stands on a moderate height above the meeting of the Devon and an arm of the Trent, with a deep ditch on the north and east sides towards the town. There was no castle here before Alexander began to build in or about 1130; and his work from the beginning consisted of a rec-tangular enclosure without a mount, in which the gatehouse had some-thing of the importance of a keep. The necessity of defending the en-trance of the castle, whatever the nature of the site might be, led to the construction of stone gatehouses at an early date ; and, at Tickhill or Lewes, the gate-towers were pro-bably constructed at a time when the mounts and embankments of the bailey were still defended by timber.

Newark ; Gatehouse

Stone curtains which display " herring-bone " masonry may generally be assumed to be early in date. It has been customary to look upon " herring-bone " masonry as indicative of pre-Conquest work, and many buildings have been described as " Saxon " on the strength of this detail alone. On the other hand, it never occurs in direct association with details which

---

[1] Harvey, *op. cit.*, p. 98, says that Newark castle " has now no trace of a keep, and possibly never possessed one." The gatehouse, however, may fairly be considered as belonging to the category of tower-keeps, and has one characteristic of that type of building—viz., the cross-wall which divides the upper stages, and is borne by an archway in the centre of the gateway passage.

13

may be regarded as definite criteria of pre-Conquest masonry; and the dimensions, apart from other features, of churches in which it is found in any quantity, usually afford suspicion of its post-Conquest origin.[1] Its use in castles, which, as has been shown, were a Norman importation into England, demolishes its claim to be regarded as a distinctive sign of Saxon work; and its employment in Normandy, especially in the donjon of Falaise, where almost the whole of the inner face of the walls shows " herringbone " coursing, may be set against any theory which would attribute it to English masons after the Conquest.[2] It was used by Roman builders, and much of it may be seen in the towers of the *enceinte* at Porchester. Saxon builders, however, did not copy Roman methods of walling, and the surest criterion of Saxon work is the thin wall, wholly composed of dressed stone, or of rag-work without facings. Norman builders, coming from a country where the continuity of Roman influence was never broken, used the ordinary Roman method of a compound wall, in which a solid rubble core was faced with ashlar on one or both sides. It is only natural that in early stone castles, which were constructed as quickly as possible, the facing should be of a rough description, of coursed rubble or of " herring-bone " courses laid in thick beds of mortar. At a subsequent date, when masonry was added to already fortified sites, the work could be pursued in a more leisurely manner. The most striking example of " herring-bone " work in an English castle is in the cross-wall of the great tower at Colchester (101), which is unquestionably a building of the eleventh century. Here the work was evidently hurried on, with the object of securing the greatest amount of strength in the least possible time, and Roman tiles were re-used in large quantities as bonding courses for the rubble walls, and for the " herring-bone " coursing of the

---

[1] The churches of Upton, near Gainsborough, Burghwallis, near Doncaster, and Lois Weedon in Northamptonshire, are examples of this type. " Herring-bone " work occurs at Brixworth, in a portion of the tower to which a pre-Conquest date cannot safely be attributed. At Marton, near Gainsborough, it occurs in a tower of " Saxon " type, which was probably not built until after the Conquest. It is found twice at York, but the date of the so-called Saxon work in the crypt of the minster is very doubtful; while the tower of St Mary Bishophill Junior, although Saxon in type, is more likely to be Norman in date. Examples of " herring-bone " work in the churches of Normandy are found, *e.g.*, at Périers and in the apse at Cérisy-la-Forêt (Calvados).

[2] The donjon of Falaise belongs to the early part of the twelfth century, and is therefore a late example of " herring-bone " work. The " herring-bone " work in the keep at Guildford is probably still later, and that in the curtain wall at Lincoln, raised on the top of earthen banks, can hardly be attributed to a very early date.

dividing wall. At Richmond, as has been noted, there is a
certain amount of "herring-bone" work in the curtain. The
castle was founded on an entirely new site by Alan of Brittany :
earthworks were out of the question, and the date of the older
masonry of the stone wall is beyond dispute.

A very remarkable example of "herring-bone" walling is
the curtain-wall at Tamworth (48). The castle was founded by
Robert Marmion after the Conquest on the low ground at the
meeting of the Tame and Anker, the town, the fortified *burh* of
Æthelflæd, being on higher ground to the north. Marmion's
fortress took the mount-and-bailey form. The bailey was a
triangular platform of earth, raised artificially above the level
of the river bank, with its apex towards the confluence of the
streams. The mount was on its west side, and was divided from
it by a ditch. The defences on the side next the town were of

Colchester ; Cross-wall

stone. Here the curtain-wall remains in very perfect condition,
crossing the ditch and climbing the mount, with a sloping
rampart-walk along the top. The inner face is composed entirely
of "herring-bone" courses, alternating with one, two, and sometimes three, layers of thin horizontal stones. This appearance
of more than one horizontal course is very unusual.[1] It is
obvious that the site, being commanded by the town, would be
materially strengthened by a stone wall on that side : on the
south side, scarping and ditching would have been sufficient, and
there is no trace of stone-work of an early period here. The
original entrance was at the north-eastern angle of the enclosure,
and probably took the form of a stone gatehouse.[2]

[1] It has also been noted in the tower of Marton church, near Gainsborough.

[2] The lodge which now occupies its site was built in 1815, while the
present main entrance to the castle, south-west of the mount, was made in
1810, and is quite outside the original *enceinte.*

Other instances of "herring-bone" work in curtain-walls that may be mentioned here are at Corfe, Hastings, and Lincoln. Corfe was built on an isolated hill, which was scarped and ditched, something after the manner of a "contour" fort of early days: the portion of the curtain in which "herring-bone" coursing is found follows the natural line of the edge of the hill. Hastings is a fortress on a steep promontory: the mount, on the east side of the enclosure, was defended by a deep ditch, and covered by a large outer bailey with formidable earthworks. The curtain, on the east and north sides of the inner ward, is chiefly of the thirteenth century; but part of the north curtain, forming the north wall of the castle chapel, is of "herring-bone" construction. Lincoln, as we have seen, was a large mount-and-bailey fortress, surrounded by earthworks, which, on the west side, enclosed portions of the wall of the Roman city. "Herring-bone" masonry is seen here and there in the west and north curtains, which have been raised on the top of the earthen banks.[1]

The battlemented parapet with which the curtain-wall of a castle is usually crowned, generally may be assigned, in its present state, to a later repair and heightening of the curtain. This is the case at Lincoln, where the parapet and upper part of the wall are of the thirteenth century. It has been seen that the edict of Lillebonne in 1080 forbade the defence of the curtain by flanking towers,[2] rampart-walks, and other aids to defensive warfare; and, as a matter of fact, the full development of the fortification of the *enceinte* belongs to a later period. At the same time, towers projecting beyond the line of the curtain are found in some of our early Norman castles of stone. The line of the early curtain at Richmond is unbroken by contemporary towers, and closely follows the edge of the rock on which it is built. But at Ludlow (96) where the inner ward is the original castle, founded probably by Roger de Lacy after 1085, the curtain is flanked by four original towers in addition to the gatehouse, which has been described. The shape of the ward is that of a triangle with convex sides, the base of which, on the side of the outer ward and the town, faces south and west. Some thirty feet to the east of the gatehouse, a tower, in the basement of which an oven was inserted at a later date, capped the south-west angle of the enclosure, projecting southwards as far as the edge of the ditch. The west curtain continued in a line with the west wall of this tower for some sixty feet, until it was

---

[1] See note 2 on p. 100.
[2] A curtain is said to be flanked when its line is broken at intervals by projections, so near one another that the whole face of the piece of curtain between them can be covered by the fire of the defenders stationed in them.

broken by a small postern tower.   At the apex of the triangle, projecting to the north-west, was another tower, the remaining tower being at the north-east angle, with its north wall in a line with the north curtain.   All these towers are, roughly speaking, rectangular in shape, but the outer angles of the north-east and

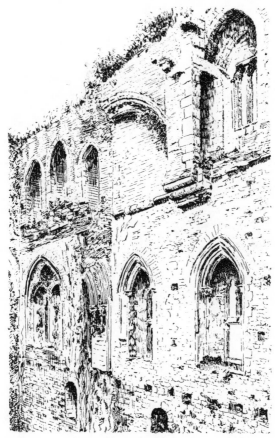

Chepstow ; Hall

north-west towers are chamfered.   The original openings were round-headed loops with wide inward splays.   Although the curtain was thus supplied with several projections, more towers would be needed to flank it perfectly, and large portions of the wall, particularly on the north and east sides, were left without more protection than could be given by their own strength.

Oxford castle is another instance of early walling, where the tall rampart tower which commanded the river and the castle mill still remains.[1]

Of the stone buildings which existed within the enclosures of early Norman castles, the traces which remain are comparatively few, and in most cases work of an altogether later period has taken their place. The great hall for the common life of the garrison, such as Robert d'Oily built in Oxford castle in 1074, would be indispensable. At Ludlow there can be little doubt that the original hall stood on the site occupied by the present hall, much of the east wall of which is apparently of the same date as the curtain. The two lower stages of the oblong keep at Chepstow are the hall (103), with the cellar below, founded by William, son of Osbern, before 1071. Although the upper stage was transformed in the thirteenth century by the insertion of traceried windows in the north wall, and of

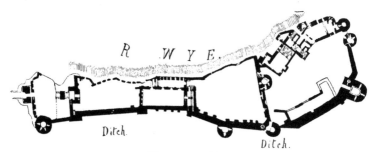

Chepstow ; Plan

an arch between the daïs and the body of the hall, the walls are of eleventh century masonry, and the plain arcade which went round them is clearly visible on the north and west sides. In the south wall of the cellar are the loops which lighted it ; these have lintel-heads with arch-shaped hollows cut in the soffits. The hall and cellar at Richmond, which occupy the south-east angle of the bailey, appear to be those built by Alan of Brittany before 1088. A few additions took place here at the end of the twelfth century,[2] but the windows in the north wall of the hall, which are of two lights, with edge-rolls in the jambs, are clearly of early date. When, for a time,

[1] Much of the curtain of Lancaster castle is of fairly early date. For the supposed Roman origin of the castle and its probable history, see note 2 on p. 327 below.

[2] These additions have given rise to the common theory that this hall is a work of late twelfth century date.

LUDLOW CASTLE : inner bailey

the great stone tower became the fashionable form of keep, a great hall formed part of its internal arrangements ; but this was the hall of the lord's private dwelling, and was used by the garrison only in time of siege. Domestic buildings, including a great hall, may sometimes have been constructed of timber within the bailey, and at the end of the twelfth century were probably superseded by permanent buildings of stone, like the halls at Warkworth or at Oakham. As at Richmond, such halls would be placed against or close to the curtain, to leave the interior of the bailey as open as possible. In case of siege, freedom of movement within the area of the castle was essential, and the bailey formed the natural base of operations. The hall at Chepstow was on the highest and narrowest part of the rocky promontory on which the castle stands, at the head of the bailey ; its south wall formed part of the curtain overhanging the great ditch between the castle and the town (106).[1]

Norman castle-builders were careful to provide chapels within their fortresses. In several cases, the chapel within the bailey appears to have been the first building of stone raised inside the enclosure. The small chapel at Richmond, in a tower of the east curtain, is almost beyond doubt that which was granted by Alan of Brittany to St Mary's abbey at York about 1085. The details are very rude in character : there is a plain wall arcade, supported on shafts, the capitals of which have rough voluting and no abaci. The same type of capital is found in the wall arcading of the original gatehouse at Ludlow (95), and also, though with more finished ornament, in that of the circular nave of St Mary Magdalene's chapel (108) within the same castle. Certain details in the chapel at Ludlow, especially the bands of chevron ornament round the arches, seem to indicate that the nave is later than the eleventh century. The arch which divided the nave from a rectangular chancel ending in a half octagon, is of advanced twelfth century date ; and it is clear that the chancel must have been built or remodelled at a later date than the building of the nave. The aisled chapel at Durham castle, which now forms part of the basement of Bishop Pudsey's building along the north side of the bailey, has groined vaults, cylindrical columns, and capitals with voluted crockets and square abaci, which may be safely ascribed to 1075 or a little later. The capitals may be compared with those of the original gateway arch at Richmond. The classical spirit which is so noticeable in them, and is derived directly from the contemporary work of

---

[1] Other examples of early stone halls will be mentioned in a later chapter.

Normandy, is also apparent in the capitals of the crypt of the castle chapel at Oxford. Oxford castle was founded in 1071, Durham in 1072. At Hastings, the first of the Conqueror's castles, there is, as has been said, much herring-bone work in the north wall of the chapel nave and in the vice or turret-stair

Ludlow ; St Mary Magdalene's Chapel

of the central tower. Such definitely architectural detail as is left, however, belongs to a rebuilding of the later part of the twelfth century.

The importance of the castle chapel in Norman times, and indeed throughout the middle ages, deserves a note. Chapels were often richly endowed, and, as at Hastings, Bridgnorth, and Leicester, were sometimes founded as collegiate establishments, with a dean and canons. The collegiate church of St Mary at Warwick, founded by Roger of Newburgh, the second Norman earl, probably had its origin in a castle chapel, removed to a new and enlarged site within the town. The greatest of these collegiate chapels, although one of the youngest, was St George's at Windsor, founded by Edward III. The chapels at Hastings, Bridgnorth, and Leicester were churches of some size and importance ; and their chapters, like those of the secular cathedrals, usually consisted of royal clerks, generally non-resident, whose duties were served by vicars. As royal chapels, they were exempt from episcopal jurisdiction ; and the term of " free chapel," which was given to them, became applied in course of time to chapels founded in private castles and even upon manors.[1] In most cases a castle chapel was served by a single priest, either the incumbent or his vicar. The incumbent of the free chapel of St Michael in Shrewsbury castle, usually a royal clerk holding his grant from the king, and inducted by the sheriff as the king's officer, held the church of St Julian in Shrewsbury as parcel of his cure.[2] Where the Norman castle and parish church stood side by side, as at Earls Barton or Higham Ferrers in Northamptonshire, the lord of the castle and his household would doubtless attend the church. But the foundation of a chapel within the castle was a common thing, even when the church, as at Ludlow or Warwick, was at no great distance ; and in later years, when chantry foundations became usual, castle chapels increased in number. Thus at Ludlow, a second chapel, served by two chantry priests, was built within the outer bailey about 1328 ;[3] and a college of eight chantry priests was founded in 1308 by one of the Beauchamps in his castle of Elmley in Worcestershire.[4]

[1] This is very noticeable in Shropshire, where a large number of parish churches, to which rectors were presented and instituted in the ordinary way, are described as free chapels in the registers of the bishops of Lichfield and Hereford during the thirteenth and fourteenth centuries.

[2] See Pat. Rolls, 18 Rich. II., pt. 1, m. 28 ; 3 Hen. IV., pt. 1, m. 6.

[3] Pat. 2 Edw. III., pt. 2, m. 4. The walls of this chapel, dedicated to St Peter, remain. In the fifteenth century it was enlarged as far as the west curtain by a western annexe, and in the sixteenth century it was divided into two floors, the upper floor being the court-house, and the lower floor the record-room of the court of the Marches.

[4] Pat. 2 Edw. II., pt. 2, m. 24.

CHAPTER VI

THE KEEP OF THE NORMAN CASTLE

WE have seen that there were two types of early Norman castle in England. There was the ordinary mount-and-bailey castle, with its defences of earthwork and timber; and there was the castle founded on a rocky site, in which there was no mount, and the defences were of stone. In the first instance, the strongest position, the mount, was occupied by the donjon or keep. In the second case, as at Ludlow, the wall was defended by a strong gatehouse and a certain number of towers; but at first there was, strictly speaking, no keep. During the first half of the twelfth century, an era of constant rebellion against the Crown, private owners constructed castles in very large numbers, for purposes of aggression and self-defence. The second half, the age of the first Plantagenets, was an era of consolidation, during which the building of castles was methodised under royal control. Unlicensed fortresses disappeared, leaving only their earthworks to mark their place. The permanent castle of stone became the rule; and to this period, the second age of our medieval military architecture, belong some of our most formidable and imposing castles. The aim of the builders, during this epoch, was to strengthen to the best of their ability that point in the plan which would form a centre of ultimate resistance to an attack from without. This point was the keep.[1]

The keep of Norman and early Plantagenet days was virtually a castle within a castle. In the mount-and-bailey castle, there was generally only one entrance to the enclosure. If the besiegers forced this and entered the bailey, a ditch divided them from the mount, the most formidable part of the defences. Here the defenders could concentrate themselves for a last struggle, in which the advantage, unless the siege could be prolonged indefinitely, was distinctly on their side. Even where the mount was of inconsiderable height, it commanded the bailey

---

[1] The word *keep* is a comparatively modern term, unknown to medieval castle-builders, to whom this part of the castle was the *donjon* or *dungeon*, or the *great tower*.

CARISBROOKE: steps to keep

and the ditch at its base. Its sides were too steep to allow of its being climbed without some artificial means of foothold. A chance arrow, tipped with burning tow, might reach the palisade round the summit of the mount, and set it alight in a dry season ; but the defending party had all the advantage of being able to discharge their missiles downward and into a large portion of the bailey. Their disadvantage lay in the possibility of a prolonged blockade by a large force, and in consequent scarcity of ammunition and victuals. The danger of fire could be minimised by covering the wooden defences with skins newly flayed or soaked in water ; but the work of renewing these in case of a long siege would be difficult.

The wooden donjon on the mount took the form of a square tower surrounded, at the edge of the mount, by a palisade, and approached, as has been described already, by a steep wooden bridge, which crossed the ditch into the bailey. But it is obvious that the existence of a castle in any given place as a permanent centre of royal influence must lead to the abandonment of wooden defences in favour of defences of more lasting material. The stone curtain first took the place of the palisade in the defences of the bailey, and was built across the ditch and up the sides of the mount, ceasing, as can be seen at Berkhampstead (42) or Tamworth, at the level of the summit. The next step was to replace the palisade of the mount with a stone wall of circular or polygonal shape. In some instances where this was done, it is possible that the old wooden tower was left within the enclosure. Cases in which a new tower of stone was built upon the mount are rare. Builders would hesitate to charge the surface of the artificial hillock with the concentrated weight of a large square tower. The encircling curtain was much better adapted to the plan of the mount, and distributed its weight more successfully over the edge of the surface. But, with the building of a stone wall round the summit, the necessity of a tower would be removed. Just as, in castles like Exeter and Ludlow, there was from the first a stone wall without a definite keep, the enclosure being virtually a keep in itself, so, in the more limited area of the mount, the encircling wall formed the keep, and, in the larger examples, sheltered upon its inner side buildings, usually of timber, which afforded the necessary cover for the defenders, while their roofs, abutting on the wall below the summit, left room for the rampart-walk and the wooden galleries which were fitted to the curtain in time of siege.

This was the genesis of the so-called "shell" keep, which converted the summit of the mount into a strong inner ward, the centre of which was clear of buildings, and gave more chance of concentration to the defenders than the narrow passage between the wooden tower and the palisade, into which the angles of the tower would have projected awkwardly. One of the best examples of the type which remains is the keep upon the larger of the two mounts at Lincoln, a polygon of fifteen faces on the outside, twelve on the inside. The wall has lost its parapet, but retains its rampart-walk; it is 8 feet thick, and keeps its height of 20 feet perfect round the whole of the enclosure. The masonry is ashlar of late twelfth century

Cardiff; Keep

character, and each of the external angles is capped by a flat pilaster buttress. The marks on the inner face of the walls indicate that the enclosure was surrounded by timber buildings, with which two small mural chambers communicated, in the thickness of the outer curtain where it joins the keep. The doorway of the keep is in the north-east face of the wall, which is pierced by a segmental-headed archway, with a semicircular covering arch on the outer face. This doorway, defended by a wooden door with a draw-bar, was approached by a stone stair made in the side of the mount. At the present day the ditch

at the foot has been filled up, and the stairs are modern, but
originally the ditch must have been crossed by a drawbridge at
the foot of the stair, which, when drawn up, would have left the
mount isolated from the bailey.   There was a small doorway
in the south-west face of the keep wall, probably intended to be
a postern, through which an exit could be gained in emer-
gencies.[1]

The shell of masonry upon the mount, however, was by
no means the universal form taken by the keep.   Sometimes,
as at York, the timber defences of the mount survived until a
comparatively late period, when their place was taken by a

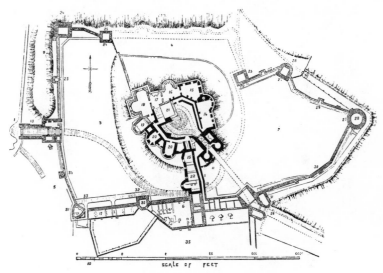

Alnwick ; Plan

tower of a form in keeping with the principles of fortification of
the day.[2]   At Alnwick (115) the base of the great mount, with
a considerable portion of its ditch, remains between the two
wards of the castle.   The present cluster of towers and connecting buildings upon the mount, surrounding a somewhat dark
and confined courtyard, is in large part a nineteenth century
reconstruction of the fourteenth century house of the Percys

---

[1] Other important shell keeps of the normal type are at Arundel, Cardiff
(114), Carisbrooke (171), Farnham, Lewes, Pickering, Totnes, and Tonbridge
—the last one of the most considerable and finest examples.

[2] Clifford's tower at York is sometimes quoted as a shell keep.   It was
actually a tower with a forebuilding.

which occupied the site. The outer and inner archways, however, of the gatehouse through which the keep is entered, are twelfth century work, and agree very well in date with the large remains of Norman masonry which can be traced in the curtains of both wards. It is probable that, about the middle of the twelfth century, Eustace, son of John, who died in 1157, surrounded the whole of the present enclosure with stone walls, and, levelling the mount to its present height, built in stone the earliest domestic buildings of the castle, upon the enlarged site of the earlier wooden donjon and palisade. The appearance of Eustace's buildings must have been very different from that of

Beaugency

the mansion of the Percys; and we may assume that he defended the summit of the levelled mound by a thick curtain, against which his hall and other domestic apartments were placed.

In France and Normandy, the rectangular donjon of stone began to supersede the wooden tower at an early date. At Langeais (Indre-et-Loire), Fulk the Black, count of Anjou, built a stone donjon as early as 992.[1] Three walls of this structure are left: it was oblong in form and was composed of a basement and upper floor. The masonry is largely faced with courses of small cubical stones, following the manner inherited by the Romanesque builders of France from their Roman predecessors: tiles are introduced in the arched heads of the windows in the upper stage, which are not mere loops, but have a considerable outward opening. This keep was obviously intended to be at once stronghold and dwelling-house. Such a building was a translation into stone of a wooden construction like the tower-house on the motte at Ardres. It is built on a promontory above a small stream, and is defended by a ditch on the landward side. Many

[1] See Enlart, ii. 500, 676: Anthyme Saint-Paul, *Histoire Monumentale*, p. 168, gives the date 993, with an expression of doubt. Fulk the Black was count of Anjou 987-1039.

of these stone towers remain in Normandy and the country round the Loire; and, as a rule, are earlier in date and larger in area than most of the similar buildings in England. The tower of Beaugency (Loiret) is an oblong on plan, measuring about 76 feet long by 66 feet broad (116): the present height is 115 feet. The date indicated by the masonry is about 1100.[1] The fabrics of the towers of Falaise (Calvados) and Domfront (Orne) may be attributed to Henry I. In or about 1119 he systematically garrisoned his fortresses at Rouen and other places, of which Falaise was one.[2] Domfront, from 1092 onwards, was his favourite castle.[3] Its strong position gave it an exceptional advantage as a base of operations; and in 1101,

Falaise

when Henry ceded his Norman possessions to his brother Robert, he kept Domfront for himself.[4] After the battle of Tinchebray (1106) Henry was lord of Normandy, and restored order in the duchy by razing the unlicensed strongholds built under Robert's weak rule.[5] The tower of Domfront, however, and possibly that of Falaise, were not built until 1123.[6] At

---

[1] Enlart, ii. 685, says "début du xiie siècle."
[2] Ord. Vit., xii. 14.
[3] *Ibid.*, viii. 19.
[4] *Ibid.*, x. 18.
[5] *Ibid.*, xi. 20: *adulterina castella* is the phrase used.
[6] Enlart, ii. 710. Blanchetière, *op. cit.*, 83, mentions Henry's operations in 1123, but believes in an earlier date for the donjon.

Domfront the castle is a large enclosure, occupying the highest point of a long hill which has a gradual eastward slope, but rises in an abrupt cliff from a narrow valley on the west, and descends steeply on the north and south. A deep ditch, through which the modern road from Caen to Angers has been carried, divided the castle from the town. The great tower lies to the east of the centre of the castle enclosure, so as to command the ditch and the town beyond. Only the north-west angle, with a portion of the adjacent walls, remains perfect. The height slightly exceeds 70 feet. The area of the whole structure is 85 feet by 70, not counting the buttresses and plinth. At Falaise (117) the great tower occupies nearly the whole of the summit of the isolated cliff on which it stands, the town occupying the hilly but lower ground on the north side. The length of the tower is a little less than that of Domfront, while the breadth is slightly greater. The height is about the same.

The tower of Domfront, like that of Beaugency, stood within a walled castle, where the capture of the bailey would have exposed the tower directly to the besiegers. It was therefore built with an exclusive view to strength, and its window openings, even upon the second floor above the basement, were small and narrow, those on the first floor being mere loops. On the other hand, the tower of Falaise stands high above the curtain-wall by which the ascent from the town was protected. Its outer face is of ashlar throughout, and the window openings of the two upper stages, far above the reach of stones and arrows, are double, divided by shafts with carved capitals. Both towers were separated into three parts by cross-walls; but the two upper stages at Falaise are now undivided, and at Domfront, above the basement, there remain only indications of such a division.

Returning to England, we may safely assert that, with very few exceptions, our rectangular towers belong to a period which bears, from the historical point of view, a close likeness to the period of Henry I.'s fortifications in Normandy. Henry II. pursued the same policy of destroying unlicensed castles and strengthening royal strongholds; and his building operations took the form of providing his castles with towers, such as already were a chief feature of the castles of Normandy and Maine, but were certainly very exceptional in England. The approximate date of several of these towers can be obtained from the entries in the Pipe Rolls for the reign of Henry II.[1]

Henry II., like the Conqueror, directed his attention to the defence of the main water-ways of his kingdom. The castles of the coast and of the Welsh and Scottish frontiers were also

[1] Rad. de Diceto, *Abbrev. Chron.*, sub anno.

chief objects of his care. The Pipe Rolls of 1158-9 and 1160-1 contain accounts of large sums spent on the castle of Wark-on-Tweed, at the extreme north-west corner of the kingdom.[1] In 1158-9 occur charges for the tower of Gloucester,[2] at the head of the Severn estuary; and in the same and following years are many mentions of the castle and tower of the great littoral stronghold of Scarborough.[3] Berkhampstead, commanding the approach to London from the north-west, was an object of substantial expense in 1159-60 and 1161-2.[4] In 1160-1 £215. 18s. 5d. was spent in the fortification of the city of Chester:[5] work was also done at Oswestry,[6] and other accounts show that attention was paid to the victualling of castles on the Welsh border at Clun and Ruthin.[7] Accounts, beginning in 1164-5, refer to the strengthening of Shrewsbury castle.[8] Sums were spent on the tower of Bridgnorth, which commanded the defiles of the Severn between Shrewsbury and Worcester, in 1168-9 and following years;[9] and mentions of Hereford,[10] Shrawardine,[11] and Ellesmere,[12] testify to the care with which the western frontier of the kingdom was protected. Of the coast castles, apart from Scarborough, Dover has a constant place in these accounts. For example, in 1168-9, 40s. 6d. was paid for the hire of ships to bring lime from Gravesend to Dover, and £34. 5s. 4d. was spent on the work for which this was required.[13] Southampton castle was repaired in 1161-2,[14] and a well was made there in 1172-3.[15] The tower of Hastings was in progress in 1171-2.[16] In 1165-6 £256. 4s. 9d. was spent upon the castle of Orford, the great stronghold of the Suffolk coast, which was an object of large yearly expense down to 1171-2.[17] On the line of the upper Thames, continual sums were spent on the palace-castle of Windsor: the wall of the castle is referred to in 1171-2 and 1172-3.[18] Work was done at Oxford and a well made in 1172-3 and 1173-4.[19] Hertford castle was maintained to guard

---

[1] *Pipe Roll Soc.*, vol. i., pp. 13, 14; iv. 23.

[2] *Ibid.*, i. 27.

[3] *Ibid.*, i. 29, 30, 31; ii. 14; iv. 36; v. 50; vi. 57, 58; vii. 11, 12; xii. 79; xiii. 31.

[4] *Ibid.*, ii. 12; v. 49. [5] *Ibid.*, iv. 35.

[6] *Ibid.*, iv. 39. [7] *Ibid.*, iv. 40.

[8] *Ibid.*, viii. 89; ix. 59, etc.

[9] *Ibid.*, xiii. 107, 108; xv. 132; xvi. 32.

[10] *E.g.*, *ibid.*, xiii. 140. [11] *Ibid.*, xvi. 32; xviii. 110.

[12] *Ibid.*, xviii. 110. [13] *Ibid.*, xiii. 161.

[14] *Ibid.*, v. 35. [15] *Ibid.*, xix. 53.

[16] Charles Dawson, *Hastings Castle*, ii. 524.

[17] *Pipe Roll Soc.*, ix. 17; xi. 18; xii. 15; xiii. 95; xv. 2; xvi. 2.

[18] *Ibid.*, xviii. 16; xix. 68.

[19] *Ibid.*, xix. 167; xxi. 77; see also xvi. 92.

15

the Lea.[1]   In addition to Dover, the castles of Rochester,[2] Chilham,[3] and Canterbury[4] protected the main routes to the narrowest part of the Channel.   The chief fortress of the vale of Trent was at Nottingham, where large sums were spent in 1171-2 and 1172-3.[5]   Of the inland castles of the north, the tower of Newcastle cost some £385 between 1171-2 and 1174-5.[6] This forms a contrast to the small sum spent on the tower of York—£15. 7s. 3d.—in 1172-3 :[7] it is clear, from the Pipe Rolls of later reigns, that this was merely a wooden structure.[8]

However, there are earlier instances of towers which are of first-class importance, and these must be briefly described before we dwell upon the characteristics of the donjons of the second half of the twelfth century.   We have seen that William the Conqueror, immediately after his coronation, began the construction of certain strongholds in connection with the city of London.[9]   His first work was probably to enclose within a palisade the undefended sides of the bailey, the east side of which was covered by a portion of the Roman city-wall.   Before the end of his reign, the White tower had been begun as a principal feature of the castle, and was completed in the reign of William Rufus, who in 1097 built a wall about it.[10]   This tower is therefore at least as early in date as most of the early square towers of Normandy and the adjacent provinces, and is considerably earlier than the towers of Falaise and Domfront.   A tradition attributes the design to the direction of Gundulf, bishop of Rochester 1077-1108, who is also said to have been the builder of the donjon-like tower at Malling in Kent, originally attached to the church of St Leonard, and of the tower, the ruins of which remain, on the north side of the quire of Rochester cathedral.

The White tower is at present 90 feet in height, and is therefore much lower than the nearly contemporary tower of Beaugency.   Its area, however, is far greater, covering an oblong of 118 feet from east to west by 107 feet from north to south. It is four stages in height, and was built of rubble masonry,

---

[1] *Pipe Roll Soc.*, xvi. 118, 119.   [2] *Ibid.*, xvi. 141.
[3] *Ibid.*, xvi. 137.   [4] *Ibid.*, xix. 81.
[5] *Ibid.*, xviii. 7 ; xix. 173.
[6] *Ibid.*, xviii. 66 ; xix. 110 ; xxii. 183.   Malcolm, king of Scots, yielded Bamburgh, Carlisle, and Newcastle to Henry II. in 1157 ; and the towers at all three places were begun within a few years of this event.   That at Bamburgh is mentioned in 1164.
[7] *Ibid.*, xix. 2.
[8] See evidence brought by Mrs Armitage, *Eng. Hist. Rev.*, xix. 443-7.
[9] Ord. Vit., iv. 1.   He calls these strongholds *firmamenta quaedam*.
[10] *A.S. Chron.*, sub anno.

ashlar work being confined entirely to the pilaster buttresses
and windows, and the plinth. Modern repairs have made the
original appearance of the tower hard to reconstruct. The
entrance was upon the first floor, and was never covered by
a fore-building : this entrance seems to have been in the western
part of the south wall. A well-stair or vice, in a round turret
at the north-east corner, was the chief means of communication
between all the floors ; but vices were also made from the second
floor to the roof in the square turrets of the north-west and south-
west angles. There is also a square turret above the place
which would ordinarily be occupied by the south-east angle ;
but the south wall, throughout its height, is continued into an
apsidal projection, which is
curved round to meet the
east wall. The two upper
stages of this projection
form the apse of St John's
chapel, with its encircling
gallery. The faces of the
tower and the apse are
strengthened by flat but-
tresses at regular intervals,
which are gathered in at a
string on the level of the
floor of the uppermost
stage, and again at the
level of the roof. There are
no window openings in the
basement, which was originally used for stores. The
window openings of the
first and second floors were

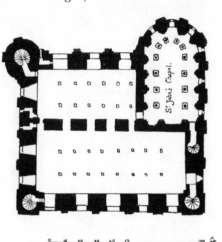

White Tower ; Plan of Second Floor

originally narrow loops, with wide internal splays, but have been
considerably enlarged, with some damage to the appearance of
strength which the tower once possessed. The openings in the
aisle of the chapel on the second floor, however, were wider than
the rest. The third floor, being out of the range of ordinary
missiles, had wide window openings : the two openings in the
south wall of the larger room on this floor are double. The
greatest thickness of the walls of the basement is 15 feet : the
walls of the uppermost stage are from 10 to 11 feet thick.

The tower is divided internally into two parts by a longitudinal wall, east of the centre, 10 feet thick.[1] Thus in the

[1] Such cross-walls, found in the larger towers, were not merely useful
as partitions between the rooms. They enabled the builders to lay their

basement there is a large western chamber, 91 by 35 feet, and
on every floor above there is a corresponding room, the dimensions of which increase with the thinning of the outer walls to
a maximum of 95 by 40 feet.   The eastern chamber, however,
is divided into two parts by a cross-wall, considerably to the
south of the centre.   There is thus in the basement and each
floor an oblong north-eastern chamber, into which access is
obtained from the main well-stair.   In the basement there is a
doorway in the longitudinal wall between this and the western
chamber ; but, on each of the upper floors, the communication

White Tower ; St John's Chapel

is maintained by five openings in the wall.   Apart from the
recesses of the loops, and the mural lobbies which lead to the
vices in the turrets, there are only two mural passages, one in
the first and one in the second stage, communicating with garde-
robes ; but the wall of the third floor is pierced all round by a
gallery, with a barrel vault, in the thickness of the wall, which

floors more conveniently, as timber of sufficient scantling for so large an
undivided space was obtainable with difficulty.   In case of the great tower
being taken by storm, the cross-wall on each floor formed a barrier to the
besiegers, shutting off the tower as it did into two halves.   This is well seen,
for example, at Porchester.

communicates at either end with the broad gallery above the aisles of St John's chapel.

The south-eastern quarter of the tower contains, in the basement, the sub-crypt of the chapel, known in later days as " Little Ease." On the first floor is the upper crypt, which, as well as the sub-crypt, has a barrel vault, and ends in an apse. The second floor is the ground-floor of the chapel and its aisle or ambulatory, which is divided from the nave by plain round-headed arches springing from cylindrical columns with capitals, those of the eastern columns famous for the Tau-shaped plaques left uncarved between their volutes, those of the western columns

Tower of London ; St John's Chapel   Christchurch

scalloped (122). The nave of the chapel rises through the third floor to the barrel vault. The aisles have groined cross-vaults : the gallery above them on the third floor is covered by a half barrel vault. This gallery, as before mentioned, is connected in its north and west walls with the mural gallery of the main chambers. The ground floor of the chapel communicated with the north-eastern chamber through a doorway in the cross-wall ; but the main entrance was through a short mural lobby from the western chamber, which led into the west end of the south aisle. At a late date a vice was made in the thickness of the wall from this lobby to a doorway in the basement, by which access was obtained to the chapel from the later domestic buildings adjoining the south side of the tower.

The well of the tower, a most necessary feature in case of siege, was in the floor of the western chamber of the basement, near its south-western angle, and was cased with ashlar. Only three fireplaces remain, all in the east wall, two on the first, and one on the second floor: the smoke escaped through holes in the adjacent wall. The use of the rooms on the various floors is uncertain, and it is possible that they may have been separated by wooden partitions into smaller rooms. The basement chambers, however, were obviously store-rooms; and the great western chamber on the third floor was used by many of our kings as a council-chamber. The first-floor rooms may have been intended for the use of the garrison, while the larger room on the second floor was probably the great hall of the tower, and the smaller room the king's great chamber. The upper room, next the council-chamber, may have been for the use of the queen and her household. Accommodation, suited to the scanty needs of the times, was thus provided for a large number of persons; and the great size of the chapel alone indicates that the tower was intended as an occasional residence for the royal family. The palace hall at Westminster, however, was in building, when Rufus made his wall round the Tower; and it is clear that the cold and dark interior of the fortress was planned mainly with a view to defence, and with little respect for comfort.

The great tower of Colchester castle (47), which is of the same date as the White tower, covers an even larger area. The internal measurements of the ground-floor, excluding the projections at the angles, are 152 feet north and south by 111 feet east and west. This, the greatest of all Norman keeps, has unfortunately lost its two upper stages, and, with them, the chapel, which, like that in the White Tower, was built with an apsidal projection covering the junction of south and east walls. The crypt and sub-vault of the chapel, however, remain. In this respect, and in the division of the floors into larger and smaller chambers by a cross-wall running north and south, the likeness between these two great towers is very marked. The rectangular projections, on the other hand, which cap three of the angles of the tower at Colchester, are far more prominent than those of the Tower of London, and form small towers in themselves; and, even at the angle where the apse of the chapel is extended eastward, the south wall has been built of a thickness to correspond with the projections at the north-east and north-west angles. That at the south-west angle differs in plan from the rest, being longer from east to west and wider on its western face than the others.   Its south face also is recessed from the level of the south wall of the tower, but projects in a large rectangular buttress at the point where it joins the main wall. This south-west tower contained the main staircase.   The entrance was on the ground floor, immediately east of the buttress just mentioned, and not, as in most rectangular keeps, upon the first floor.   The ashlar with which the exterior of the tower was cased has been stripped off, and the rubble core of the walls, with its bonding courses of Roman tiles, is now exposed.   Below the ground floor the walls spread considerably : this can be seen upon the north and west sides, where the hill drops towards the river, and the upper part of the solid foundation is above ground.   Between the angle towers the walls are broken, on the east and west sides, by two rectangular buttresses of slight projection : on the north side there is only one, and on the south side none.   The ground floor and first floor were lighted by narrow loops, splayed inwardly through about half the thickness of the wall.   In each of the east, north, and west walls of the ground floor there are three of these.   The south wall has only two : one lights the well chamber on the east of the entry, while the other, at the opposite extremity of the wall, lights the sub-vault of the chapel.   The wall between the two, being on the side of the tower most open to attack, is of great solidity, and is unbroken by opening or buttress.   In each face of the first floor, exclusive of the angle towers and apse of the chapel, there were four loops.   The window openings of the upper stages were probably larger.   One of the most striking features of this tower is the plentiful use of Roman tiles among the masonry, especially in the cross-wall, where they are arranged in a very regular and beautiful series of "herring-bone" courses (101).   This employment of Roman material gave rise to a tradition, not yet wholly extinct, that the tower was a Roman building.   It need hardly be said that nothing would be more natural than for the Norman masons to adopt the economical principle of applying to their own use material which lay ready to hand among the ruins of the Roman station.

The towers of London and Colchester are exceptional in their date and in the hugeness of their proportions.   Although the towers of the later part of the twelfth century have many features in common with them—the division by means of cross-walls, the well-stairs in one or more of the angles, the pilaster buttresses projecting from the outer walls, and the mural galleries and chambers—no tower was subsequently attempted upon their scale.   The tower of Rochester (frontispiece), which appears to have

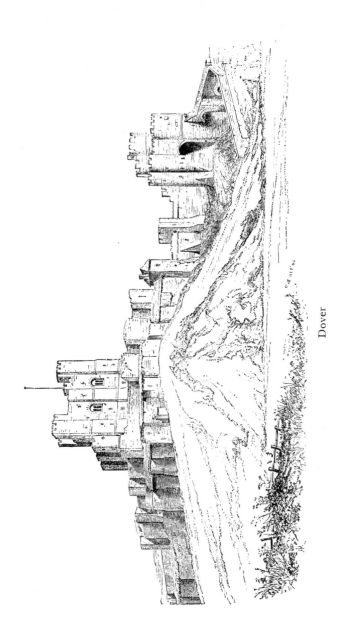

Dover

been begun somewhat earlier than 1140, and is therefore intermediate in date between these two exceptional examples and
the later towers, is 113 feet high to the top of the parapet,
and is 70 feet square (exterior measurement) at its base. The
tower of Dover (126), built in the early part of the reign of Henry
II., measures 98 by 96 feet at the base. The walls, however, have

Clun

the exceptional thickness of 24 to 21 feet, so that the internal
measurements are considerably reduced, while the height to
the top of the parapet is only 83 feet. The towers of London
and Colchester are also exceptional in the importance given
to the chapel in their plans. The great prominence of the angle
turrets at Colchester is an unique feature, while the position of

16

the main entrance upon the ground floor, although not unique, is very unusual.

The later towers differ from those of London and Colchester in the fact that they were additions to enclosures already existing, instead of being the nucleus of a castle founded for the first time. Although they have a general family likeness, neither their position on the plan, which was necessarily dictated by the nature of the site, nor the details of their arrangements, are uniform. Most of the castles in which they occur are divided by a wall, built across the enclosure from curtain to curtain, into an outer and inner ward or bailey. The tower, standing at the highest point of the inner ward, was placed so as to command both these divisions of the castle. If the outer ward were

entered, the besiegers were confronted by a second line of defence, the wall of the inner ward, in conjunction with which the great tower, with its superior height, could be used by the defenders. Finally, if the inner ward were taken, the tower still remained as a formidable refuge for the garrison.

Where a new tower keep was added to castles of the usual type, whose main defences consisted of an earthen mount and banks, it was often raised, as at Canterbury and Hast-

Guildford

ings, on a new site, independent of the mount, which was probably avoided as affording insufficient foundation. Thus, at Rochester, the old mount of the eleventh century castle, now known as Boley Hill, remains at some distance from the later enclosure. But there were cases, and possibly more than are generally recognised, in which the mount was utilised for a tower. At Christchurch the comparatively small keep was built entirely upon the artificial mount. The keeps of Norwich and Hedingham (135), two of the grandest of their class, were built upon mounts, which, if in great part natural hills, had been scarped and heightened by art. The mounts at Guildford and Clun (127) are artificial. In both these last cases the summit of the mount was converted into a shell keep, surrounded by a wall ; but on the eastern side of this enclosure a tower, of respectable if not large dimensions, was made. The tower at Clun was built against the east slope of the mount, the basement being entirely below the level of the summit of the earthwork. This is also partly the case at Guildford (128), where the tower is placed across the eastern edge of the mount. The inclusion at Kenilworth of artificial soil within the basement of the keep has led to the suspicion that the mount of the castle was reduced in height, and the tower built round the lower portion (132).

At Guildford and Clun the combination of a shell of masonry

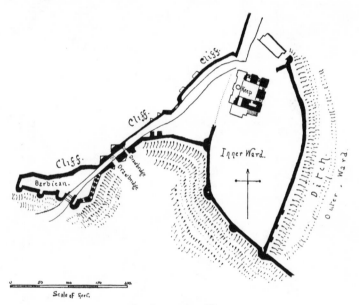

Scarborough ; Plan

with a tower keep produced the effect of a small inner ward—which is virtually what a shell keep is—with a tower upon its *enceinte*. Frequently, as at Scarborough (129) and Bamburgh the tower keep stood upon the line of the curtain between the two wards. At Scarborough it actually stands athwart that line, but its greater projection is towards the inner ward, from which, of course, it was entered. The towers at Norham (157) and Kenilworth fill up a corner of the inner ward, but have no noticeable projection beyond the curtain. This is also the case at Porchester (131), where the north-west angle, in which the keep stands, is also the north-west angle of the Roman

Map of Rectangular Keeps

station.[1] Some, however, of the finest of these towers, Rochester, Dover, and Newcastle, stood wholly detached within the inner ward, although, as at Rochester, near enough to the curtain to enable the defenders to command the outer approaches from the upper stages.

From the point of view of dimensions the towers may be divided into two classes. There are the towers proper, such as Clun, Corfe, Guildford, Hedingham, Helmsley, Newcastle, Porchester, Richmond, Rochester, and Scarborough, in which the height is greater than the length or breadth. Such towers are approximately square; and to them must be added Dover, in which, however, owing to the immense thickness of the walls, the height is less than the length or breadth. In one case, Porchester (131), the measurement from north to south exceeds that from east to west by 13 feet, and at first was also in excess of the height; but the tower was raised to nearly twice its height not long after the completion of the original design.

Porchester

The second class is composed of keeps, of which one or both of the dimensions of the ground-plan exceed the height, without the exceptional circumstances which governed the proportions of Dover. Such keeps are noticeably oblong in shape. At Castle Rising and the tower of Bowes in Yorkshire the height is less

[1] At Norham and Kenilworth the towers are at an angle of the inner ward where the two wards are adjacent. At Porchester it is at an outer angle of the inner ward, so that two of its sides are on the outer curtain of the castle.

than either the length or breadth.   At Kenilworth (132) the length from east to west exceeds the breadth by nearly 30, and the height by 7 feet.   Middleham, from north to south, measures approximately 100 feet by 80 from east to west: its height is only 55 feet, which, though it surpasses the 50 feet of Bowes and Castle Rising, is much less than the 80 feet of Kenilworth.   Its length and breadth, however, make up an area far surpassing the 87 by 58 feet of Kenilworth, the 82 by 60 feet of Bowes, and the 75 by 54 feet of Castle Rising.   The foundations of another keep of this class remain at Duffield in Derbyshire.   Bamburgh, 69 by 61 feet, but only 55 feet high, is another member of the

Kenilworth

class.   Another great Northumbrian keep, Norham, although its height is 90 feet, is oblong in plan; and its measurement from east to west comes within 4 feet of the height, so that it stands on the border between the second and the first class.

The internal divisions of the keeps are not uniformly the same, and do not always correspond to the height.   The usual arrangement in the loftier keeps, as at Hedingham, Porchester, Rochester, and Scarborough, is a basement with three upper floors; but at Corfe, which is 80 feet high, as at Guildford, which is only 63 feet high, there are only two upper floors. At Dover, 83 feet high, and Newcastle, 75 feet high, the second floor was surrounded by a mural gallery, high above the floor-level, so that the second and third floors were combined into one lofty room.[1] At Norham, however, there were four upper floors. Kenilworth, only 10 feet lower, had a lofty basement with only one floor above it. At Bowes there were two floors. At Middleham and Castle Rising, there was one main floor; but, by the subdivision of the rooms on this stage, a second floor was made in portions of the building. As a rule, the walls grow thinner as they rise: this was achieved by rebating the inner face at each floor to provide a ledge for the floor timbers. In exceptional cases, there is an off-set on the exterior of the tower; and at Rochester the walls are thinned from 12 feet at the base to 10 feet at the top by a slight exterior batter. At Porchester the walls are 11 feet thick at the base: this is reduced to 7 feet at the first floor, and, by an off-set at the level of the original roof, to 6 feet in the upper stage. The thickest walls, next to those at Dover, appear to be at Newcastle, where their thickness at the first floor is 14 feet.

Many of these towers, such as Rochester and Dover, are built of rag-stone or coursed rubble, with dressings of ashlar. The masonry at Guildford (128) is extremely rough, and "herring-bone" coursing is extensively used: the date of the tower, however, to judge by its internal details, is not earlier than the third quarter of the twelfth century.[2] On the other hand, not a few have their walls cased with ashlar. Hedingham and Porchester are noble examples from the east and south of England; Bridgnorth and Kenilworth from the midlands. Of the towers of Yorkshire, Bowes, Richmond, and Scarborough have ashlar casing; Middleham is of rubble with ashlar dressings. Ashlar facing is used throughout at Bamburgh, Newcastle, and Norham: at Norham the ashlar is of two distinct kinds, small cubical stones being used in one part, and larger stones in another.[3] As at Colchester, Dover, and Kenilworth, the foundations of the larger towers spread considerably, and rise above ground in a battering plinth, into which the buttresses at the angles and on the face of the walls die off without interruption. At Newcastle there is a roll

[1] At Hedingham and Rochester there are mural galleries above the level of the second floor, the height of which therefore corresponds to that of two external stories. Both towers are exceptionally lofty, Rochester being 113, Hedingham 100 feet high.

[2] We know from the Pipe Roll for 1173-4 that work was being done at Guildford in that year (*Pipe Roll Soc.*, xxi. 3).

[3] This points to two separate dates for the structure. The earlier masonry has been attributed to Bishop Flambard, who founded the castle in 1121; the later to Bishop Pudsey, who made additions to the castle about 1157. If this is so, the history of the tower is parallel to that of Porchester —a low stone tower, possibly of the reign of Henry I., heightened in the reign of Henry II.

string-course above the plinth, and at Bamburgh (91) the plinth is moulded with a very imposing effect. Where the tower is built on an uneven site, as at Middleham or Scarborough, the plinth appears only on the faces where the ground falls away from the tower.

The angles of the tower were always strengthened by rectangular pilaster buttresses of the ordinary twelfth century type, formed by thickening the two adjacent walls. In most cases these meet, forming a solid exterior angle. Occasionally, as at Guildford, Hedingham, and Rochester, a hollow angle is left between them, which, at Castle Rising and Scarborough, is filled by a shaft or bead. Above the line of the parapet the angle buttresses are continued into square turrets. Within one or more of these angles, there was a vice. At Newcastle (139) the angle buttresses are of such breadth and projection as to form distinct towers: this is even more noticeable at Kenilworth, where there are angle towers not unlike those at Colchester. On the faces of the tower between these angles there were usually one or more pilaster buttresses of slight projection. These varied in number according to the plan and site of the tower. At Dover there is one on each face, with the exception of the side which is covered by the forebuilding. At Kenilworth there are four on one face, three on another, two on a third : the remaining wall has disappeared. At Porchester there is one on each of the west and north faces, none on the east or south : when the tower was heightened, neither angle nor intermediate buttresses were continued upwards. It is worthy of note that one of the angle towers at Newcastle is polygonal, not rectangular, in shape. This points to a transition in methods of fortification, of which more will be said hereafter. The south-east angle at Rochester is rounded ; but this is the result of a repair of the tower which took place in the thirteenth century.

As the main object of these towers was defensive, their external architectural features were generally confined to their excellent masonry. A moulded plinth, as at Bamburgh, is of very rare occurrence. At Norwich and Castle Rising a wall is arcaded or recessed : this, however, is quite contrary to the usual practice. String-courses, where they were used, were generally confined to the buttresses, as at Kenilworth ; although in a few cases, as at Richmond, they were continued along the wall. The necessary window openings were few and small. Here, however, a distinction must be made. It has been remarked already that the donjon of a castle sometimes formed the residence of its lord as well as a strong tower in time of war. The towers of London and Colchester were certainly planned upon their liberal scale with this double end in view ; and, destitute of comfort as they

HEDINGHAM : great tower

seem to us to-day, the upper floors of the White Tower were at any rate well lighted. Similarly, at Rochester, there was a large provision of single-light windows in the floors above the basement. And, as a rule, while the basement was lighted by a very few narrow loops, set high in the wall, and the first floor, which was not above the range of missiles, was lighted sparingly by narrow loops with wide internal splays, the second floor, which formed the main apartment, had much larger windows. These, as in the Tower of London, or at Dover, Hedingham, and Scarborough, were sometimes of two lights, divided by an intervening shaft or piece of wall. At Newcastle, where the second floor, owing to the thickness of the walls, in which separate chambers are contrived, is very dark, there is a wide single opening in the intermediate buttress of the east face, which externally has a moulded arch and jamb-shafts (139). At Richmond, a tower the single object of which seems to have been defence, the window openings, with one exception, are narrow loops with internal splays ; and, of all twelfth century towers, this was probably the darkest and least comfortable (93).[1]

The main entrance of the tower was usually on the first floor, although sometimes, as at Dover, Newcastle, and Norwich, it was on the second floor, and led directly into the main apartment. It was obviously unsafe to make an entrance in the basement, where the doors could be easily forced or burned. At the same time, there is, as we have noticed, a basement entrance at Colchester, where the approach was protected by a strong ditch.   The rocks on which Bamburgh and Scarborough stand made the position almost impregnable, and in both cases the main doorway of the tower is on a level with the soil of the ward in which it stands.[2] When the outer opening of the original gateway at Richmond was removed to make way for the new tower, the inner opening was left, forming a direct communication between the interior of the castle and the basement : this also was permitted by the natural strength of the site ; but the main entrance to the tower was in the south-east corner of the first floor, from the rampart-walk. At Ludlow, both openings of the gateway were walled up (94), and a stair was made to the first floor against part of the west wall of the tower.[3]

[1] Porchester, in spite of its great size, is a tower which was apparently built for exclusively military purposes. The floors are feebly lighted, and there is no fireplace in the building.

[2] Both these castles belong to the class of cliff strongholds which were walled from their earliest foundation.

[3] Further alterations were made in the fifteenth century, when a new stair was inserted in the north-east angle, and the outer stair against the west wall was removed.

17

Even in the tower on the mount at Guildford, the main entrance was on the first floor (128). Where the doorway led into the chief apartment of the tower, it received special architectural treatment. That at Newcastle is a wide opening with a semicircular arch of three orders and shafts in the jambs: it has been rebuilt, but probably follows the original design closely. On the other hand, the first-floor entrance at Kenilworth, which led into the main room, is exceedingly plain, with a segmental arch, and a semicircular relieving arch in the wall above.

Entrances on upper floors were necessarily approached by stairs, which were habitually placed against the wall, at right angles to the entrance, and sometimes, as at Dover, Newcastle, and Rochester, turned the angle of the wall in their descent. These were usually covered by a structure known as the fore-building, which provided a formidable covered approach to the main entrance. The fore-building formed a substantial annexe to the tower, and has some variety of plan. Indications of it are found in its simplest form at Scarborough, where it was of two stages. The lower stage was a vaulted passage against the south wall, from the end of which the basement doorway was entered at right angles; the upper stage was entered by a doorway from the first floor of the tower. The entrance passage was closed by wooden doors; if these were forced, an attacking party would still have some difficulty and danger in breaking into the tower, while missiles, hurled upon them through a hole in the floor of the upper stage, would make retreat from the passage a delicate matter. The fore-building at Kenilworth was also of two stages, enclosing an entrance stair, which led to the doorway on the first floor. The arrangement at Rochester was more complicated. Here the stair began against the north-west angle buttress, where it was covered by a small tower of two stages, the lower containing the doorway, the upper communicating with a vaulted chamber in the angle of the first floor of the tower. The stair then turned the angle, and, protected by an outer wall some 6 feet high, rose along the north wall of the tower to a drawbridge, with a deep pit below. At the further side of the drawbridge, the east part of the north wall was covered by a building in three stages. The middle stage, entered from the drawbridge, contained a chamber, in which was the main entrance to the first floor of the keep. The lowest stage was a vault, which communicated with the basement of the tower; the upper stage, entered from the second floor of the tower, contained a room, which may have been a chapel. At Dover and Newcastle the fore-buildings were even more elaborate, including a lower tower which

NEWCASTLE : great tower

protected the entrance and right-angled turn of the stair, a middle tower which covered the stair half-way up, and an upper tower at the head of the stair, beyond the platform from which the second floor was entered. The basement of the fore-building at Newcastle was the castle chapel; the lower tower was, as at Rochester, simply a gate-tower; the middle tower formed a covering to a second gateway on the stair; and the upper tower contained a vaulted guard-room commanding the platform of entrance. At Dover, the upper tower, solid at the base, had vaulted chambers on the first and second floors; the middle tower enclosed a well, the mouth of which was contained in a chamber entered from the platform in front of the main doorway of the keep; while the lower tower formed a large projection at the south-west angle of the keep, containing upon its first floor a covered landing for the stair, from which opened to the east a room, probably an oratory, and to the west a porter's lodge. Upon the second floor was the chapel of the keep, entered from the main apartments. A vault in the basement of the lower tower of the fore-building communicates with the basement of the keep through another vault, which is common to the keep and fore-building. Similarly, the vault at the first-floor level of the upper tower communicates with the main first floor through another common vaulted chamber. The Dover fore-building is thus an integral portion of the keep.

Of all existing fore-buildings, that at Castle Rising (143) is in the best state of preservation. Here the main entrance to the keep is on the east face of the building, near its north end. The stair, which had a timber roof, ascends by the side of the east wall, straight from the ground. There is a gateway at its foot, and another gateway at a landing half-way up. The upper flight of stairs, which was also roofed with timber, passes through a third gateway into the upper floor of a tower, which, as at Rochester and Norwich, covers the main doorway of the keep, and is not placed, as at Dover and Newcastle, beyond the doorway. Each of the doorways of the fore-building has a rounded arch with an edge-roll, and shafts with cushion capitals in the jambs. The main doorway of the keep has five orders, the four outer orders being shafted, and the arch having rich late Norman mouldings. The chamber at the head of the stair is vaulted in two bays, but originally had a timber roof. There is a vaulted chamber beneath it.

There is an exceptional arrangement at Porchester (131), where the stair, instead of being covered by the fore-building, is set outside it, against its eastern face. From the landing at the head there is a straight passage, between the first-floor rooms of the fore-building, to the main entrance of the tower; while, from the same landing, another flight of stairs leads to the northern rampart-walk of the castle.   Another exceptional fore-building is found at Berkeley (142). Here, however, the exception consists in the fact that it is a fore-building, not to a tower, but to a shell-keep of peculiar construction.   The mount of the early Norman castle was reduced in height, and its base, forming a platform some 20 feet above the ground, was enclosed within a wall, 8 feet thick, which is strengthened by pilaster but-tresses and rises to a height of 60 feet.   Against the south-east face of this wall is a narrow fore-building.   The stair, which was covered by a timber roof, passes through the lower stage of a gateway-tower, and ascends to a platform, from which, after another gateway has been passed, the interior of the shell is

Berkeley

entered.   The room upon the first floor of the gateway-tower is entered from the platform by a narrow ledge above the stair.

As the main doorway of a tower-keep was set in the outer face of a thick wall, a narrow passage had to be traversed before the interior of the tower was reached.   At Castle Rising, the wall is comparatively thin, and the doorway is recessed deeply, so that the tower is entered directly.   In most cases, the keep was divided internally into two parts by a cross-wall, which reached from the basement to the summit.[1]   This wall was often central, as at Porchester, Rochester, and Scarborough; but in towers which are oblong in plan, as at Castle Rising and Middleham, it divided the keep into two unequal rect-angles.   At Bowes, as also in the Norman keep of Domfront,

[1] For the reason, see note on pp. 121, 122.

CASTLE RISING : stair of forebuilding

it was so far from being central that it cut off only a narrow
oblong from the interior, the large main room on the first
floor of Bowes being left nearly square.   In a square keep,
the cross-wall was frequently opposite the main entrance, and
parallel with the fore-building.   At Hedingham, Lancaster,
Porchester, and Scarborough, it is at right angles to the fore-
building, so that the main entrance is, as in the oblong keep of
Castle Rising, in an end, and not in a side of one of the rooms.
The cross-wall at Scarborough was not continued to the second

Rochester ; internal cross-wall

floor ; and, on the first floor, a transverse arch took its place,
throwing the two main rooms into one.   A great transverse arch,
perhaps the finest architectural feature in any of our tower-keeps,
also spans the second floor at Hedingham, in place of the cross-
wall (147).   On the second floor at Rochester, the cross-wall is
represented by two pairs of rounded arches, divided by a central
block of wall containing the well-shaft (145).   But a cross-wall was
not an universal feature of a tower-keep.   Neither Clun nor Guildford, towers of moderate size, have one ; and, of the greater keeps,

Newcastle, Richmond, and Kenilworth have undivided interiors. This is remarkable in a keep of the area of Kenilworth: at Newcastle and Richmond the walls are so solid that the interior space is comparatively small, while at Newcastle additional room was supplied by unusually spacious mural chambers. At Castle Rising, in addition to the main cross-wall, each of the divisions of the keep has a smaller cross-wall at its extremity, cutting off additional apartments from the main rooms, and allowing in one place the insertion of an upper floor.

Of the divisions of the tower, whether divided by a cross-wall or not, the basement was probably used for the storage of arms and provisions. It sometimes contained the opening of the well of the keep.[1] The first floor, where there was no other, contained the main apartment or hall. In the loftier type of keep, this was on the second floor, and, as we have just seen, the substitution of an arch or arcade for the cross-wall sometimes converted this floor into one large apartment. At Dover and Porchester, as in the Tower of London, the division into two apartments was maintained, and there is only a small doorway through the cross-wall. The second room, in these instances, probably formed the "great chamber" or private apartment of the lord of the castle when in residence. Where the hall was on the second floor the first floor was probably set apart for the garrison in time of siege and for the servants. The provision for private bedrooms was, in those days of publicity, extremely small; but where, as at Dover and Newcastle, the thickness of the wall allowed of several large mural chambers, some of them may have been devoted to this purpose; and in some keeps, as at Hedingham, an upper floor above the main apartments was provided, which doubtless served this end.[2]

For the purpose of communication between the floors, the example of the towers of London and Colchester was followed. A well-stair was constructed in one of the angles from the basement to the summit of the tower, and had an entrance to each floor through a short passage in the thickness of the wall, or sometimes in the embrasure of one of the windows. This single stair was the only means of approach to the basement. At Dover there are two such stairs; and, in a few instances, there are small outer doorways to the basement,

---

[1] Legends about the cruelties practised on prisoners, often connected with these basement chambers, need not be believed too readily. Specially constructed prison chambers in castles usually belong to a period later than the twelfth century. On the origin of the word "dungeon" see Chapter III.

[2] See the description of the tower at Ardres in Chapter III. Such upper floors were probably divided into rooms by wooden partitions.

HEDINGHAM : second floor of great tower

HEDINGHAM : doorway of great tower

which may be original, like the postern, high above the ground at Newcastle, or may have been cut at a later date, like the entrance to the basement from the fore-building at Kenilworth. The two stairs at Dover are diagonally opposite to one another. At Rochester a second stair, also diagonal to the other, begins at the first floor and ascends to the roof. The main stair at Guildford starts in an angle of the first floor : the basement was probably entered by a trap-door and ladder, but later, probably in the thirteenth century, a doorway was cut through the wall into the basement below the main entrance. At Scarborough, although the main entrance was at the basement level, it merely opened on a stair leading to the first floor : the stair to the basement, if there was one, seems to have been in one of the angles which has been destroyed. In the keeps of Richmond and Ludlow, owing to the preservation of the older gatehouses in whole or in part, the arrangements are exceptional. The basement at Richmond (93) had, as we have seen, its own entrance from the interior of the castle ; but there was also an inserted stair, now blocked, in one of its angles from the first floor. The main stair of the tower, however, started to the left of the main entrance on the first floor, and continued upwards straight through the south wall to the level of the second floor, where it stopped. The stair from the second floor to the roof started from a point above the first floor entrance, and also ran through the whole thickness of the south wall above the lower stair, opening on the rampart at a point above the entrance to the second floor.[1] At Ludlow, as a consequence of the transformation of the gatehouse, the original straight stair from the basement to the floor above, in the thickness of the east wall, was blocked up, and the basement was entered only by a trap-door in the first floor.[2]

The various floors of the tower-keep were of timber, and vaulted chambers, even in the basement, were an exception. The basement at Newcastle has an original vaulted roof, on eight ribs springing from a central column : the vaulting of the basement at Richmond, also from a central column, is an insertion. At Norham the basement is divided by the cross-wall into two parts, one of which has a cross-wall of its own, dividing it into two chambers, both barrel-vaulted : the other division has four bays of groined vaulting, divided by plain

---

[1] It was thus impossible to reach the roof from the first floor without passing through the second-floor chamber—a precaution which was adopted also in the cylindrical tower at Conisbrough.

[2] Here the basement was probably used as a prison. The upper part of the original stair still remains.

transverse arches.   The basement at Bamburgh was also vaulted
in three chambers, the largest of which had a central arcade of
three arches, from which ribs were struck to the outer wall and
cross-wall.   The two chambers of the basement at Middleham
were also vaulted, one from a central arcade of five bays.   But
these northern examples are quite exceptional ; and, even at
Castle Rising, where the architectural treatment of the various
portions of the building is unusually elaborate, and the larger
chamber of the basement is divided by a row of columns,
vaulting was confined to the small subdivisions which support
the lesser first-floor chambers already mentioned.

Mural chambers, made in the thickness of the wall, were
necessarily vaulted, the usual form employed being the barrel-
vault, which sprang from the wall without any dividing string-
course.   Otherwise, the only apartment which had a stone roof
was the chapel, frequently found in connection with the tower-
keep.   It must be added, however, that the chapel hardly ever
occupies any part of a main floor in the keep, and that at Castle
Rising, where it is in an angle of the first floor, the chancel alone
is vaulted, and is constructed in the thickness of the wall.   Chapels
on the scale of those of London and Colchester were never again
attempted in a keep.   According to the usual theory, chapels
in castles and houses were planned so that no room used for
secular purposes should be above them ; and their position in
a keep was usually upon the upper floor of a tower in the
fore-building, communicating with the adjacent floor of the main
structure.   The altar was always placed against an east wall,
and the distinction between nave and chancel was usually kept.
Thus at Rochester, where all three stages of the tower of the
fore-building are vaulted, the top floor was probably a chapel,
the nave of which was entered directly from the second floor
of the keep through a mural passage, while the chancel communicated through a small vaulted lobby and a short stair
with the main stair of the keep.[1]   At Dover the chapel, with
ribbed vaulting, and a chancel arch of two orders with chevron
moulding and jamb-shafts, occupies the upper floor of the lower
tower of the fore-building.   The walls of chancel and nave are
arcaded, which is a very usual feature in a castle chapel, but
does not appear at Rochester.   The entrance from the second
floor of the keep at Dover was through a mural chamber and
a passage along the west wall of the chapel, which led to the
chapel doorway on the left hand, and a small vaulted room,
possibly a vestry, on the right.   At Porchester, again, the south

---

[1] There are indications, however, of a second chapel in the keep itself,
occupying the south-east angle of the third floor.

NEWCASTLE : chapel

chamber on the first floor of the fore-building was the chapel, approached from the passage which led through the fore-building to the main doorway. The chapel at Newcastle (152) is in an unusual position, in the basement of the fore-building, and is entered through a passage from the foot of the main stair. It also had originally an outer doorway, which communicated directly with the outer stair of the fore-building near its foot— another unusual feature. The ribbed vaulting, wall-arcading, and chancel arch, are of remarkably excellent workmanship, and the "water-leaf" ornament of the capitals of the wall-arcade bears a close resemblance to that of the capitals of the contemporary Galilee of Durham. As the fore-building at Newcastle is against the east wall of the keep, the longer axis of the nave of the chapel runs north and south, and is at right angles to that of the chancel. The chapel is thus T-shaped : the altar was placed on one side of the chancel, against the east wall, and was practically invisible from the nave. It is probable that the constable of the castle and his family or friends occupied the western part of the chancel, facing the altar, while the nave was used by the garrison and servants.[1]

Roomy chapels, like those at Newcastle and Old Sarum, were not merely the chapel of the great tower, but of the whole castle. On the other hand, the ordinary chapel of a tower-keep provided less accommodation, and seems to have been intended for the lord of the castle or his deputy and their immediate household. At Guildford the chapel of the keep is a mere oratory, formed by two mural chambers at right angles to one another, in the southwest angle of the first floor. The main body of the chapel, covered with a barrel-vault, is in the west wall ; the space for the altar, arranged so that the priest faced eastwards, is in the south wall, and is covered by a half-barrel-vault set at right angles to the longer axis. The nave, which is thus quite out of sight of the altar-chamber, has a wall-arcade of late twelfth-century character, supplying a valuable clue to the real date of this rudely built and archaic-looking keep. Although a chapel or oratory in the keep was not uncommon, it was on the whole a luxury. At Richmond and Ludlow no provision was made for one ; the chapels of the castles, which remain in both cases, were of earlier date than the conversion of the gatehouse into a tower. It is not unlikely that the name of chapel may have been given in later days to rooms in

---

[1] The recently excavated chapel of the great tower of Old Sarum was a vaulted building occupying the south-eastern part of the basement of the tower itself. It was entered directly from the bailey, and had no direct communication with the first floor of the tower.

18

keeps and fore-buildings which were intended for quite other purposes.[1]

Although, in time of siege, cooking in the keep itself would sometimes be necessary, no special part of the tower was set aside as a kitchen. Castle Rising is an exception, where the room cut off at the north-west angle of the first floor seems to have served this purpose, and a circular chimney-shaft was hollowed out in the angle itself.[2] Fireplaces are found in most tower-keeps, though not on all floors. Rochester and Dover were well provided in this way, while, on the other hand, the tower of Porchester was without any apparent means of artificial warmth. The fireplaces at Dover in the cross-wall are of great size; those at Rochester are numerous, but small, and have arches decorated with the thick and roughly-cut chevron ornament which also appears in the arcade of the cross-wall on the second floor. The original fireplaces at Newcastle are in the large mural chambers on the first and second floors. The main apartment here was probably warmed by a brazier on the floor; and this may have been a common method, as it was in the halls of private houses. A vent for the smoke must have been made in the roof.

Water, in view of the straitened circumstances of a siege, was a necessity in a keep, and, where there are no remains of a well, it is safe to assume that one has been filled up. In a mount-keep like Guildford, the well may have been inside the shell which walls in the front part of the mount. The wells of the Tower of London and Castle Rising were in the basements. At Colchester there is a well-chamber in the south wall of the basement, to the right of the entrance-passage. But in the later keeps the pipe of the well, a cylinder lined with ashlar, was often carried up through the thickness of a wall to the upper floors, which thus received their supply of water directly, without the necessity of a journey to the basement. At Kenilworth it was in the south wall, close to the south-west angle, with an opening on the basement and first floor. It is in the east wall at Newcastle, near the north-east angle: it has only one opening, at the well-head on the second floor, and is reached by a mural passage from the main apartment. There are two wells at Dover, one in the middle tower of the fore-building, with an opening at the level of the second floor, the other in the south wall of the keep, with its only opening

[1] Such as the so-called oratories in the fore-buildings of Dover and Newcastle.

[2] At Old Sarum, the room in the basement, west of the chapel, was probably the kitchen.

on the second floor, in a mural chamber to the left of the main entrance. The pipe at Rochester is in the centre of the cross-wall, and was carried up to the third floor, with an opening in the north chamber of each stage.

Mural chambers have been noticed incidentally. Some keeps, even of the largest size, have their walls unpierced, save for window openings : this is the case with Corfe. Porchester, in spite of its great size, contains only two, which were used for the common and necessary purpose of garde-robes or latrines. On the other hand, the exceptionally massive walls of Dover contain a large number of such chambers, most of which are of considerable size : the position of the garde-robes here is not easy to determine. At Newcastle advantage was taken of the thickness of the walls to construct large chambers in connection with the first and second floors : that in the south wall of the second floor, known as the "king's chamber," has an original fireplace, and is well lighted. A doorway at its north-west corner leads into a garde-robe in the west wall. The number of mural chambers at Newcastle is small compared with that at Dover, but the walls were freely pierced with passages and galleries. A stair, made through the upper part of the south and west walls to the ramparts, seems to have been abandoned during the progress of the work : the notion that it was deliberately intended to lead a body of the enemy, who might have entered the tower, into a *cul-de-sac*, is fanciful, but it certainly might have had this unintentional effect. At Dover, Hedingham, Newcastle, Norwich, and Rochester, where the hall or apartments on the second floor were of unusual height, galleries were made in the walls round the upper part of the stage. The gallery at Dover was not continued round the north-west angle of the tower, but a passage, now blocked, was made through the cross-wall from north to south, so that the east room on this floor was completely surrounded by a gallery. The gallery at Rochester surrounds the whole tower, communicating with the vices in the south-west and north-east angles, and opening upon the interior of the tower in no less than fourteen places, each of which corresponds to a loop in the outer wall. Where the arcade which, on the second floor, takes the place of the cross-wall, joins the east and west walls, the floor of the gallery is raised by a few steps, to provide the adjacent arch with a solid abutment. The arrangement of the mural galleries at Bamburgh, which, owing to the modern alterations of the interior of the tower, is rather obscure, seems to have been very like that at Dover, with a passage through the cross-wall between two divided rooms upon the second floor. The gallery at Hedingham, like that at Rochester, is complete, and this floor, which is still roofed, is admirably lighted (147). In cases where a mural chamber served as a garde-robe, as at Guildford, Porchester, and the tower of the Peak, the outer wall, in which the seat was contained, was slightly thickened and corbelled out at this level, and a vent made below the seat. At Kenilworth the north-west turret seems to have been used entirely as a garde-robe, the lower part of the basement forming a pit for the refuse.[1] The garde-robes at Castle Rising are contained in a vaulted chamber in the west wall of the first floor, the vents opening upon the recesses by which the outer face of the wall is broken up.

The roof of the tower-keep was of timber with an outer covering of lead, and was some feet below the level of the encircling rampart-walk on the top of the outer walls. The rampart-walk had a parapet upon its outer face, which at regular intervals was lowered to form embrasures. The solid portions of the parapet were of much greater breadth than the embrasures: the familiar type of battlemented parapet, in which the embrasures are of equal width with the solid "cops" or *merlons* between them, belongs to a later date. From the rampart-walk stairs led into the summits of the angle turrets, which were some feet above the level of the parapet. The original arrangement of the roof can be gathered only from the marks left against the inside of the walls. In towers with a cross-wall, like Rochester, each of the divisions was covered, as a general rule, by a roof of more or less high pitch. A central gutter ran along the top of the cross-wall, and side gutters along each of the lateral walls, which were drained through spout-holes made in the outer walls, which carried the rampart-walk. At Porchester, where, as already noted, the tower was heightened, there was originally a high-pitched central roof, with lean-to roofs against each of the lateral walls, and gutters above the centre of each of the two interior chambers. This curious arrangement seems to suggest that the cross-wall itself was added when the tower was heightened, and that the gutters originally were supported by timber struts in the second or attic stage of the tower. When the tower was raised, a flat roof was planned and possibly laid, and, by a curious and unique device, for which it is hard to find an adequate reason, the parapets of the east and west walls were slightly gabled. The present roof, however, is formed in the usual way, with two gables and central and side gutters. In towers without a cross-wall, like Ludlow, Newcastle, and

---

[1] *Cf.* the employment of one of the angle towers at the later castle of Langley in Northumberland as a garde-robe tower. Some of the late medieval pele-towers of the north of England, *e.g.*, Chipchase and Corbridge, provide excellent examples of mural garde-robes with corbelled-out seats.

NORHAM : great tower

NEWARK CASTLE

Richmond, the covering was a single high-pitched roof. In any case, the roof was below the level of the rampart-walk, and was not intended to form a free field for the defence of the tower : the occupation of the roof of the tower for purposes of defence was not contemplated until a somewhat later period than that at which the rectangular tower-keep was in general fashion. At Rochester, and probably in many other instances, the inner side of the rampart-walk was protected by a rear-wall, lower than the parapet. The parapet at Rochester was 2 feet broad and 8 feet high : the rear-wall had a breadth of 3 feet, and the rampart-walk of 4 feet. A foot of wall was left for the springing of the roofs and for their side-gutters. The roof at Newcastle was re-laid in 1240 ; but here and at Dover the insertion of comparatively modern vaults makes the original arrangement difficult to trace. The present roof of Richmond is modern, with a skylight to give light and air to the dark room on the second floor : the height of the outer walls above the roof suggests that the original roof was of unusually high pitch or rose above an intermediate attic. The angle turrets formed elevated platforms, approached from the rampart-walk by stone stairs. Their elevation afforded a greater command of the proceedings of the enemy at the foot of the tower ; and their solid construction may sometimes have allowed the defenders to employ them for stone-throwing engines, without interference with the operations of the soldiers on the somewhat narrow rampart-walk.

It has already been shown that, if the main object of these towers was defensive, many of them seem to have been planned with a degree of comfort which indicates that their builders had an eye to their permanent use as the principal residence within the enclosure of the castle, and that, in the towers built during the reign of Henry II., a compromise between their military and domestic character was effected. It is clear, however, that, in the cases of Richmond and Ludlow, the converted gatehouse-towers were planned simply as military strongholds. Their position, in both these instances, was exposed to direct attack, while the early domestic buildings occupied a more sheltered position on the further side of the inner ward. The tower-keep can never have formed a convenient residence, even where, as at Hedingham, it was well lighted, or, as at Dover, was unusually roomy. New methods of fortification led to its general disuse, and although, in certain parts of England, the type persisted upon a small scale until the end of the middle ages, the period during which the fashion of building rectangular tower-keeps was pursued was comparatively short.

CHAPTER VII

THE PERIOD OF TRANSITION: CYLINDRICAL TOWER-KEEPS

THE development of the castle during the twelfth century was governed, as has been explained, by the methods of attack which its defenders had to meet. The strong fortresses of the reign of Henry II., with their stone curtains and rectangular keeps, opposed to the enemy a solid front of passive strength which defied attack. Sufficiently provisioned, a small garrison was capable of holding out against a long blockade, and tiring the patience of the assailants, whose artillery could make but little impression upon the masonry of the castle. At the same time, the stone castle with the rectangular tower-keep does not represent a final point in the perfection of fortification. The early Plantagenet castles were, on the contrary, merely a departure from the ordinary type of castle, composed of earthwork and timber, in the direction of an organised system of permanent stone castles. They belonged to a transitional period; for, even while they were being built, improvements upon their most striking feature, the rectangular keep, were suggesting themselves. During the last twenty years of the twelfth century, lessons learned by the Crusaders from the traditional methods of fortification employed in the Eastern empire exercised a profound influence upon the military architecture of France and England; and the application of these lessons during the thirteenth century entirely altered the defensive scheme of the castle, until the plan of masterpieces of fortification like Caerphilly and Harlech presented an entire contrast to the plan of defensive strongholds like Norham and Scarborough.

The first necessity which had governed the development of fortification was that of enclosing the defended position so as to present an adequate barrier to attack. The bailey was surrounded with its palisade; while the palisaded mount, with its wooden tower, commanded—that is, overlooked—the operations of the defenders within the bailey, and provided a second line of defence, if the bailey were taken. As siege-engines increased in strength, stone-work took the place of stockading. The bailey was encircled by a stone wall with a certain number of towers on its circumference. It was sometimes divided into an outer and inner ward by a cross-wall, or, as at Ludlow (96), a large outer bailey was added to it, which formed a courtyard for barracks and stabling, and a protection in time of war for dwellers on the outskirts of the castle and for their flocks. A wall superseded the palisade round the mount, or a strong tower was built, either in connection with the mount or on a new site, which commanded the whole enclosure. Thus the passive strength of the castle was ensured. But stone walls and towers, however strong, were in themselves an insufficient protection, unless the defenders could keep themselves fully informed of the movements of the enemy. It was necessary that they should be able to command the field in which the besiegers worked, and especially the foot of the wall or tower on which the attack was concentrated. The battering-ram, the scaling-ladder, and the mine must be kept under constant observation. A first step towards this was the establishment of projecting towers along the wall at intervals. These flank the wall—that is, the outer face of the wall between them can be overlooked and protected by bodies of men posted upon the projection on either flank. At first, however, the system of flanking was far from perfect; and therefore the next step was in the direction of improving it, so that every portion of the outer surface of the *enceinte* might be covered by the fire of the defenders. This improvement, which we are about to trace, was effected gradually, (1) by a change in the form of the flanking defences themselves; (2) by their multiplication at more frequent intervals. The first of these changes begins to be noticeable during the later years of the twelfth century: the second was brought to pass in the first half of the thirteenth century, and led to further developments in the arrangement of the lines of defence.

The rectangular form of the keep and of the towers on the curtain was in two respects a drawback to the defence of the castle. In the first place, the salient angles of the masonry were liable to destruction by sap and mine. The parallel jointing of the stonework made the removal of fragments of stone by the bore or pick at these points a comparatively easy, if still laborious, task. In the second place, the angles of a tower or curtain, which were thus points of danger, were precisely the places which the defenders were least able to command satisfactorily. Each face of a rectangular tower commands the field immediately in front of it: the range of shot, from the point of view of each marksman, is in a direction at right angles to the face of the tower. Strictly speaking, the foot of the whole curtain and its towers lies within a "dead angle," as vertical fire from the rampart is impossible; but the wooden galleries attached to the rampart obviated this difficulty. But, if the lines of two adjacent faces of the tower are produced, it will be seen that the space contained by these is out of the defenders' range, and within it miners can work securely, while the main attack is directed against the faces of the rectangle. One obvious concrete illustration of this is seen at Rochester. When King John, in 1215, besieged the castle, he directed against it his stone-throwing engines. Finding that progress by this means was slow, he set his miners to work. A breach was made in the outer curtain, and the miners continued their operations on the tower, and eventually, after much difficulty, broke their way through it.[1] We can see to-day that the south-east angle of the tower has been rebuilt, and that the form of the reconstructed turret is round, and not square. This, no doubt, marks the place where the breach was made: the repairs are evidently part of the work taken in hand by Henry III. in 1225.

A further weak point in the defences of the castle was the insufficient flanking of the curtain. In the eleventh century, as we have seen, flanking towers were discouraged by feudal over-lords, who rightly recognised the danger which a strongly fortified castle, in the hands of rebels, might mean to themselves. As time went on, stone curtains were provided with towers; but these were not many in number, and, so long as the rectangular form of tower continued in fashion, long spaces of straight wall were left between the projections. The risk of providing too many salient angles was probably recognised by military engineers. From the flanking towers the adjacent part of the wall could be covered by the artillery of the defence; but, where a long interval existed between two towers, the wall mid-way was out of effective range. To protect these unflanked points in time of siege, a body of defenders would have to be kept on each spot. A twelfth-century castle, therefore, to be thoroughly defended, needed a large garrison to cover its numerous weak points. Any attempt to concentrate the defence upon one threatened spot might lead to the weakening of the defence at other points, of which the enemy would not be slow to take advantage.

Added to this was an inherent drawback in the normal plan of the castle. Its wards and keep provided a system of successive lines of defence, which caused an enemy immense trouble

[1] Roger of Wendover, ann. 1215.

to pierce, but could not offer a combined resistance to him. In many castles, like Norham or Barnard Castle, the inner ward and keep were placed at a distant angle of the enclosure, and were protected from external attack by steep outer slopes and a river at their foot. In such cases, the wall of the outer ward offered the first resistance: the inner ward did not come into action until the enemy had entered the outer ward, and the defenders had to retire to the inner enclosure. If the inner wall was breached or stormed, the keep gave the defence its last shelter. At Château-Gaillard, as has already been described, the chief feature of the siege was the capture of ward after ward: the defenders, in despair, did not even attempt to resort, as a final resource, to the keep. Château-Gaillard was in its own day a model of scientific fortification. Its fall was therefore

Château-Gaillard ; Plan

a very striking example of the disadvantage of successive lines of defence, of which only one could be effectively used at a time. It is true that here and there, as at Rochester, the keep was placed so near the curtain of an outer ward that the exterior of the castle could be commanded from its battlements, and its artillery could be brought into play over the heads of the defenders of the curtain. At Richmond, the great tower commands the one side of the castle from which attack was possible, and was thus placed in the very fore-front of the defence. But such arrangements were happy ideas which occurred to individual engineers, and do not imply any systematic advance in the science of defence.

The experiences of the earliest Crusaders brought the warriors of the west face to face with methods of defence far superior to those employed in England and France. The city-wall of

Antioch gave them an example of a perfect system of flanking defences ; and, in the triple *enceinte* of Constantinople they saw how successive lines of defence could be used in co-operation. At Antioch the wall was flanked at frequent intervals by fifty towers.   Each of these, rising above the curtain, commanded not only its space of intermediate wall, but the rampart-walk as well. The rampart-walk, moreover, passed through the towers, which were protected by strong doors.   To gain the whole line of wall, therefore, it was necessary to occupy the towers, each of which could be converted into a separate stronghold, isolating the intermediate rampart-walk.   The siege was badly conducted, the Crusaders limiting themselves to a strong position between the city and the Orontes, and allowing the defenders to hold their communications on two sides of the city open for some five months.   Posts of observation were eventually established on the two neglected sides ; but the actual capture of the city was due to the treachery of one of the commanders of the Turkish garrison, who admitted a body of Franks into one of the towers in his charge.   They made their way into seven more towers, and so gained access to the city.[1]   The three walls of Constantinople surrounded the whole city : each was higher than the one outside it, so that all three could be used simul-taneously by the defenders.[2]   Against such a system of concentric defence, the besiegers were manifestly at a disadvantage.

These lessons from the east, stimulating though they were, did not produce their full practical effect for some generations in the west.   Our engineers had to pass through a long epoch of gradual experiment before they could arrive at a finished system of flanking or of concentric lines of defence.   The traditional mount-and-bailey plan provided the foundation of the plan of the stone castle.   The traditional importance of the keep as the ultimate place of refuge dictated the arrangement of ward behind ward, culminating in the great tower.   Meanwhile, the improvement of flanking defences led more and more to the concentration of engineering skill upon the curtain, so that the keep gradually took a place of secondary importance.   As an obvious result of further improvement, the keep was dispensed with, and the whole attention of the engineer was directed to combining the defences of the castle into a double or triple line of simultaneous resistance to attack.   These steps took time : the transition from one to the other was effected by no sudden revolution, but by work along old lines, a work of revision and

[1] See the description of the fortifications of Antioch in Oman, *Art of War*, pp. 527-9 ; plan facing p. 283.
[2] *Ibid.*, 526-7.

improvement, until the finished product formed an almost complete antithesis to the source from which it was derived.

The earliest signs of transition in England are seen in the strengthening of the masonry by the reduction and elimination of salient angles. It is obvious that, if a rounded or polygonal form is given to a projecting tower, or if the angle of a rectangular tower is rounded off, a wider field will be commanded by the artillery of the defence. The new range will be a large segment of a circle radiating from the centre of the tower, instead of a rectangle in front of each face. The sectors at the angles within which an attacking party can work securely will be thus eliminated, and the chances of the success of a mine will be less. The masonry also will offer much greater resistance to the battering or boring engines of the enemy. The joints are no longer parallel, but radiating, so that it becomes much harder work to force out stones and effect a breach. The obtuse angles of polygonal towers, with the joints of the masonry in the alternate faces running in oblique directions to each other, have a much greater power of resistance than the right angles of the ordinary twelfth-century tower.

The general use of circular and polygonal forms is first found in connection with the principal tower of the castle, the keep. The main object was at first, no doubt, the greater cohesion imparted to the masonry : the scientific advantages, from the point of view of artillery, probably were not realised till later. In France the cylindrical donjon appeared at an earlier date than in England : that at Château-sur-Epte (Eure) is said to have been begun in 1097.[1] The tower of Houdan (Seine-et-Oise) is a cylinder flanked by four cylindrical turrets : it was built during the reign of Louis VI. (1108-37),[2] and the form shows that the builders looked, not merely to the strength of the masonry, but to the reduction of the enemy's chances of successful attack. The majority, however, of such donjons in France belong to the second half of the twelfth century and the beginning of the thirteenth, and were contemporary with our rectangular towers. But the engineers of Henry II., to whom we owe so many of our stone keeps, were certainly acquainted with the possible benefits of forms other than square. The keep of Orford in Suffolk was probably built between 1166 and 1172,[3] and is therefore earlier in date than many rectangular keeps.

---

[1] Enlart, ii. 504.

[2] *Ibid.*, ii. 508 : it is attributed to Amaury, count of Evreux (1105-37) : the masonry (*ibid.*, 461) is of coursed rubble with bonding-courses of ashlar.

[3] See note 17, p. 119. The keep of Orford is described at some length by Harvey, *Castles and Walled Towns*, pp. 106-111.

Internally, it is cylindrical; externally, a polygon of twenty-one sides, with three very large rectangular turrets projecting from it. It has a basement and two main floors, and is entered by a two-storied fore-building, which forms a southward continuation of the eastern turret. The sloping base of the tower is continued round the turrets, and greatly strengthens their angles; while the turrets themselves are so placed as to flank the whole tower and fore-building very effectively, and to provide additional room in the interior. This combination of the rectangular and polygonal forms is, for its date, an unique departure from the ordinary type of English tower-keep. But it must be re-membered that the shell-keep on the mount usually took the

Conisbrough ; Keep

form of a cylindri-cal or polygonal wall strengthened by but-tresses; and at Or-ford, where the tower appears to stand upon the base of a levelled mount, we may have a conscious adapta-tion of this form to the heavier and loftier tower. At Gisors (Eure) the older don-jon was an octagonal tower, built on a mount, and sur-rounded by a circular wall. The tower was probably built by Henry II. between 1161 and 1184,[1] within the somewhat earlier shell, and took the form which was best suited to the artificial soil on which it stood. But there are at least two instances of English rectangular keeps in which a slight departure from the normal form was made for obvious purposes of additional strength, without reference to an artificial site. At Newcastle the north-west turret is octagonal, with very obtuse angles. In the small tower of Mitford, on the Wansbeck above Morpeth, the north wall is built with an obtuse salient angle, so that the tower forms an irregular pentagon. The date of this tower cannot be fixed with certainty, but it probably belongs to the second half, at any rate, of the twelfth century;

[1] Enlart, ii. 505.

and it can hardly be doubted that the object of this peculiar device was to give the defenders better command of the angles of the tower which were exposed to attack from the inner ward.

Somewhat later than these is the noble cylindrical keep of Conisbrough (166), which is attributed to Hamelin Plantagenet,

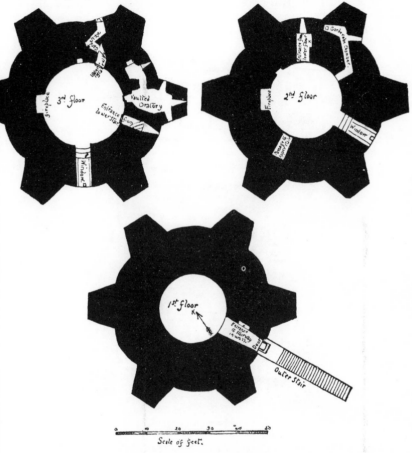

Conisbrough ; Keep. Plans

a natural brother of Henry II., and husband of Isabel, heiress of William, earl of Surrey. Hamelin died in 1201 : the tower was built, as the architectural details show, during the last quarter of the twelfth century. It is a regular cylinder ; and to its circumference are applied six bold buttresses, which narrow slightly out-

wards, and rise above the parapet in turrets.   The whole is built
of dressed stone in large rectangular blocks, the fine condition
of which, after more than seven hundred years, is extraordinary.
The construction is unusually solid : the thickness of the wall in
the basement exceeds 20 feet.   On the first floor it is just under
15 feet : in the two upper floors it is reduced by internal off-sets,
until, at the rampart level, 75 to 80 feet above the ground, it
is 12½ feet.   In addition to this the buttresses, which project 9

Conisbrough ; Fireplace

feet at the basement level and 8 feet above, are not used, like the
turrets at Orford, to contain additional rooms, but are built solid.
The chapel, however, was formed by constructing a chamber in
the eastern buttress upon the third floor.

The tower of Conisbrough, like that of Orford, was intended
for residential as well as defensive purposes ; but light and
comfort were sacrificed to military necessities.   The entrance,
as usual, was upon the first floor, but there is no trace of any

fore-building, nor is the original means of approach at all clear. The basement was simply a domed well-chamber and store-room : the only approach to it from the first floor was an opening in the centre of the guard-chamber, over which was probably the windlass by which buckets were lowered into the well.[1] The first floor was a guard-chamber : there were no windows, and the only means of admitting daylight was through the open door on the far side of the passage through the wall. On the right-hand side of this passage, a curved stair mounts through the thickness of the wall to the second floor, which it enters by a landing in the embrasure[2] of a loop on the north side. This floor was the hall of the keep. There is a large fireplace (168) in the west wall, with a spreading chimney-breast, and a lintel of joggled stones resting on triple shafts with carved capitals. In the wall between the fireplace and the entrance is a rectangular recess, containing a small sink, which was drained through the wall. There are two windows, the loop close to the entrance, and a double window opening to the south-east. The embrasures are barrel-vaulted : that of the double window has a stone bench on all three sides, and stands three steps above the floor of the hall. This window was not glazed : the upright between the two rectangular openings has at the back a rounded projection, through a hole in which the bolt of the shutters passed, and the fastening was further secured by a wooden draw-bar. On the north-east side of the hall a winding passage with two turns and a flight of steps leads through the thickness of the wall to a garde-robe.

To reach the third floor, the hall had to be crossed to a recess in the direction of the south-west buttress. From this point a curved staircase mounted through the wall to the embrasure of a loop in the south-east face of the third floor. The apartment on this floor contained a smaller fireplace, immediately above that on the second floor, and treated with similar architectural ornament. The flue of the lower chimney runs up through the wall behind that of the other : the common chimney-top projects from the rampart-walk above. There is also upon this floor a trefoil-headed recess with a sink. There are two windows, the loop in the south-east face, and a double opening, similar to that below, looking south. This room corresponded to the "great chamber," which is found in the larger houses of the middle

---

[1] Possibly there was a trap-door in the centre of each floor : see below. All the floors are gone above the entrance stage.

[2] An embrasure is the splay or inner opening of a window. The word is also applied to the openings between the *merlons* or solid pieces of a crenellated parapet.

ages. On its east side the chapel, an irregular hexagon, vaulted in two ribbed bays with a transverse arch between, was constructed in the eastern wall and buttress. The details of its beautiful capitals, like those of the fireplaces, show elementary foliage of the water-leaf type, such as is found in the chapel of the tower at Newcastle (152). Chevron is used in the stilted transverse arch and round the outside of the arch of the loop at the east end. The quatrefoil openings north and south of the chancel bay, and the trefoil-headed *piscinae* in the same walls, are of an advanced transitional character; and, by comparing these details, a date approximating to 1185-90 may with some certainty be given to the tower. In the north wall of the chapel a doorway leads into a small vestry or priest's chamber, lighted by a loop. The stairway to the rampart-walk mounts through the wall above this chamber, and its head is above the western bay of the chapel. It is entered from a recess in the north-east wall of the second floor, and from this recess there is also a zigzag passage to a garde-robe, the seat of which is corbelled out in the angle between the north-east buttress and the north wall of the tower. The two lower stairways and the two garde-robe chambers are each lighted by a small loop.

In the roomier arrangement of the keep at Orford, the stair is a vice in the turret or buttress to which the fore-building is annexed. The chapel is upon the first floor of the fore-building, and, being on a level of its own, not corresponding to the levels of the tower, is approached from the stair by a separate passage. The entrance to the chapel is a doorway on the left of this passage, which is continued through the south-east wall of the tower to a priest's room in the south turret.

The defensive side of the arrangements at Conisbrough must now be considered. The tower stands close to the north-east corner of a large bailey, the shape of which follows that of the knoll on which it is built: the north segment of the tower, with the two adjacent buttresses, continues the line of the curtain; but five-sixths of the circumference, with four of the buttresses, are within the enclosure. On the north and east sides the steepness of the hill made access nearly impracticable, and the natural point of attack was from the south and south-west. The position of the keep is at the point furthest removed from attack, and the capture of the inner ward, as will be seen in a later chapter, was rendered very difficult by a well-guarded approach.[1] The tower stood on higher ground than the rest of the ward, and the entrance, on the south-east side, was sheltered by the east curtain. The south and south-west faces were fully

[1] See pp. 217, 230, 233.

exposed to an attack from the inner ward, and it was on this side, therefore, that the defenders needed full command of the sides and base of the tower. Accordingly, when we mount to the rampart-walk, and examine the tops of the buttresses, we find that the two which are upon the north curtain, and were not exposed to attack, contain cisterns. The two on either side of the main entrance were not necessary for flanking purposes, as the entrance itself would be defended by some kind of plat-form in time of siege. One, therefore, above the chapel, was employed as a house for carrier-pigeons ; while the other con-tained an oven, in which stones and arrows could be heated. The remaining two buttresses are raised platforms which effectively flanked that part of the circumference which was otherwise insufficiently guarded, and lay open to catapults and mining operations. The spreading base of the tower and buttresses served further to keep the battering-ram and bore from direct contact with the main wall of the tower, and improved the flanking position of the defenders ; while missiles dropped from the summit upon this talus **or** sloping surface would rebound upon the enemy with deadly effect.

Above the talus the solidity of the main wall defied the force of catapults. These engines, however, had increased in strength and range, and it was no longer safe to give light to the tower in the somewhat lavish method adopted by the engineers of some of our large keeps. At Conisbrough, as we have seen, the walls of the first floor, save for the entrance passage, are absolutely solid. The loops in the upper floors are very few in number, and the one on the most exposed face is almost concealed by a buttress. The double window on the second floor is immediately over the main entrance, on a side which it would be difficult to command with a large siege-engine. That on the third floor is placed upon an exposed face, but would probably be out of range.[1] The garde-robe vents are on the side where the tower crosses the line of the curtain.

In time of siege the larger windows would be shuttered and barred. The defence would be conducted from the top of the tower, while a body of the garrison would be told off to protect the main entrance. The whole summit would be utilised. The defence was not confined, as in a rectangular keep, to the rampart-walk ; but there was a rear-wall to the walk, through which openings probably gave access to a covered round-house

---

[1] It may also be noted that the practice of placing windows immediately above one another would be naturally avoided, as tending to weaken the masonry of the whole wall at these points. This is well seen in the irregular position of the numerous loops which light the vice of the donjon at Coucy.

above the third floor. To this room, which, to judge from contemporary instances, had a conical roof, arms and missiles could be hauled up, through trap-doors in the floors below, from the guard-room and the store-chamber in the basement. There was no vaulted roof in the tower above the basement, so that the flat roof could not be used as a platform for catapults. There is no indication that hoarding was employed outside the rampart. The tower and its buttresses were finished off with a battlemented parapet in the usual way ; the buttresses, as has been shown, were so constructed and so near together that additional wooden defences were practically unnecessary.

In France the treatment of the donjon was pursued with more variation than in England. To the middle of the twelfth century belongs, for instance, the donjon of Etampes (Seine-et-Oise), which takes the form of a quatrefoil (172). The donjon of Provins (Seine-et-Marne) is of much the same date, the ground-plan forming an octagon flanked by four cylindrical turrets. Although both these towers have analogies in England, they were constructed nevertheless by French engineers at a period before even the rectangular tower had become common with ours.[1] They are also only two out of many diverse experiments. The cylindrical form, however, commended itself to the builders of the finest French examples.

Etampes ; Donjon. Plan

Château - Gaillard (163) follows closely upon Conisbrough in point of date, having been begun by Richard I. in 1196. The donjon is not, as at Conisbrough, a tower to which the line of a somewhat earlier curtain has been adapted, but is part of a homogeneous scheme of fortification. The site of the castle is the top of a very steep and almost isolated hill on the right bank of the Seine : the west slope is a precipice, and the only practicable attack could be made from the ridge joining the hill to the high ground on the south. The donjon is set so that its west face projects from the curtain of the inner ward, upon the very edge of the precipice. The interior forms a regular cylinder, and the west face is a segment of a circle. On this side the solidity of the masonry is increased by a tremendous outward slope or batter, the whole

[1] Enlart, ii. 735, gives the date of the donjon (Tour Guinette) at Etampes as about 1140.

GOODRICH CASTLE : buttery hatches

GOODRICH CASTLE : round tower with spur at base

height of the basement and adjacent curtain. Towards the inner
ward, however, the cylinder is strengthened by a covering spur,
also battered, so that, while the interior of the castle was commanded from the rampart, the tower offered to the besiegers an
angle of immense thickness and strength, immediately opposite
the gateway of the inner ward. A possible prototype in France
of this form of defence is the donjon of La-Roche-Guyon (Seine-
et-Oise), higher up the Seine, where the spur covers about a quarter
of the circumference of the tower. Philip Augustus adopted the
same device a few years later in the White tower at Issoudun
(Indre).[1] It is seen at Goodrich (174), Chepstow, and elsewhere.

As the upper portion of
the tower of Château-
Gaillard is gone, its in-
ternal arrangements are
difficult to decipher. It
was purely a tower of de-
fence ; but the inaccessible
nature of the west side
allowed of large windows
being made in that face
upon the first floor. There
was probably a low second
floor, above which was the
roof and rampart-walk. The
rampart was defended with
the aid of a device, unusual
at the time, although very
general at a later period.
The sides of the tower
within the ward were fur-
nished with narrow but-
tress projections above the
battering base, which gradually increased in breadth

Château-Gaillard

as they went higher. These divided the face of the tower into a
series of recesses spanned by low arches, on the outer face of
which the parapet was carried. The top of each recess, between
the parapet and the wall, was left open, so that the defenders
could use the holes for raining down missiles upon their opponents.
Such holes, formed by corbelling out a parapet in advance of a wall
or tower, are called machicolations (*mâchicoulis*),[2] and gradually

---

[1] Enlart, ii. 674, gives the date of completion at Issoudun as 1202.

[2] Or *mâchecoulis*. *Coulis*=a groove. The first part of the word is probably derived from *mâcher*=to break or crush, and implies the purpose
effected by missiles sent through those openings.

superseded the external gallery of timber. Holes in stone roofs
for the same purpose are found at an earlier date, as in the fore-
building at Scarborough ; and, as early as 1160, they appear in
connection with the parapet of a donjon at Niort (Deux-Sèvres).[1]
The general tradition is that they were invented by the Crusaders
in Syria, where wood for hoarding was not easily obtained ; and
this is probably true.[2] They appear in a state of perfection,
which testifies to a long course of previous experiment, at the
great Syrian castle of Le Krak des Chevaliers (176), begun in
1202. But hoarding continued in use in Europe long after the
building of Château-Gaillard, and even the donjon of Coucy
(Aisne), by far the finest of all cylindrical donjons, was garnished
with timber hoarding carried on stone corbels—an interesting
example of the transition from one form of defence to another.

The cylindrical form of donjon was brought to perfection in

Le Krak des Chevaliers

France under Philip Augustus (1180-1223). At Gisors, which
came into his hands in 1193, he built a new circular tower on
the line of the curtain, which superseded Henry II.'s octagonal
tower on the mount. His fortification of Gisors led directly
to the building of Château-Gaillard by Richard I., to cover
the approach from French territory to Rouen.[3] But in 1204
the capture of this great stronghold delivered Rouen into
Philip's hands ; and in 1207 he built the donjon, now known
as the Tour Jeanne d'Arc, at Rouen. Here we meet with the

---

[1] Drawing in Enlart, ii. 504. Here there are two rectangular towers,
with rounded angle-turrets, connected by a lofty intermediate building.

[2] The same cause undoubtedly led, at an earlier date, to the covering of
Syrian churches with roofs of stone.

[3] Château-Gaillard was on the French side of the Seine, in territory
purchased by Richard I. from the archbishop of Rouen.

tower vaulted from basement to roof, with a strongly defended entrance at the level of the ward in which it stands, of which the most perfect example is found at Coucy.[1] Coucy, the work of a powerful vassal of the crown of France, represents a degree of scientific fortification to which none of our cylindrical donjons attains. The castle was constructed, like Conway at a later period, in connection with the defences of a walled town.[2] It consists of two wards, a large outer ward or base-court and an inner ward of irregular shape, with four straight sides of unequal length and round towers at the angles. In the middle of the east side, between the two wards, is the donjon (177), a cylinder of some 200 feet high—90 feet higher than the tower of Rochester. It stands isolated from the curtain of the inner ward, from the line of which about one-third of its circumference projects, and is surrounded by a ditch, originally paved with stone. To this ditch there was no external access. On the outer edge of

Coucy

the ditch, joining the east curtain of the inner ward at two points, was a strong wall or *chemise*. Outside this was the

---

[1] E. Lefèvre-Pontalis, *Le Château de Coucy*, pp. 48, 49, shows that the donjon forms part of the latest work undertaken by Enguerrand III., lord of Coucy, the founder of the present castle, who died in 1242 : it was evidently completed about 1240.

[2] The town walls appear to be rather earlier than the castle (*ibid.*, 34).

ditch dividing the inner ward from the base-court. Within the inner ward, a low wall took the place of the *chemise* of the donjon, and access to the tower was provided by a bridge across the stone-flagged ditch. The bridge was worked by a windlass, and, when not in use, remained drawn up on the threshold of the tower.

The donjon of Coucy is built in three stages, and has a large apartment, originally vaulted, on each floor. There is no basement chamber below the level of the entrance. In order to facilitate vaulting the various floors, each chamber was planned with twelve sides, lofty niches being left between the abutments of the vault.[1] Without giving a detailed description, we may notice the points in which this great structure resembles and improves upon the tower of Conisbrough. (1) The isolation of the tower, defended by its own ditch and, towards the field, by its own curtain, makes an entrance on the ground floor possible. In this respect, the builders of Coucy followed the example of Philip Augustus at the Louvre and at Rouen. (2) The defences of the entrance are more elaborate than at Conisbrough, where the doorway was closed merely by a strong wooden door, reinforced by two draw-bars, and a straight passage led into the guard-room on the first floor. At Coucy there was a similar door, but in front of it was an iron portcullis, worked from the first floor of the tower, and sliding through grooves at the back of the jambs of the doorway. The portcullis was defended further by a machicolation or open groove in the floor above. The entrance passage behind the wooden door was closed by a hinged grille at the entrance to the guard-room. (3) The stair, as at Conisbrough, was on the right of the entrance passage, but, instead of following the curve of the wall, was a vice, which led straight to the roof, communicating with the two upper floors on the way. The device adopted at Conisbrough, by which the stair ends at each floor, and, in order to ascend further, the floor has to be crossed, was adopted in the lesser towers at Coucy,[2] but not in the donjon. The Conisbrough method has the advantage, very desirable in a tower, of keeping the approach to the roof under direct observation throughout its entire distance : we find it used in the stairs of the rectangular keep at Richmond. (4) The tower of Coucy, as already noticed, was

---

[1] On the third floor, these niches are divided into two stages and connected by an upper gallery which pierces the abutments of the vault, and surrounds the whole apartment. The method of vaulting this gallery behind the abutments, so as to give additional resistance to the masonry of the tower, is described by Lefèvre-Pontalis, *op. cit.* 94 : see plan *ibid.*, p. 93.

[2] In the angle-towers at Coucy, however, the stairs take the form of vices, and do not curve with the wall, although ceasing at each floor.

defended by a lofty parapet, pierced with arches, which, in time
of siege, gave access to an outer wooden gallery supported by
stone corbels.[1] The form of the corbels is that which became
general in later times: each is composed of four courses of stone
projecting one above the other, with their outer ends rounded.
(5) The well at Coucy was in one of the niches between the
abutments of the ground-floor vault. (6) There are garde-robes
at Coucy on the left of the entrance-passage, and in a similar
position at the entry to the first floor. (7) We have seen
that at Conisbrough arms were probably transported from the
basement to the roof through a series of trap-doors in the floors.
At Coucy there was a circular opening left for this purpose in
the crown of the vault of each floor. (8) The solidity of the
tower of Coucy is emphasised by the absence of large windows,
even more noticeable than at Conisbrough; and, although the
tower contains fireplaces, its purely defensive character is unmistakable. It provided accommodation for an enormous
garrison, but for residential purposes, it would have been uncom-
fortable to the last degree. It contains no trace of a permanent
chapel: when the tower was in use, an altar might have been
set up in one of the niches on the first floor; but the regular
chapel was in the inner ward, and was connected with the
domestic buildings.

In the walls of the tower of Coucy can still be seen the holes
which served to attach the scaffolding during construction. The
spiral course which they take shows that the scaffolding, rising
with the tower, formed an inclined plane of a moderate slope,
up which the necessary materials could be wheeled. The
advantage of a cylindrical tower from this point of view is
obvious. Another structural feature is the provision of gutters
for the drainage of the roof in the stonework at the back of the
vault-ribs of the second floor. The absence of any effective
provision for draining the centre of the roof at Conisbrough
points to the probability that it was sheltered, as already
explained, by a conical roof of its own.

The introduction of the cylindrical donjon in England coin-
cides with a period at which the keep was already beginning to
disappear from the castle. The principal examples, which may
be attributed to the early years of the thirteenth century, are
on the frontier and in the south of Wales. Chief among them
is the fine tower of Pembroke (180), which was probably built
by William Marshal, earl of Pembroke and Striguil, about 1200.

[1] The gabled coping of the parapet formed the central support for the
sloping roof of the outer gallery and of the corresponding *coursière* on the
inner side.

The castle of Pembroke was of great importance, owing to its situation upon an arm of Milford haven,[1] and its command of the passage to Ireland.   The keep was probably the first completed portion of the present castle, the stone-work of which, as it stands to-day, is very largely of the late twelfth and early thirteenth century.[2]   It is a round tower, with a basement and three upper floors, standing just within, but not touching, the curtain which divided the inner and higher from the outer ward. The height is 75 feet ; the floors were of wood, but the uppermost stage was vaulted by a dome, which still remains, rising in the centre of the tower above the rampart-walk.   The stair is a vice in the west wall, from the basement to the summit : the main entrance was upon the first floor, but there is also a basement entrance, which seems to have been pierced not long after the building of the tower.   The whole structure batters upwards, and the walls are slightly gathered in at each stage on the outside, a method the reverse of that pursued at Conisbrough : the masonry is roughly coursed rubble.   On each of the first and second floors there is,

Pembroke

towards the inner ward, a two-light window with pointed openings, the spandrils between which and the enclosing arch are pierced with plate tracery.   The third floor was lighted by windows pierced in the dome.[3]   Commanding, as it does, the

[1] It stands on a promontory between two creeks at the head of the inlet known as the Pembroke river.

[2] The domestic buildings may be in part earlier, but were largely reconstructed in the thirteenth century.

[3] The tower is sometimes described as being of five stages : the dome, however, was merely a vault, and did not form a separate stage.

whole interior of the castle, this tower is remarkably grand in situation; and its thick walls offered considerable resistance to artillery. It shows, however, no advance upon the defence of Conisbrough. The rampart-walk is narrow, and the dome in the centre prevented the employment of the roof as a platform.

The cylindrical donjon in England and Wales was simply an experiment attempted here and there, as an improvement upon the rectangular tower, but was never carried to the general perfection which it attained in France. Its isolation at Coucy,

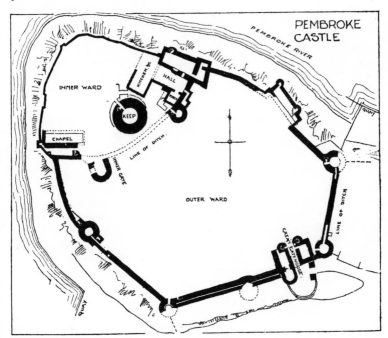

Pembroke; Plan

upon the outer face of the inner ward, protected by its own inner ditch, and covered by a strong curtain of its own, are signs of a perfection of engineering skill to which our builders did not attain. In one case, at Flint, we find a round tower which is isolated within its own ditch at one corner of the castle, but stands outside the main wall, and had no separate curtain of its own.[1]

---

[1] An account of Flint castle is given by Harvey, *Castles and Walled Towns*, p. 123 *seq*. Speed's map of Flintshire, made *c*. 1604, shows that the tower was joined to the adjacent curtain by a wall, the rampart-walk of which probably gave access to the entrance on the first floor of the tower.

The plan strongly suggests a mount-and-bailey fortress, the isolated tower occupying the site of the mount, and the bailey walled in, leaving the moat, which was marshy and was filled with water at high tide, clear. The construction of this keep is peculiar: it is composed of an outer and inner circle of masonry, with barrel-vaulted passages between the two. Its actual date is unknown.[1] But, as a rule, where the keep stands upon the outer line of defence, it is joined by the curtain of the bailey. Thus at Caldicot, near Chepstow, the castle is simply a mount-and-bailey enclosure surrounded by a stone curtain of the thirteenth century. The keep is a round tower at one corner, standing upon the partially levelled mount; and the curtain crosses the ditch to join it on both sides. At Conisbrough, where the keep was on the line of the curtain; at Pembroke, where it stood just within the line, there was no ditch round it: the high ground on which it was placed seems to have been thought a sufficient protection.

There are, however, a few round towers which, although they have not their own curtain in the sense of Coucy, are yet within defences of a peculiar nature, and therefore stand in a class apart. The most remarkable of these is Launceston, where the tower stands upon the summit of a lofty artificial mount of early Norman origin, and is approached by a steep and well-defended stair, ascending the face of the mount to the main entrance. Round the outer edge of the mount remain the lower courses of a stone wall, concentric with the keep. Within this is another and higher circular wall, which was crowned by a rampart-walk, approached by a stair in the thickness of the wall, to the left of the entrance. Inside this enclosure is the tower itself, which now consists of a basement and a ruined upper floor. The narrow space between the tower and the encircling wall was evidently roofed over at the height of the first floor of the tower: holes for joists still remain.[2] This double circle of masonry recalls Flint, where, however, the intermediate passage was vaulted, and the outer circle was probably the whole height of the tower.[3] Flint does not possess the low outer wall which existed at Launceston. The nearest analogy to Launceston is

[1] In 1277 the castle of Flint was a timber structure, so that the present work cannot be earlier than the end of the thirteenth century. The masonry is composed of large blocks of yellow sandstone, decayed where they are exposed to the tide. There was an outer bailey, the platform of which alone remains, with a ditch between it and the castle proper.

[2] These holes do not, however, surround the tower, so that the passage may have been only partially roofed.

[3] The keep of Launceston was probably built about the close of the twelfth century : that at Flint later, as already noted.

at Provins (Seine-et-Marne), where the octagonal keep has its own outer curtain, and is composed of an outer octagon with cylindrical turrets at the angles, commanded by an inner octagon rising two stages higher. The upper stage at Provins is surrounded by a lofty crenellated wall, on which rests a conical roof.

Another case is the keep of Tretower in Breconshire, which stands on a slightly elevated site near the confluence of the Rhiangol with the Usk. Here the arrangement is very curious. The keep, a round tower with a basement and three upper

Dolbadarn

stages, stands within the ruins of an approximately rectangular enclosure. This enclosure bears a close resemblance to the outer wall of a rectangular keep, but has two octagonal projections from the south face, one of which contains a vice, and the other a large fireplace. The tower itself seems to be somewhat earlier than the year 1200 : the fireplaces on the first and second floors have architectural decoration recalling that of the fireplaces at Conisbrough, shafts with capitals carved with foliage of a very elementary kind. The solution which suggests itself is that a rectangular tower, of a somewhat original plan, was begun and raised to a certain height, and that the builders then changed their minds, built a circular tower within the unfinished keep, and left the outer walls to serve as a curtain for the new structure.

The keep at Tretower, in its ordinary features, may be compared with the tower of Bronllys, only a few miles distant, on the other side of the pass through the Black mountains, at the southern foot of which Tretower stands. This tower also seems to be a work of the end of the twelfth century, but its architectural details are much plainer: both seem originally to have been between 70 and 80 feet high, and each contained a basement and three floors. Each has a battering base, and above this the wall at Tretower batters slightly to the summit; the diameter of Tretower exceeds that of Bronllys throughout. The original entrance in each case was on the first floor, from which at Tretower a vice led to the top of the building. The basement at Tretower had its separate stair in the wall opposite the entrance. At Bronllys the basement has a pointed barrel vault, and was entered by a stone stair and ladder from a trap-door in one of the window recesses of the first floor. The stair from the first floor to the second opened from another window recess, and curved through the wall, as at Conisbrough; there was, as also at Conisbrough, a separate stair to the third floor. The wall of the basement at Bronllys has been broken through in two places, and in one of these a hollow in the wall has been disclosed, in which originally a great beam was inserted to give coherence to the masonry. The same feature is seen in the outer building at Tretower. This device was frequently employed in the construction of medieval walls, but its traces are not often so clearly seen.

Dolbadarn ; Interior

One feature of the tower of Bronllys is that, like that of Caldicot, it stands upon an artificial mount, which occupies the ordinary position of such earthworks, at the head of the enclosure. The more roomy, but lower, tower at Hawarden, the upper floor of which is internally an octagon, almost surrounded by a mural passage, is built upon a lofty mount. At Skenfrith in Monmouthshire the tower, nearly equal to Bronllys in diameter, but not higher than Hawarden, stands upon a very low mount, and is placed in an isolated position, nearly in the centre of a trapezoidal enclosure. Here the lowness of the mount and the absence of indications of a normal earthwork plan suggest that it was raised to strengthen the foundations of the tower, and is not the mount of an earlier castle. The knoll, on the other hand, on which the round tower of Dolbadarn (183) stands, between the two lakes at the foot of the pass of Llanberis, is natural. The details of this tower are very plain, but it was probably built during the thirteenth century. There is no trace of any castle in connection with this small military outpost, which, like the not far-distant rectangular keep of Dolwyddelan, on the eastern slopes of Moel Siabod, bears some analogy to the "pele-towers" of the north of England,

York ; Clifford's Tower

and may have been built by a Welsh chieftain upon an English model during the reign of Henry III.

None of the towers in England and Wales mentioned in this chapter have the inner spur which has been noticed as characteristic of French towers. It appears, as has been said, at Goodrich and Chepstow. Other instances are a tower in the outer curtain at Denbigh, and the spur on the inward face of the great tower at Barnard Castle. Here the work is not earlier than the time of Edward II., and the tower is little more than a large mural tower added to a large shell-keep standing on a high rocky point. The spur here is a half pyramid, the apex of which dies away in the face of the tower. Of an octagonal tower we have one example at Odiham in Hampshire, which may be of the end of the twelfth century. This has the feature,

anomalous for so early a date, of angle buttresses which project
4 feet, but are only 2 feet broad.

Of donjons which were built in England during the reign
of Henry III., the most interesting, by virtue of their plan, are
those of York and Pontefract. The tower of York (185), raised
upon the mount of the northern of the two castles, was
built possibly about 1230, and assumed the quatrefoil shape
which is found in France at Etampes. This keep, presumably
because it is built on a mount, is usually called a "shell"; it
was, however, a regular tower, and the entrance, in the angle
between two of the leaves of the quatrefoil, is guarded by a
rectangular fore-building, on the first floor of which was the

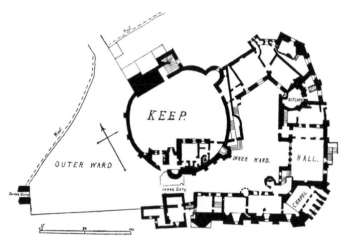

Berkeley Castle ; Plan

chapel. As at Etampes, the quatrefoil plan is preserved internally,
but the angles formed by the meeting of the four segments are
chamfered off: there was no vaulting, as at Etampes, but the
floors were of wood. A quatrefoil plan was also adopted at
Pontefract, with some slight variation, owing to the irregular
shape of the rocky mount. This keep is in a state of complete
ruin, although some idea of its former shape may be gathered
from a bird's-eye view preserved among the records of the duchy
of Lancaster.[1] We can see, from what is left, that it was not
built upon the top of the mount; but that, on three sides, the
mount was enclosed by walls of revetment,[2] which formed

---

[1] Reproduced in *Memorials of Old Yorkshire*, 1909, opposite p. 256.
[2] *I.e.*, retaining walls used to face (*revêtir*) a sloping surface.

the base of the segments composing the quatrefoil. This process recalls the walling-in of the mount at Berkeley, where, however, the lower part of the mount was left, and the space between the slope and the wall filled in with earth. At Pontefract the slope of the mount must have been much reduced before the walls of revetment were added : the sandstone upon which the castle was built is soft, and would lend itself easily to such an operation.

The bird's-eye view of Pontefract just mentioned cannot be regarded as absolutely trustworthy, but it gives us the relative position of the various towers of the castle. It shows us a curtain flanked by a formidable row of mural towers ; the keep, a complicated erection of several segments, with bartizans [1] projecting from the battlements in the angles formed by the junction of the segments, is still the dominant feature of the castle ; but our attention is equally claimed by the defences of the curtain and the domestic buildings which it encloses. And, in pursuing our subject, we must first trace the growth of domestic buildings within the castle area, and then turn to that strengthening of the curtain which led eventually to the disuse of the keep.

[1] A bartizan is a small turret or lookout corbelled out at an angle of a tower or on the surface of a wall. The word is connected with "brattice" (*bretèche*) ; and such turrets, like the machicolated parapet, are the stone counterpart of the bratticing and hoarding of timber applied to fortresses at an earlier date.

CHAPTER VIII

THE DWELLING-HOUSE IN THE CASTLE

THE castle needed, among its chief requirements, a dwelling-house which might be occupied by the owner and his household. Thus the stronghold of the lord of Ardres upon its mount was planned as a capacious dwelling, with a kitchen attached ; and where, as in this case, the keep was the castle, it necessarily served the double purpose of fortress and residence. Enough has been said of the rectangular and cylindrical forms of tower-keep to show that the domestic and military elements were often combined in their arrangements. But the use of the tower-keep as the principal residence within the castle was a fashion of comparatively short duration. The example of its double use had been set in the great towers of London and Colchester, and in the rectangular towers of Norman and French castles. Of the towers of Henry II.'s reign, those which, like Castle Rising, are low in proportion to the area they cover, generally have the best provision for living purposes. Lofty towers, like Newcastle or Conisbrough, can never have been comfortable residences ; and it is not surprising to find that at Newcastle, about half a century after the building of the tower, a more commodious dwelling-house was built within the castle area.[1] But we have seen already that in early castles, as at Oxford, a hall for the lord or his constable was generally, if not always, built within the bailey. The practical necessity of this is obvious in mount-and-bailey castles, where the tower on the mount, or the stone shell which took its place, was reserved for the main purpose of a final refuge in time of siege. No one who examines the sites of castles like Lincoln, Launceston, or Clare, with their formidable mounts, can fail to realise that the mount was an inconvenient place of residence, and that domestic buildings would be naturally provided in the annexed bailey. Bishop

---

[1] Ventress's model of the castle, made in 1852, shows the great hall near the north-east corner of the outer ward, its west end being nearly opposite the main entrance of the castle. The outer ward nearly surrounded the small inner ward, which contained the keep.

Bek's thirteenth-century hall at Durham, built against the western curtain of the bailey, stands upon the substructure of a far earlier building. The domestic buildings in the bailey at Guildford appear to be of earlier date than the stone tower on the mount; while at Christchurch in Hampshire (123), the dwelling-house next the river and the tower on the mount appear to be almost contemporary.

Castles which, for reasons already explained, were surrounded from the beginning with a stone wall, and had at first no regular keep, contain even better examples of the existence of a separate hall. The eleventh-century hall at Richmond is almost perfect, although some additions, made nearly a century later to the upper part of the structure, have led to the mistaken attribution of a later date to the whole building.[1] At Ludlow, mingled with the fabric of the fourteenth-century hall, are clear indications of the earlier stone hall, built, as at Richmond, against the curtain on the least accessible side of the inner ward. The fabric of the great hall at Chepstow, much enriched and beautified in the thirteenth century, is contemporary with the foundation of the castle in the eleventh century. Part, at any rate, of the sub-structure of the hall at Newark belongs to the castle founded in the twelfth century by Bishop Alexander, although the whole building on that side of the enclosure, with the exception of an angle-tower, bears witness to reconstruction and repair at two later periods. At Porchester, again, the substructure of the hall contains a considerable amount of early Norman work, which may be attributed to the time of Henry I.

The situation and plan of the hall remained very much the same throughout the middle ages. What we find at Richmond, Ludlow, Chepstow, or Durham, we find also at Manorbier, Caerphilly, Harlech, and Carnarvon, at Warwick and at Naworth. The domestic buildings were placed against the curtain on one side or at an end of the inner ward, and preferably where a precipice or steep slope made the assault of the curtain on that side difficult or impossible. This position is well illustrated in the fortified thirteenth-century house of Aydon in Northumberland. Here there was, on the side of entrance, a large walled outer ward, or, as it was called in the north of England, a "barmkin."[2]

---

[1] At Richmond the hall and its adjacent buildings were unusually complete for their date, and the tower-keep was not planned as a dwelling-house. None of our tower-keeps, Porchester excepted, are so purely military in character.

[2] The origin of this term is doubtful; some think it to be a corruption of "barbican"—a work covering the entrance to the house or castle proper. Large outer baileys, as at Ludlow (96) and Coucy, correspond to the "barmkins" of the north of England.

The house was built round two sides of a walled inner courtyard, the hall and main apartments standing on the brink of a deep ravine, where they were safe from approach or from the peril of siege-engines. The curtain was therefore pierced with window-openings of a fairly large size, which gave the house more light and comfort internally than would have been possible upon a more exposed face of the site. The hall at Warkworth (49) was built against a solid curtain upon the steepest side of the peninsula occupied by the castle, and, although there were no window-openings in the curtain at the level of the hall, it was pierced by a postern, through which the kitchen could be supplied, at the end nearest the tower. Castles on comparatively level sites show the same disposition. At Cardiff (191), the domestic buildings are on the west side of the enclosure, built against the curtain, and protected by the river, and bear the same relation in the plan to the main entrance and the shell-keep on the mount, as the hall at Warkworth bears to the gateway and the mount with its later strong house.[1]

The plan of the hall and its adjacent buildings was, and continued to be, that of the ordinary dwelling-house. The *aula* of Harold at Bosham in Sussex is represented in the Bayeux tapestry (36) as a house with a basement, apparently vaulted, and an upper floor approached by an external staircase. No division of the upper floor is shown: it consists apparently of one large room. This plan, with the division of the hall by a cross-wall into a main and smaller chamber, is precisely what we find, at the end of the century after the Conquest, at the large town house in Bury St Edmunds known as Moyses hall, or at the manor-house of Boothby Pagnell in Lincolnshire. It is represented in manor-houses of the later Gothic period at the so-called "Goxhill priory" in Lincolnshire or at the house of the bishops of Lincoln at Liddington in Rutland. Its most familiar survival in non-military architecture is in the halls of several of the Oxford colleges, like Christ Church or New college. In the plan of the monastery, the frater or dining-hall followed the same lines of an upper room upon a vaulted substructure. Similarly, the hall of a castle was simply an ordinary *aula* placed within an enclosure walled for military purposes. The hall

---

[1] At Arundel, Cardiff, and Warwick, mount-and-bailey castles which are still inhabited, the present great halls stand on sites which were doubtless occupied by the original halls built by the founders. All three were largely rebuilt at a later date, and have been further restored in modern times. Warwick was one of the Conqueror's earliest castles ; Arundel was founded before 1086, Cardiff about 1093. A large portion of the *enceinte* at Cardiff follows the line of the curtain of the Roman station (see *Archæologia*, lvii. pp. 335-52).

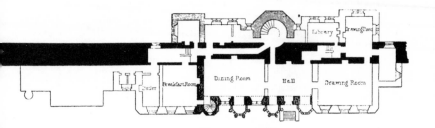

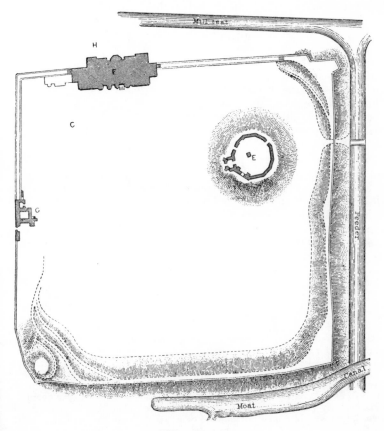

Cardiff Castle ; Plan

at Christchurch is the exact counterpart of Harold's *aula* in the Bayeux tapestry. It is a rectangular building, probably of the third quarter of the twelfth century, with a basement, originally vaulted, and lighted by narrow loops. The first floor formed one large apartment, and was well lighted with double window openings, one of which, at the south end, received special architectural treatment. There was a fireplace in the east wall, on the side next the stream: the cylindrical chimney-shaft still remains. The entrance, near the south end of the west wall, was probably approached by an outer stair at right angles to the wall, and led into the lower end of the hall, opposite the daïs for the high table. The fireplace, set diagonally to the entrance, warmed the daïs and the body of the hall: the end near the doorway, corresponding to the "screens" of the ordinary hall, was probably left free for the coming and going of the servants. The basement was simply a cellar and storehouse. It had a doorway in the west wall, while in the east wall was a gateway communicating with the water. The elevation is nearly identical with that of the house at Boothby Pagnell; but at Boothby Pagnell a cross-wall divides both upper floor and basement into larger and smaller chambers; while at Christchurch there was at the south-east corner a rectangular garde-robe turret, built out into the stream, which kept the vents from both basement and upper floor continually flushed.[1]

The division of the first floor into a larger and smaller apartment corresponds to the division of the ordinary dwelling-house into hall or common-room of the house, and bower or withdrawing-room and sleeping apartment for the chief members of the family.[2] In the developed plan of the medieval private house, the small vaults below the bower became the cellar, and, as at Manorbier, a vice was provided by which wine could be brought directly from it to the high table. The bower or solar[3] itself was known in large houses as the great chamber, and access to it was obtained

[1] At Boothby Pagnell there is a cylindrical chimney-shaft very similar to that of the hall at Christchurch.

[2] The usual arrangement even in small cottages: *cf.* Chaucer, *Cant. Tales,* B. 4022 (the house of the dairy-woman in the Nonne Preestes Tale), "Ful sooty was hir bour, and eek hir halle."

[3] The word "solar" or "soller" (*solarium* = a terrace exposed to the sun) was used indiscriminately of any room, gallery, or loft above the ground-level of a building: *e.g.*, the loft or gallery above a chancel-screen was commonly known as a "solar," and the same word should be applied to the chamber, inaccurately called a "parvise," on the first floor of a church porch. The word, however, is sometimes applied to a well-lighted parlour facing south, without respect to the floor on which it stands, *e.g.*, the abbot's solar at Haughmond (*Archæol. Journal,* lxvi. 307) and at Jervaulx (*Yorks. Archæol. Journal,* xxi. 337).

through a door near one end of the cross-wall behind the daïs. There was, however, a variation upon this plan in which the hall and bower are on a different floor-level, and this appears at a fairly early date. In this case the hall occupied the whole height of the basement and first floor, and was entered from the ground-level of the bailey: the cellar, in this case, was on a level with the floor of the hall, and the solar was reached from the daïs by a stair. This plan became very common in the later Gothic period ; and is well illustrated in manor-houses like Haddon and Compton Wyniates, and in the colleges of Cambridge, where the common-room or parlour took the place of the cellar, and the solar was occupied by the master's lodging. But it is also found in castles and fortified houses, as at Berkeley and Stokesay. An indication of its employment at a date not long after the Norman conquest is found in the story of the insult offered to Robert of Normandy by William Rufus and Henry I. They came to visit him, about the year 1078, at the castle of L'Aigle, where he was staying, either in the constable's house or some dwelling near the castle. William and Henry played dice "upon the solar," and indulged in horseplay, which took the form of making a deafening noise, and pouring water on Robert and his followers, who were below. Robert lost his temper, and rushed into the dining-hall (*cenaculum*) to punish his brothers : the quarrel, stopped for the time being by their father, was the beginning of the long feud which ended for Robert in his confinement at Cardiff. The mention of the "solar" distinctly implies a room upon the upper floor, probably at some elevation above the hall.[1]

This alternative plan supplied more direct communication with the kitchen than was possible, where the hall was upon an upper floor ; and in connection with it, a kitchen and its accompanying offices are very frequently found at the lower end, near the entry of the hall. This became, in manor-houses and in the colleges of Cambridge, the normal position of the kitchen, buttery, and pantry, divided from the body of the hall by the "screens." Most of the cooking in the earlier castles must have been done either in temporary sheds or in the open air: the basement of the hall, which, in later manor-houses, was some-times used as a kitchen, was not so used at an early period. The apartment in a corner of the cleverly planned first floor of the

[1] Ord. Vit., iv. 19 : "Super solarium . . . tesseris ludere ceperunt." The word "solarium" may be used, of course, in this passage with reference merely to the site of the house—*i.e.*, it may mean "the first floor above the ground." In this case William and Henry may have been playing dice in the hall itself, which, as at Christchurch, may have occupied the whole "solarium." Robert was evidently outside the house.

keep at Castle Rising was probably a kitchen, and is a rare instance of a room set apart for this purpose before the end of the twelfth century. It must be remembered, however, that the domestic buildings of castles were very often, as at Ludlow, enlarged and entirely rebuilt, until they became, as at Cardiff and Warwick, splendid mansions; and details with regard to the original arrangement of the lesser apartments are thus hard to recover.

At Warkworth (49), probably a little before 1200, a house of considerable extent, including more than one private apartment and a kitchen, was built against, and at the same time with the, west curtain.[1] Up to this time, the castle had been an ordinary mount-and-bailey stronghold with timber defences, and no earlier stonework remains. The new house was much beautified by additions made in the fifteenth century, but the plan was little altered. Its central part was the hall, parallel with the curtain which it joined. The entrance was in the side wall next the bailey, and led, as usual, into the lower end of the hall, which occupied the full height of the house, and thus formed the only internal means of communication between the lord's and the servants' quarters. An unusual feature of the hall, which cannot have been well lighted, was an eastern aisle, over which the sloping roof was probably continued. At the upper end, behind the daïs, the cellar was entered directly from the hall: a straight stair next the curtain gave access to a landing, from which a doorway gave access to the great chamber. The great chamber communicated with a polygonal angle tower, called by the curious name of "Cradyfargus,"[2] the first floor of which, next the great chamber, may have been the chamber of the master of the house, while the upper floor was probably used by the ladies. Nearly at right angles to the great chamber, against the south curtain, was a chapel, of which enough remains to show us that the ground-floor, entered from the bailey, was used by the servants and garrison: while the west end was divided into two stories, the upper one of which was entered from the private apartments, and was a gallery for the use of the lord and his family. It is difficult to speak positively of the arrangements of the kitchen, which stood against the west curtain at the other end of the hall. It may originally, like the kitchen at Berkeley, have had no direct com-

---

[1] Bates, *Border Holds of Northumberland* attributes the walling, etc., of Warkworth castle "on its present general lines" to Robert, son of Roger (1169-1214), who obtained in 1199, for 300 marks, a confirmation of the grant of the castle and manor from John.

[2] So called in Clarkson's survey, made in 1567. One explanation of the name is that the tower was similar to one in Carrickfergus castle, on Belfast Lough. Clarkson describes its polygonal form as "round of divers squares.'

LUDLOW : interior of building west of great hall

munication with the hall: the passage and offices between, in
their present state of ruin, are fifteenth-century additions or
reconstructions. But all the elements of the larger English
house are here. The chief alterations in the fifteenth century
were the building of a porch and gateway-tower in front of the
hall entrance, and the insertion of a lofty turret, with a vice and
vaulted vestibule to the great chamber, to the north-eastern
angle of the hall, where it blocks the last bay of the aisle.

An aisled hall, as at Warkworth, was a very exceptional
feature. There are, however, a few existing examples of a hall
with a nave and two aisles, the most famous of which is the
thirteenth-century hall at Winchester. The midland castles of
Leicester and Oakham also had aisled halls: that at Leicester
was divided by arcades of timber, and still exists, although many
of its original features, including the timber columns, have been
removed or obscured. The hall at Oakham has been more
fortunate. This castle, upon a flat site which had no strategic
advantages, was really an *aula* or manor-house, enclosed by a
strong earthen bank, and was probably not surrounded by a wall
until the thirteenth century. Within this enclosure Walkelin de
Ferrers, towards the end of the twelfth century, built an aisled
hall of four bays, the architectural details of which are of unusual
beauty, and of great importance in the history of early Gothic
art in England. The building runs east and west, the original
entrance, from the ground-level of the bailey, being, as usual, in
the last bay of a side-wall, in this case the easternmost bay of the
south wall.[1] The daïs was at the west end; and two doors,
which probably communicated with the kitchen and buttery,
remain in the east wall. The aisles would doubtless be kept
clear of tables, to facilitate the service from the kitchen.[2] At
either end of the building, the arcades spring, not from responds,
but from corbels. Semicircular responds would have interfered
with the benches behind the high table, and with the free passage
of the servants between the kitchen and the aisles.[3] The columns
are slender cylinders of Clipsham stone: the capitals are tall,
and carved with a great variety of stiff-stalk foliage, with which
are mingled bands of nail-head and dog-tooth. The arches
are rounded: dog-tooth is used in the hood-mouldings, which

[1] This entrance has been blocked, and the modern entrance has been cut
through a window-opening, in the adjoining bay to the west.
[2] The aisle-walls are low and the whole building is covered by a single
high-pitched roof, so that there is no clerestory.
[3] The same feature occurs at the west end of the great hall at Auckland,
where the daïs was placed: there are regular responds at the east end, but
the eastern bay was made somewhat wider than the rest, to give room for
the screens.

rest upon figure-corbels. The classical character of the foliage, and the refined sculpture of the figures and heads in the corbels throughout the hall, have analogies in one or two other buildings of the district: they recall very closely the early Gothic work of the Burgundian province, and its English derivatives at Canterbury and Chichester. Nothing, however, is known of the masons employed; and the fabric has no documentary history. In the low side-walls are double window-openings, each with a sculptured tympanum beneath an enclosing arch: the pier dividing each of the windows is faced with a shaft, and the jambs are adorned with elaborate dog-tooth. These windows may be compared with those of the aisled hall of the episcopal palace at Lincoln, built about a quarter of a century later, where the arcades at both ends sprang from corbels. A close parallel to the arrangements of the hall at Oakham is provided by the contemporary hall, built by Bishop Pudsey at Auckland castle, near Durham. Here, again, the so-called castle was simply an *aula* without the strong earthworks which give Oakham a military character. The proportions of the Auckland hall are larger, and its architecture more simple, but with even more advanced Gothic characteristics. At the end of the thirteenth century, considerable alterations were made in the structure, and at the Restoration the hall was converted by Bishop Cosin into a chapel.[1] This involved the blocking up of the original entrance, the position of which exactly corresponded to that of Oakham. A new doorway was made in the west wall, and the bay which originally was set apart for the daïs was converted into an ante-chapel. In neither case do any other contemporary buildings remain: the mansion at Auckland, on the west side of the old hall, is a building of several periods, of which the earliest existing portion is not earlier than the reign of Henry VII.

Hugh Pudsey (1153-95), the prelate responsible for the hall at Auckland, did much to increase the splendour of the episcopal castle at Durham (199). Durham castle is an excellent example of a mount-and-bailey fortress on a strong triangular site, with precipitous natural defences on the north and west. The entrance was on the one accessible side, from the plateau on which the cathedral and monastery stood. At the apex of the site, on the right of the entrance, was the mount, with a shell-keep on its summit; while to the left, along the west side of the bailey, was

---

[1] Bishop Bek (1284-1311) probably heightened the aisle-walls and inserted traceried windows. Cosin (1660-72) rebuilt the greater part of the outer walls, renewed Bek's windows, and added the present clerestory and roof: the splendid screen, which divides the chapel from the ante-chapel, was also part of his work.

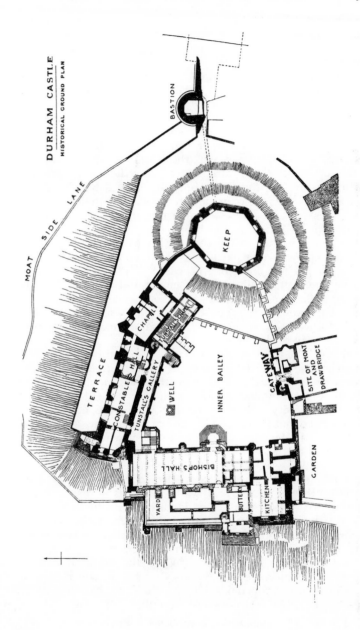

the original hall.   The eleventh-century chapel was on the north
side of the bailey, nearly opposite the entrance.   Pudsey's chief
work was the construction of a long building of three stories in
connection with the north curtain.   The eastern part of the
basement was formed by the early chapel ; the rest was probably
devoted to store-rooms and cellars.   On the first floor was a great
hall, entered by a doorway (201) which may fairly be called the
most magnificent example of late Norman Romanesque art in
England.   Above this, on the second floor, approached by a
vice in the south-east corner, was another hall, known as the
Constable's hall, and to-day as the Norman gallery.   The walls
of this upper structure were lightened by their construction as a
continuous arcade, the arches forming frames to window-openings, and the piers between them being faced with detached shafts
in couples (203).   The internal arrangements of this building
are now much obscured by the partition of the lower hall into
several large rooms ; while the south part of the upper hall has
been cut up by smaller partitions.   Early in the sixteenth century
a new chapel was built on the east side of the lower hall, and
against the south wall of the basement and first floor was made
a stone gallery of two stories.   The outer stair to the lower hall
was then taken away ; but Bishop Pudsey's doorway was left,
and light was thrown upon it by a large mullioned window in
the outer wall of the gallery.[1]

Meanwhile, about the end of the thirteenth century, Bishop
Bek, who also improved upon Pudsey's work at Auckland, raised
against the west curtain, and upon the substructure of the early
hall, the great banqueting-hall, which is now used as the dining-
hall of University college.   This hall, again, has inevitably been
much altered, but its actual plan and arrangements are very fairly
maintained to-day, and the long two-light windows with simple
geometrical tracery in the side walls represent, with some restoration of stone-work, its original lighting.   The entrance, up a
flight of stairs and through a porch added by Bishop Cosin, is
in the south end of the east wall, and leads into screens roofed
by a gallery, on the south of which are the kitchen and servants'
offices.   A doorway in the east wall led from the daïs to the
bishop's private rooms ; but at this end the older arrangements
were altered by the construction of Tunstall's gallery in the
sixteenth century, and, later still, by the addition of Cosin's
splendid Renaissance staircase—alterations which provided
covered access from Bek's hall to Pudsey's building at right
angles to it.   The buildings just described are some of the most

---

[1] The work of this late period is attributed to Bishop Tunstall (1530-59).
Cosin at a later date made additions to the chapel.

Durham Castle ; Doorway

beautiful and instructive remains of domestic architecture in England, and have no military characteristics. The strength of the castle, however, was not forgotten. No English castle, even when Bamburgh and Richmond are remembered, presents a more formidable defence than the curtain, pierced by a few spare openings and by the narrow western windows of Bek's hall, which revets and crowns the cliff above the Wear; while, in the fourteenth century, Bishop Hatfield (1345-81) replaced the older keep by a new and probably more lofty polygonal shell.

At Durham the buildings of Pudsey and Bek alike stand upon basements, which were used as cellars and store-rooms; and the preference for first-floor halls in castles was doubtless due to the necessity of providing plenty of room for magazines, both for provisions and arms, within a confined space, and keeping the muster-ground in the centre of the bailey as clear as possible. At Newark (157), where the ground fell away towards the river, the hall was built on the slope, and was entered from the level of the bailey, the slope being utilised for the construction of a large vaulted basement, lighted by loops from the river side, and communicating with the water by a sloping passage and a gateway opening on a small quay. The use of every available space for storage is illustrated at Carew castle in Pembrokeshire, where the whole space beneath the lesser hall and its adjacent buildings is occupied by cellars, while the basement of the greater hall, on the opposite side of the courtyard, appears to have been used as stables. At Pembroke a large natural cavern below the hall and its adjacent buildings was turned to use as a lower store-house. A vice was constructed in the rock from a ground-floor chamber north of the hall, and the mouth of the cavern was closed by a wall, in which was a gateway, opening upon a path from the water-side.

If Henry II. may be given the chief credit for the construction of rectangular keeps in castles, Henry III. was almost as active in building halls. The finest example of his work now remaining is at Winchester. At the Tower of London, at Scarborough, and at Newcastle, the name alone of his halls, rectangular buildings with high-pitched roofs, remains. But, in and after his reign, the hall and the adjacent domestic buildings became a fixed feature of the plan of the castle. In castles which, up to this time, may have possessed small and inconvenient halls, or possibly halls built merely of timber, new and more permanent domestic buildings were constructed. Thus, at Rockingham castle, the beautiful doorway of the thirteenth-century hall (205), with deeply undercut mouldings and jamb-shafts with foliated capitals, still forms the entrance to the house of the sixteenth

DURHAM: arcading on south side of Constable's hall

and seventeenth centuries, the hall of which is probably of the
exact dimensions of its medieval predecessor.[1]   In castles which
are the most perfect examples of fortification, such as Caerphilly
or Conway, the hall forms an integral part of the plan, filling its
natural place in the
design; and of these,
Caerphilly was com-
pleted   about   the
end of the reign of
Henry III.   The en-
thusiasm of Henry
for fine architecture,
domestic as well as
ecclesiastical,   was
imitated by many of
his   powerful   sub-
jects; and it is ac-
tually   from   this
period that we may
trace that promin-
ence of the domestic
element in our castles
which was eventually
cultivated at the ex-
pense of fortification.
    In the dwelling-
houses, often of pala-
tial size, which grew
up   within   castles,
and   reached   their
perfect development
in the thirteenth and
fourteenth centuries,
the main apartments,
in addition to the
hall, were the great
chamber, the kitchen
with its offices, and

Rockingham Castle ; Doorway of hall

the chapel.   The normal plan, as already shown, was that of the
first-floor hall, with the great chamber at one end, and the kitchen

----

[1] At the fortified manor-house of Drayton, some fourteen miles south-east
of Rockingham, the great hall is a fabric of the later half of the thirteenth
century, although the date has been obscured by later alterations.   The
vaulted cellar at the east end of the hall (*c.* 1270) is almost intact ; but the
great chamber above was rebuilt about the end of the seventeenth century.

at the other. The plan of the chapel was not fixed, but, where it formed part of the block of buildings, it is usually found in connection with the great chamber end of the hall.

The main points of the hall may be briefly recapitulated. The entrance was invariably in the side wall next the bailey, at the end nearest the usual place for the kitchen. This end was screened off from the hall by curtains or by a wooden partition containing one or more doors. This shut out draught; while the passage thus formed was generally covered by its own ceiling, the space above forming a gallery, which was entered from a vice at a corner of the end wall. At the further end of the hall was the daïs with the high table, at right angles to which were placed the long tables in the body of the hall. The hall was covered by a high-pitched timber roof, the principals of which were borne by corbels in the side walls. In early examples, warmth was supplied by a large hearth in the middle of the floor, a little below the daïs, the smoke from which escaped through a louvre in the roof above; but it became customary to make a fireplace in one of the side walls.[1] Light was admitted through window-openings in the side wall next the ward; but, where the outer wall of the castle was secure from attack, as at Warwick or Ludlow, windows were made there also. These windows were usually of two lights, divided by a mullion, with simple tracery in the head. They also had a transom, below which they were closed by shutters, the upper part of the window alone being glazed. In the hall at Ludlow, the date of which is about 1300, there were three two-light windows next the ward, while the curtain was pierced by three single-light openings. The hearth stood in the body of the hall just below the daïs, and was carried by a pier in the cellar beneath. In the fifteenth century the middle window next the ward was blocked, and a fireplace inserted : the hearth was then removed. The hall formed the chief living-room of the house, and in it the majority of the lord's retinue not only had their meals, but slept.

The great chamber, as time went on, became the nucleus of a number of private apartments. In the most simple examples, it is a rectangular apartment behind the daïs, communicating with it directly through a doorway on one side of the end wall. Where the hall occupied the ground floor, a vice, or, as at Warkworth, a straight stair, furnished an entrance to it. At Ludlow, where the kitchen was a detached building, and at Stokesay (207), there was a first-floor chamber at both ends of

---

[1] As at Penshurst. The hearth-stone remains at Stokesay. At Haddon the great fireplace in the west wall was inserted several years after the hall was built.

the hall. The domestic buildings at Ludlow are very symmetri-
cally arranged, the hall, in the middle, being slightly recessed
between two projecting blocks of building, each with a chamber
on the first floor (195). Of these, that at the east end of the hall,
behind the daïs, was evidently the more important ; and, in the
fifteenth century, it was on this side that an additional block
of private apartments was built. From each floor of the great
chamber block a large garde-robe tower was entered : this tower
projects from the north curtain of the castle, and was added

Stokesay

when the earlier hall was remodelled and the hall and its
adjoining blocks assumed their present shape.

Manorbier castle contains an interesting example of the
enlargement of domestic buildings, with a solar block at either
end of the hall. The castle stands on rising ground in a deep
valley, about half a mile from the sea. The inner ward or castle
proper is surrounded by a curtain, with a gatehouse in the east
wall. The dwelling-house is upon the west side of the ward, at
the end opposite the main entrance, and consists of two distinct
portions. The earlier consists of a first-floor hall and great chamber above cellars. There was a floor above the great chamber,
probably forming a bower for the ladies of the household, the

hall corresponding in height to these two upper stages. The present entrance to the hall is in the side wall at the end next the great chamber, and was probably made, with the outer stair against the wall, in the thirteenth century. The hall itself with its adjacent buildings appears to be originally of the later part of the twelfth century : the cellars below have semicircular barrel vaults. In the second half of the thirteenth century a new block of buildings was made at the opposite or south end of the hall. It was now probably that the new entrance was made. The position of the daïs seems to have been reversed, and a window in the south end-wall of the hall blocked by a fireplace. Behind

Manorbier Castle ; Outer stair to Chapel

this wall, and entered by a doorway in its west end, was the new great chamber, a long, narrow building, with its principal axis at right angles to that of the hall, and with a floor above. At each end of the south wall of this apartment is a passage. That at the west end passes along the line of the curtain to a garde-robe tower which projects at the south-west angle of the castle : the passage is still roofed with flat slabs on continuous corbelling, and is well lighted by loops in the curtain. The other passage, at the south-east corner of the great chamber, forms a lobby to a large chapel, which was built across the south-west angle of the ward, so that a small triangular yard was left between it and the curtain.   There is a separate outer stair to the chapel (208), placed, like the stair to the hall, at right angles to the wall.   The whole group of buildings, with its two outer stairs, is unexcelled for picturesqueness in any castle.

The kitchen at Manorbier was placed, at any rate when the thirteenth-century alterations were undertaken (probably about 1260), at right angles to the hall and older great chamber, against the north curtain.   Owing to the confinement of the space within the curtain, and the growing necessity of private accommodation, the position of the kitchen was not fixed so regularly in the castle as in the ordinary dwelling-house.   At Berkeley (186), where the hall was built against the east curtain of the inner ward, the kitchen is a polygonal building, divided from the screens by a buttery, and occupying a more or less normal place in the plan.   At Warkworth (49), as we have noticed, the kitchen is in its proper place, near the entrance end of the hall, but may have been at first a separate structure.   The original position of the kitchen at Cardiff (191) seems to have conformed to this plan.   The desirability of placing the kitchen within easy reach of the hall is obvious. At Kenilworth, where the magnificent hall, built towards the end of the fourteenth century, occupies the whole north side of the inner ward, and is on a first floor above a vaulted cellar, the private apartments formed a wing against the west curtain of the ward, while the kitchen was against the east curtain, and was within easy reach of the stair to the hall, and the passage below it which led into the cellar.   The kitchen at Ludlow (106) was a separate building, opposite the entrance to the hall and the western solar block, and placed against the north outer wall of the small courtyard which covers the keep.   In the two great Edwardian castles of Conway and Carnarvon, where the halls were large and the space limited, the kitchens were built against the curtain opposite the hall.[1]

The chapel was also a variable factor in the plan.   It has already been remarked that, in some early castles, the chapel was a collegiate church, standing separately within the precincts of the castle, and sometimes, as at Hastings, filling up, with the houses of the dean and canons or their deputies, a very considerable part of the enclosure.   Indeed, nearly all the ruins left within the curtain at Hastings are those of the large cruciform church and the buildings in connection with it.   At Ludlow the Norman chapel was a detached building in the inner ward (106). This was the private chapel of the lord of the castle, and in the

---

[1] At Harlech the kitchen was at right angles to the hall, against the south curtain.

24

sixteenth century was joined by a gallery to the block of buildings at the east end of the hall : the nave was then divided into two floors, so that the first floor formed a private gallery or solar, while the household used the ground-floor. This method of division of the west end of the chapel into two floors is very usual : it was employed twice at Warkworth, both in the chapel attached to the domestic buildings already described, and in the chapel of the later tower-house on the mount. It may also be seen in the chapel at Berkeley, and in many manor-houses, as at Compton Wyniates. At Ludlow we have noticed that there was a second chapel for the garrison in the outer ward, built in the fourteenth century : with this the arrangement at the Tower of London may be compared, where the royal chapel of St John is in the White tower, but the garrison chapel of St Peter was built on the north side of the inner ward. The chapel at Kenilworth was against the south wall of the outer ward. There was a chapel on the south side of the inner ward at Alnwick. As a rule, however, only one chapel would be provided. The chapels found in tower-keeps have already been discussed : with the exception of Newcastle and Old Sarum, they were, as a rule, private chapels or mere oratories.

In later castles, two considerations determined the planning of the chapel. It was placed so that the altar should be as nearly as possible against the east wall, and so that there should be direct access from the private apartments to the gallery at the west end. These conditions are met both in the earlier and later chapels at Warkworth : they can be traced in the plan of Bodiam and other late medieval castles. At Berkeley (186) where the solar block was at right angles to the hall, against the south, or, more correctly, the south-west curtain, the chapel fills the angle between the buildings, and the entrance is masked by a vestibule from which a vice led to the private apartments. The altar is placed rather north of east, against the wall at the back of the hall daïs, and the gallery at the opposite end was entered from the great chamber. The main axis of the chapel is at an obtuse angle to that of the hall, and a vestry was made in the south-east corner, where the wall dividing it from the hall is thickest. In the plan of the great Welsh castles of the later part of the thirteenth century the chapel was usually in close connection with the domestic buildings. At Conway, where there is also a beautiful oratory, with a vaulted chancel, on the first floor of the north-east tower, the chapel was formed by screening off the eastern portion of the great hall. At Harlech the chapel was built against the north curtain, the solar block probably occupying the angle between chapel and hall. The chapel at Kidwelly was in the two upper stages of the south-east tower of the inner ward, and was in close communication with the hall and the apartments adjoining it. The position of the beautiful little chapel at Beaumaris is somewhat isolated, on the first floor of the tower in the middle of the east curtain of the inner ward. The only communication with the hall block on the north side of the court was through a long and narrow passage in the thickness of the curtain; and the chapel is too small to have served for the devotions of a large garrison. It was so arranged, however, that, if the entrance to the tower were left open, the service might be followed by worshippers in the bailey below. Ample room, however, was given to the congregation in most cases: the first-floor chapel at Manorbier is a chamber of considerable size. It has a pointed barrel-vault and stands above a cellar, which also has a pointed barrel-vault and contains a fireplace. The fashion of founding collegiate establishments in castles did not cease until the end of the middle ages. The chapel—the third within the castle—which was begun during the fifteenth century at Warkworth bears witness to an intention of this kind on the part of one of the earls of Northumberland; but the actual details of the proposed foundation are not known, and probably were never placed on paper.

CHAPTER IX

CASTLES OF THE THIRTEENTH CENTURY: THE FORTIFICATION OF THE CURTAIN

THE keep had a traditional importance in the scheme of the castle, and the main energy of the castle-builders of the twelfth century was directed towards strengthening its power of resistance. But the improvement of siege artillery naturally turned their attention to the strengthening of the outer defences as well. The day of the palisade was past, and the stone curtain called for more scientific treatment than it had yet received. In the thirteenth century, then, military engineers began to concentrate their ingenuity upon the outer walls and entrances of the castle. Their interest was transferred by degrees from the keep to the curtain, while, at the same time, the domestic employment of the keep ceased in favour of the more comfortable quarters against the castle wall. In this way, as scientific fortification developed, the keep dropped into a secondary position, or was left out of the plan altogether.

In tracing this gradual disappearance of the keep, it should be kept in mind that the stone keep, when we first meet with it, is actually a supplement of more permanent material added to a palisaded enclosure. In early walled enclosures, like Richmond or Ludlow, the stone defences made the special provision of a keep unnecessary: the whole castle, protected by its stone wall, had in itself the strength of a keep. It was only when it became likely that the stone curtain might show less resistance than its builders anticipated, that, in both the castles just mentioned, a tower-keep was provided. In both cases, the tower stood in the forefront of the defence of the principal ward of the castle. In the first instance it protected the curtain, while, if all else failed, its use, the primary use of such buildings, as an ultimate place of retirement for the defenders, could be demonstrated. During the reign of Henry II., the stone keep, whether a tower or a shell on the mound, was the dominating feature of the stone-walled castle. At Conisbrough and Pembroke (181) the great tower still keeps its pride of place, but the curtains of the ward in which it

PEMBROKE: inner side of gatehouse

stands have been built or reconstructed with a view to effectual flanking; while the two semicircular towers which guarded the southern curtain of the inner ward at Pembroke were evidently an addition, after the keep had been built. In castles like Manorbier, the oldest parts of which are of the later part of the twelfth century, the builders returned to the original keepless plan of Richmond and Ludlow. The care, which, in the earlier castles, had been expended upon a single rallying point in the scheme of defence, was now applied to the whole outer wall of the castle, so that it began to offer a connected front to an attack.

During the transition, however, the keep, as we have seen, received its full share of attention. At Château-Gaillard (163) it was an integral part of one united design, the outer defences of which remain to be described. The great tower is at the highest point of the inner or third ward, which forms an irregular oval. But, before reaching this ward, two outer lines of defence had to be forced. There was only one possible approach for a besieging army, along the isthmus on the south-east side of the cliff. On this side the castle proper was protected by a powerful outwork, which offered a sharp angle to the isthmus. When Philip Augustus began to use his machines against the castle in February 1203-4, the round tower at the apex of this horn-work[1] was the main object of his attack. The sloping sides of the angle were flanked by two smaller round towers, while the entrance, close to the north angle, was covered on one side by a cylindrical tower, to which there was probably a corresponding tower in the opposite curtain. The horn-work was surrounded by an outer ditch. The strength of the curtain seems to have been little affected by the siege-engines. Breaches, both here and in the inner ward, were not made until Philip's miners had weakened the masonry by boring galleries beneath it. A very deep ditch with perpendicular sides, cut in the chalk, stretched across the whole ridge, and divided the outwork from the middle ward, which was capped at the angles by cylindrical towers, and contained buildings of which the substructures, and some cellars excavated in the chalk, are left. The curtain of this ward was continued along the face of the precipice and the north-eastern slope, so as practically to enclose the inner ward. The two wards, however, were not concentric, for the inner ward occupied one end of the space enclosed by the middle ward, from which

[1] The words "horn-work," "demilune," or "ravelin," were applied in later fortification to flanked outworks which presented a salient angle to the field, *i.e.*, on the side of attack. To such defences in the middle ages the general name of "barbican" seems to have been given.

it was divided by a ditch. The wall of the inner ward was the most remarkable and original of the defences of the castle. Its whole outer face, save on the side next the precipice, was formed of a series of convex curves intersecting with each other, so that no flat surface was left. The wall is solid, and, looking at its fluted outer surface, we may well admire Philip's military skill, which found it a not too formidable obstacle. A gateway in the east face gave access to the inner ward from the narrowest portion of the middle ward, and the ditch at this point was originally crossed by a stone causeway. The projecting spur of the great tower faced the gateway. The whole formidable design was perfect from the point of view of flanking, while the plan was a step towards the concentric arrangement of one ward within another. The prominence of the keep in the plan was, however, an archaic feature ; and the history of the siege of 1204 shows very clearly that the great tower was practically a superfluity, and that the last hopes of the defenders were centred in the wall of the inner ward. When Philip's miners had endangered its stability, and his engines were brought to play upon the weakened stonework, their hope was lost.[1]

The inventive skill shown in the inner wall of Château-Gaillard was not displayed again in the same form. But a step in the flanking of the curtain by round towers is seen in the wall of Conisbrough (217). Here the inner ward is nearly oval, and the southern half of the curtain, in which is contained the entrance from the outworks, is strengthened by small solid towers with battering bases, projecting some two-thirds of a circle from the wall.[2] Such solid projections for flanking purposes are found at Scarborough and Knaresborough, and could be easily added to an earlier wall, when necessity required. For the convenience of the defenders, however, larger towers with rooms on each floor were desirable ; and the actual improvement of the defences of the curtain is seen in the multiplication of such towers, so as to leave no part of the wall unflanked. The circular or polygonal form was almost universally adopted for them.

---

[1] The mining operations, so successful at Château-Gaillard, were not without their own danger to the miners. In the siege of Coucy by the count of Saint-Pol in 1411, the traditional method was used to undermine one of the towers of the base-court. A party of the besiegers descended to admire the preparations. The wooden stays, however, were not strong enough to support the weight of the tower, which fell unexpectedly, and buried the men in the mine. Their remains have never come to light.

[2] These are additions to the wall, probably made soon after the building of the great cylindrical tower. The wall seems to be of the earlier part of the twelfth century, and may have enclosed the bailey from the first. No traces of a mount remain.

CONISBROUGH : barbican of inner bailey

MANORBIER CASTLE from south-west

Warkworth (49) is an example of a twelfth-century castle in which an approach was made to an adequately defended curtain, although with long distances between the towers. The arrangement, however, is a complete contrast to the haphazard projection of towers from earlier curtains, as at Ludlow. The castle stands high on the right bank of the Coquet : the river bends round it, so that the only level approach is from the plateau on the west side, and the town climbs the tongue of land between the castle and the river.[1] The mount is at the apex of the castle site, immediately above the town. On the west side of the enclosure the curtain, which is strong and thick, is unbroken by any tower : against the inner face are the domestic buildings. The south wall, which contains the gatehouse, is flanked by two angle-towers, on the west by the tower known as " Cradyfargus," and on the east by a square tower, called the Amble tower. In the east wall, which commanded the ascent from the town, is a half-octagon tower, in each face of which is a huge loop for a cross-bow, so that a few archers could effectually rake the path outside with their fire. Of these towers, Cradyfargus projects into the castle enclosure with a blunt angle, its walls on this side being a mere continuation of the curtain. The basement was entered from the cellar behind the hall, the first floor from the great chamber above, and the second floor by a stair in the thickness of the wall from the vestibule or landing, west of the great chamber. The projection of the eastern tower is entirely outward : its internal face was flat. There was a basement and two floors : the first floor had an external stair from the ward, but it does not appear how the second floor was reached, though the jamb of a door may still be seen. The east tower had a garde-robe near the entrance of the basement and on the first floor : in Cradyfargus there are only traces of garde-robe arrangements. Although the space enclosed by the walls was large, and the flanking by no means perfect, the two most assailable sides of the fortress were very secure. The gatehouse, a building of about the year 1200 (221), formed an intermediate projection in the south wall between Cradyfargus and the Amble tower : the gateway is recessed between two half-octagon turrets. The preference of polygonal forms for the defences of this castle is rather characteristic of the north of England. There was, however, a conservative spirit in this district, which is seen in the retention of the rectangular form for the Amble tower. Even in a fourteenth-century castle like Dunstanburgh the angle towers are rectangular in form ; while the "pele-tower" of the

[1] The position of Appleby town and castle, within a great sweep of the Eden, is somewhat similar.

northern borders, throughout the middle ages, shows no important variation from the square form.

The importance given to the gatehouse at Warkworth was a sign of the times. We have seen how, at Lewes and Tickhill, the first thought of the builders was to provide their earth-works with a stone house of entry. Norman gatehouses were very simple in construction. The gatehouse at Warkworth, on the other hand, was anything but simple in its arrangements, and all the forethought possible was taken for its defence. There are three stories, the lowest of which is the vaulted hall of entrance to the castle, flanked, in the ground-floor of the half-octagon towers, by guard-rooms described in the survey of 1567 as a porter's lodge and a prison. The defences of the passage need close attention. The entrance was closed by a gate which opened outwards, and stood about 4 feet in advance of the portcullis : the space between was commanded by arrow-loops in the walls of the guardrooms. The herse of the portcullis seems to have been worked from the second floor of the gate-house :[1] the upper and broader portion ran in a groove which ceases at the level of the string-course below the vault of the passage, while the lower descended to the ground. Beyond the portcullis, the passage was kept under observation through cross-loops in the side walls. The vault stopped 5 feet short of the inner gateway, and the passage was covered by a wooden roof. On each side of the inner gateway were the entrances to the guard-rooms, which flanked the whole passage.

The plan of the castle gatehouse at Warkworth was that of the great majority of medieval gatehouses, whether in castles or in the walls of fortified towns. The ground-floor of the main block of building, which generally had two upper floors, contained the hall of entry, and was flanked by two cylindrical or octagonal towers, the lowest stories of which were guard-rooms, and were pierced with loops commanding the approach and the passage. Usually the gateway was placed at the back of an arched recess, which formed a porch. The position of the gate and portcullis at Warkworth was rather exceptional. Ordi-narily the portcullis descended in front of the gate, which opened inwards, and was secured, when closed, by one or more draw-bars. This, however, was impossible, where the gate, as at Warkworth, opened outwards, so that the usual arrange-ment had to be reversed. But, while the actual plan of the gatehouse kept its general characteristics with little change, the

---

[1] Apartments, known as the Constable's lodging, were on the first floor of the gatehouse : the portcullis probably descended through the thickness of the south wall of this floor, which was not pierced for a window.

WARKWORTH : gatehouse

WARKWORTH : tower on mount

defences of the entrance were multiplied.   Thus the Byward tower, the outer gatehouse of the Tower of London, had an outer portcullis in front of a wooden door opening inwards, behind which was a second portcullis, blocking the entrance to the inner and wider portion of the passage, which had a timber ceiling.   In addition to this, between the outer portcullis and the gate, the vault was crossed by a rib, pierced with three holes, which allowed the defenders to harass an attacking party from above, and also could be used for strengthening the gate in time of siege by a timber framework, the upper ends of which were fixed in the holes.   Such holes, which were not merely machicolations in the vault, are found elsewhere, as in the gatehouses of Pembroke and Warwick castles and the west gatehouse of the town of Southampton.   In this last case, a single rectangular gate-tower projected from the inner face of the wall only, next the town.   The gate of the passage through the ground floor was defended upon its outer face by these holes alone : there were two portcullises, but both were upon the inner side of the gate.   It is possible that such holes were originally left to fix the centering of the vault when it was first built : they converge towards one another, and probably were not filled up afterwards, in view of their defensive use.[1]

One prominent feature, however, of the defences of a gateway, as time went on, was the provision of machicolations, in the shape of long rectangular slits, in the vault of the passage and in the arch in front of the portcullis.   In some cases where they occur in connection with a portcullis, they may have been used for a heavy wooden frame, which could on occasion reinforce the iron herse of the portcullis.   At Warkworth there is no original arrangement of this kind : the wall of the first floor above the gateway projects slightly upon a row of corbels, but this was done merely to give it additional strength.   At a later date, however, the parapet at the top of the gatehouse was corbelled out, and the spaces between the corbels left open for machicolations.   From the later part of the thirteenth century onwards, the usual arrangement, as at Chepstow or Tutbury, was to carry the parapet upon an arch in advance of the main face of the gatehouse, from one tower to the other, and to leave the space between the parapet and the main wall open, so that it commanded the field immediately in front of the portcullis. The effect of recessing the front of the gatehouse within a tall

---

[1] The common idea that molten lead was poured through these holes on the besiegers is a mere legend.   This valuable material would hardly have been employed for this purpose.   Powdered quick-lime, however, may have been used, with even more deadly effect.

25

outer archway is magnificent, from the point of view of design. The design of gatehouses reaches its highest point in the great gatehouse of Denbigh, with its octagonal gate-hall, and in the King's gateway at Carnarvon, where the enclosing arch, recessing the two lower stages of the gatehouse, bears the outer wall of the upper floor (253).

In some instances, as at Pembroke (224) and Kidwelly (225),

Pembroke Castle ; Interior of gateway

where the gatehouse passage was defended by inner and outer portcullises, there are as many as three chases or slots in the vault between the outer and inner entrances. At Pembroke, where the gatehouse has the unusual feature of two flanking towers (213), of semicircular projection, on the side next the ward, an arch was thrown out from one tower to the other, some distance in advance of the inner archway. It is difficult to see how this inner barbican, as it may be called, was intended to be of use to an already strongly protected gateway ; but the space within it may have been covered by a wooden platform, accessible from the first floor of the gatehouse, from which the interior of the castle could be commanded, and an enemy who had forced an entrance could be seriously annoyed.   The vault of the entrance passage was generally a pointed barrel-vault, strengthened by transverse ribs at intervals ; but the broader space in the centre

of the passage was often ceiled, as in the Byward tower, with timber. The entrance passages of the inner gatehouses of Harlech (274) and Beaumaris (236) were roofed with wooden ceilings, supported by transverse ribs of stone set with only a narrow interval between them.

The ground-floors of the flanking towers of the gatehouse were usually vaulted. The lodges from which the towers were entered, upon each side of the inner passage, had stone ceilings when the passage itself was vaulted through its whole length, or when they formed one room with the ground-floors

Kidwelly Castle ; Interior of gateway

of the towers.   The ordinary plan, however, was to treat the flanking tower as an outer guard-room, approached from the inner lodge.   If it was cylindrical in plan, the interior was arranged as a polygon, and vaulted with ribs springing from shafts in the angles.[1]   This

---

[1] This applies, of course, to almost all vaulted towers which are cylindrical in plan, and not to gatehouse towers alone : *e.g.*, the towers of the inner ward of Coucy.   But, even where there is no vaulting, the interior plan of cylindrical towers is sometimes polygonal—*e.g.*, in the western angle-towers at Harlech, on all floors as well as in the basement.   In the eastern angle-towers of the same castle, the interior of the basements is cylindrical. Clark, ii. 73, describes these angle-towers inaccurately.

plan may be seen in the Byward tower and Middle tower of the
Tower of London.   In both towers the inner part of the passage
was ceiled with timber, and the adjacent chambers formed lobbies
to the vaulted ground-floors of the towers.   In the Middle tower,
however, the left-hand lobby was occupied by a vice leading to
the first floor ; and in the same position in the Byward tower
is a square rectangular chamber with a ribbed vault.

A good normal gatehouse, which may be taken as typical of
the period, is that of Rockingham castle (226). Its details indicate
that it belongs to the later part of the reign of Henry III.   It
is upon the east side of the enclosure, and its projection is almost
entirely towards the field.   The plan is, as usual, a rectangle
with a passage through the centre, and with semicylindrical

Rockingham Castle ; Gatehouse

towers projecting on either side of the outer entrance.   No
vaulting was used.   The passage is entered through a porch
beneath a drop arch—that is to say, a pointed arch whose two
segments are drawn from centres below the springing line—
and was guarded, just within the arch, by a portcullis in front
of a wooden door.   At the inner end of the passage was another
door.   Openings in the side walls of the passage communicated
with rectangular chambers ;[1] and in the east walls of these were
doorways into semicircular chambers within the towers.   There
was only one upper floor to the gatehouse and its towers.   In

[1] The entrances to such guard-rooms, where great thickness was given
to the outer wall, took the form of narrow elbow-shaped lobbies, which
would be a source of difficulty and deception to an attacking force.

this simple building, one is reminded at once of the rectangular stone gatehouse of the early Norman castle, with its upper chamber. Improvement is seen in the substitution, for the original entrance, of a central passage flanked by chambers upon the ground-floor; in the addition of flanking towers of scientific form; and in the protection of the timber doors by an iron portcullis.

The gatehouse at Newcastle, known as the Black gate (227), which became the entrance to the castle in the thirteenth century, is an example of a more elaborately constructed and exceptional type. The ground plan is simplicity itself, a central passage flanked by towers containing guard-chambers. The towers, however, are not merely projections from a rectangular body, but flank the whole gateway with a wide convex curve. There is a large single vaulted chamber on the ground floor of each, lighted by loops which enabled the occupants to command the castle ditch. The architectural details of the gateway are very simple, but there is a short arcade of trefoiled arches in each of the side walls, and the vaulting of the guard-rooms presents some ingenious peculiarities. The upper portion of the gatehouse was much altered in the seventeenth century. The original design, with its great seg-

Newcastle; Black gate

mental flanking towers, may have been the prototype of the even more noble gatehouse of Dunstanburgh, which is a work of nearly three-quarters of a century later.[1]

The upper floors of the gatehouse may be reserved for discussion until we come to the concentric plan, in which the gatehouse became a building of exceptional importance. For military purposes the one necessary upper chamber was that in which the machinery controlling the portcullis was worked. In the floor of this room was the upper end of the groove, through which, by means of a pulley in the ceiling, the iron frame was

[1] The Black gate was built in 1247 : the entrance was protected by an outer barbican in 1358.

Walled town in state of siege

drawn up or down, hanging here when it was not in use to close the entrance below.   Many examples of a portcullis chamber remain, as at Berry Pomeroy and in Bootham bar at York.[1]

The entrance of the castle, under improved conditions of fortification, was defended by an outwork or barbican.   The term "barbican," which seems to be of eastern derivation, was used indiscriminately to denote any outwork by which the principal approach to a castle or a gateway of a town was covered.   The word "barmkin," which is possibly, as already noted, a corruption of "barbican," was applied in the north of England to the outer yard of a "pele," or fortified (literally, palisaded) residence.   In many castles, as at Ludlow, Denbigh, or Manorbier, the outer ward was an addition or supplement to the plan of the castle, guarding the approach to the inner

York; Walmgate Bar

ward or castle proper, and its curtain was subsidiary to the strongly fortified curtain of the inner ward.   Such outer wards or base-courts resemble the northern "barmkins," an exact parallel to which is seen in the base-court of the fifteenth-century fortified house of Wingfield.   Covering outworks were by no means uncommon, and also served the purpose of a barbican.   As at Château-Gaillard, they might take the form of a walled outer ward, or, as at Llandovery, they might be horn-shaped earthworks, thrown out at an exposed point in the defences ; in either case, they had their own ditch, an extension of the main ditch of the castle.   But the barbican proper was a walled extension of a gatehouse to the field, confining the

[1] Holes in the masonry for the beam to which the pulley was fixed may be seen, *e.g.*, in the gateways at Conway and Rhuddlan.

approach to the limited area of a narrow passage. The most simple instance is the barbican in front of Walmgate bar at York (229), where a gatehouse, originally of the twelfth century, was strengthened by the addition, upon the outer side, of two parallel walls at right angles to the sides of the gateway. Thus, in order to force the gates, an attacking party would have to traverse a long and narrow alley between high walls, in which they were exposed to the missiles of the defenders concentrated upon them from the ramparts of the gatehouse and the adjacent wall.

The barbican was, in fact, an application to the main entrance of the castle of the form of defence hitherto applied most scientifically to the fore-building of the keep.[1] Its general employment as an outer defence was the direct consequence of the removal of interest from the keep to the curtain. Not merely had the wall itself to offer a stout resistance to attack, so that every point was simultaneously engaged in active defence; but the main approaches had to be so arranged as to involve an enemy in perplexity. In the protection of the main avenues of access to the town or castle, we arrive at an unconscious reproduction in stone of the methods employed by prehistoric builders of earthwork. Experience taught the engineers of the thirteenth and fourteenth centuries the lessons which she had taught the makers of Maiden Castle, and the adoption of the concentric plan of fortification followed as a matter of course.

The contraction of the main entrance of the castle by a barbican is well seen at Bamburgh, Conisbrough (217), and Scarborough (129). In the first two instances, owing to the isolated position of the fortress, and the nature of the ground outside, the main approach would have to be in any case by a path made up the steep face of the hill, and immediately below the curtain. Bamburgh was unusually well aided by nature, and the gateway, flanked by two slender round towers, is at a level considerably lower than that of the summit of the rock; in this case, the rising road within the gateway, cut in the basalt, and commanded by the curtain and the keep within the curtain, was the barbican of the castle. The hill on which Conisbrough was set is merely a steep knoll, with a wide outer ditch on its less precipitous side. The outer ward, on the south-west side of the ditch, was apparently an earthwork without stone walls.[2]   A

---

[1] At Sandal (86) there was a barbican guarding the entrance to a shell-keep.

[2] Conisbrough is virtually a castle of one ward set on an isolated hill, not unlike Restormel in Cornwall.

WARWICK : barbican

gatehouse was set on the edge of the ditch, in advance of and at a lower level than the curtain of the inner ward. Its arrangements, so far as they can be traced, were not greatly superior to those of early stone gatehouses. Its lateral walls, however, were prolonged up the edge of the slope to the entrance of the inner ward. The left-hand wall joined an angle of the curtain half-way up the passage ; the wall on the right hand was continued so as to cover the inner gateway, which was at right angles to the passage thus formed.[1] As at Bamburgh, the approach in this case is a narrow gangway between high walls, commanded throughout from the rampart of the inner ward, and, for the second half of the distance, passing immediately beneath it. A passage of this type, with a right-angled turn at its far end, might easily become a death-trap for a besieging force.

At Scarborough the castle cliff is almost entirely separated from the town by a deep ravine, and the approach is along the narrow ridge between this chasm and the northward face of the rock. The gatehouse, flanked by rounded towers, forms part of a small and irregularly shaped walled outwork or barbican placed upon the outer curve of the ravine. From this *tête-du-pont*, as it may be called, a straight passage, walled on both sides, crosses the head of the ravine, passing over a bridge on its way, and skirting, on the left hand, the sheer edge of the cliff. On the further side, the space widens into the outer ward, commanded and nearly blocked by the rectangular keep. The wall on the left is continued along the edge of the cliff, while that on the right, which, as being more open to attack, is much the thicker, bears away with the curve of the slope, and joins the south curtain of the inner ward upon its west face.[2]

The examples already given illustrate the precautions which thirteenth-century engineers took to guard their castles from surprise and storm ; and the arrangements found in the Welsh castles of Edward I.'s reign are even more remarkable. It will be noticed that in the three castles just mentioned the main gatehouse is thrown forward to the outer end of the barbican, which forms a narrow passage uniting the gatehouse to the inner entrance. In late thirteenth and fourteenth century castles, however, the barbican was, as we see it at Walmgate bar in York, an addition to the front of a gatehouse. This method of covering gateways by outer defences is seen at Kenilworth, where the approach to the outer ward of the castle, across the

---

[1] The entrance may be compared to the more perfect plan of the barbican and platform at Conway (254).

[2] The wall of *enceinte* at Scarborough is probably in great part the wall which defended the castle from its foundation.

26

lake formed by the damming-up of two rivulets, was broken up into sections by three lines of defence. First, an outer earthwork, segmental in shape, and strengthened by round stone bastions, guarded the approach to the first gatehouse. Beyond this gate-house, which formed a *tête-du-pont* like the Middle tower at

Warwick Castle; Barbican

London, a long causeway or dam, with a wall on its eastern face, crossed the lake to the strong gatehouse known as Mortimer's tower, which, guarded by two portcullises, stood upon the end of the dam, in advance of the curtain. But the ordinary barbican, which was characteristic of the castles of the fourteenth and fifteenth centuries, was not a long and elaborately

protected line of outer defences, but a stone building thrown out
in front of a gatehouse, so as to concentrate the attacking force
into a small space, and prevent a combined rush on the principal
gateway.   The contracted approach thus made was usually, in
the later examples, as at Warwick (231), Alnwick (243), and
Porchester, all barbicans of the fourteenth century, a straight
lane between walls.   At Porchester it is set in front of the
twelfth-century gatehouse of the inner ward, which was covered
in the early fourteenth century by a rectangular projection,
pierced by lateral doorways opening upon the scarp of the
inner ward outside the curtain.

The barbican proper, somewhat
later in date, is composed of two
parallel walls, guarding the drawbridge from the base-court or
outer ward.   A loop cut obliquely
through the west wall of this passage opened towards the west
gateway of the base-court, so that
a surprise of the barbican could
be prevented.   In this case, as at
Alnwick, the approach to the
barbican was a drawbridge; but
at Alnwick, where the drawbridge
crossed an outer loop of the castle
ditch, the ditch proper was crossed
by a second drawbridge within
the barbican.

At Lewes, about the end of
the thirteenth century, a barbican
was added to the front of a
Norman gatehouse which was of
much the same character as the
gatehouses at Porchester and

Mont-St-Michel; Châtelet

Tickhill.   The addition here took the shape of a short passage
with a wall on each side, finished at its outer end by a new
and lofty gatehouse, rising from the middle of the outer ditch
of the castle, and approached by a mounting roadway.   The
shape of the new gatehouse is an oblong, with its main axis
perpendicular to the road, but its angles were capped by round
turrets, corbelled out at a point near the spring of the entrance
archway (98).   Such turrets are known as bartizans, and are
common in French military architecture of the thirteenth and
fourteenth centuries.   They were not so usual in England, and
are seldom found on such a scale as at Lewes: smaller bartizans,

corbelled out at a point nearer the battlements of the building
in which they occur, may be seen in the gatehouse at Lincoln,
and at the angles of the towers of Belsay (313) and Chipchase in
Northumberland.[1] The parapet of the barbican gatehouse at
Lewes is brought forward from the wall on a row of corbels
so as to allow room for six formidable machicolations. The
work bears some resemblance to the *châtelet* which covers the
main entrance of the fortified abbey of Mont-Saint-Michel (235).[2]
In France an outer gatehouse like that at Lewes, or an outer
enclosure like that at Scarborough, bore the name of *châtelet* or
bastille. All such defences in advance of a gateway, whatever
the special name they may bear, may be classed under the head
of barbicans.

Beaumaris Castle; Gateway

In the highest ex-
amples of military skill
in fortification—at
Conway (254) and
Beaumaris (236), for
instance—the greatest
care was taken to cover
the gateways with ob-
lique or right-angled
approaches, so that
straight access should
be impossible to an
enemy. The same
method of hampering
the path of an enemy
with right angled turns
is noticeable in French
examples of fortifica-
tion, and notably in the gateways of Carcassonne (239). In
England, however, an entrance defended by a barbican in a
straight line with it was generally preferred; and, even in
castles like Caerphilly and Harlech, the strength of the entrances
depended upon the disposition of the concentric wards of the
castle, and they were guiltless of the devices and traps which
are one leading feature of Beaumaris A good example of an
oblique approach to a thirteenth-century castle is at Pembroke,

---

[1] They appear to have been a feature of the keep at Pontefract; *cf.* also
Micklegate, Monk, and Bootham bars at York, which have bartizans at the
outer angles. At Lincoln the wall of the upper floor of the gatehouse,
between the bartizans, presents an obtuse angle to the field.

[2] The main gatehouse (Belle-Chaise) was built under abbot Tustin
(1236-64); the *châtelet* was added under Pierre Le Roy in 1393.

TUTBURY : gatehouse

YORK : Micklegate bar

where the main gateway is covered by an open barbican, forming
a rectangular vestibule, the entrance to which is in a wall nearly
at right angles to the gateway.   The west gate of Tenby is
covered by an almost semicircular barbican, the original entrance
to which, with a groove for a portcullis, is on the north side,
so that an angle had to be turned before the gateway was
reached.   At a much later date other openings were pierced in
the outer wall of the barbican, and the curious arrangement is

Carcassonne

known to-day by the misleading name of the " Five Arches."
The east side of the chief ward of Carew castle was protected
by a rectangular outer court, entered from the field by a small
gatehouse.   The gatehouse of the inner ward is in the south
half of the east wall, and is flanked by a round angle-tower
and a tower which projects from the middle of the wall.   The
outer faces of these two towers were joined by a wall which
thus covered the gatehouse, and was pierced by a doorway,
set a little to the north of the main entrance, with its jambs

sloping to the left. This gave access to a walled-in passage, with an upper floor, leading obliquely to the inner entrance. As this side of the castle was on level ground and was much exposed, special care was taken to guard the approaches; there was, however, only one portcullis, at the inner end of the main gateway; but the wooden doors, four of which had to be passed before the portcullis was reached, were of great strength, and each was closed with several very massive draw-bars.

The town gateway at Tenby may be compared to the Porte de Laon at Coucy, which was also covered by a semicircular barbican. While, however, the Tenby barbican was directly attached to the wall, the barbican at Coucy was separated from the gateway by the town ditch and a bridge, and was altogether more elaborate. The bridge itself crossed the ditch in two

Tenby; West Gate

sections, describing an obtuse angle, at the apex of which was a round tower. The road passed through the tower, and turned the angle at its inner gate, from which the second section of the bridge passed straight to the actual gateway. At Coucy all the resources of fortification were displayed; while at Tenby the application of the same principle was simple and unpretending.[1] Equally masterly is the oblique entrance to the castle of Kerak in Syria, beside which the entrances to Pembroke and Carew are of small account.[2] The long rectangular castle of Kerak is divided into two nearly equal wards by a wall parallel to its major axis. The main gateway is on the east side of the junction of the cross-wall with the outer curtain; but, instead of leading directly into the castle, the path turns to the left after passing through the gateway, and

[1] The fortifications of Coucy were built in the thirteenth century: the round tower in front of the Porte de Laon was superseded in 1551 by a bastion of pentagonal form. The southern gate of Coucy (Porte de Soissons) was made in a re-entering angle of the town wall: the southern gate at Conway (Porth-y-Felin) shows the same disposition. The walls of Tenby were originally built early in the reign of Edward III.: letters patent, granting murage for seven years to the men of Tenby for the construction of their walls, were issued 6th March 1327-28 (Pat. 2 Edw. III., pt. 1, m. 22).

[2] Plan in Oman, *Art of War*, opposite p. 530.

is confined within a long inner barbican, from the end of which a gatehouse at right angles gives admission to the interior of the upper ward.

The importance attached, from the thirteenth century onwards, to the gateway and its approaches, and the prominence of the gatehouse in the concentric castle of Edward I.'s reign will now be understood. It now remains to speak of the defences of the exposed face of curtain between the towers, and of the towers themselves. The progress towards effective flanking has been traced already, and the towered curtains at Dover (126) or the Tower of London are examples of scientific flanking achieved by long experiment. The towers rose above the level of the curtain, and were entered on the first floor from the rampart-walk, which they commanded. The walk, in fact, passed through the towers, as it may still be seen passing through the gatehouses at York. Thus each tower was the key to a section of wall; and, as the Crusaders found at Antioch, the wall could be taken only by the capture of several towers, each of which guarded a separate section.

Outer stair to tower and rampart-walk in town wall

The rampart-walk between the towers occupied, as from the earliest times, the top of the wall, and was defended by battlements upon the outer, and sometimes by a low rear-wall on the inner side.[1] The chief access to it was by stairs in the towers,

[1] The northern rampart-walk at Coucy was widened by the building of an arcade of thirteen pointed arches against the inner face of the wall, connecting a series of internal buttresses. Part of the western wall of the town of Southampton was widened, some time later than the actual building of the wall, by the addition of eighteen arches upon the outer face (293). The soffits of the arches were pierced by long machicolations—a necessary precaution in so exceptional an arrangement.

but sometimes, as at Alnwick, there was a stair from the interior of the castle, built at right angles to the wall (241). In the shell-keep on the mount at Tamworth, there is a small stair which ascends in the thickness of the wall. The principal alterations which took place with regard to the rampart-walk were concerned with the treatment of the parapet. The division of the parapet into merlons or solid pieces by embrasures has been explained already, and it has been seen that, in the first instance, the embrasures are pierced at rather long intervals. The tendency

Carcassonne

grows, however, to multiply embrasures and narrow down the merlons between them, on the theory that the archer, discharging his arrow through the embrasure, can shelter himself and re-string his bow behind the merlon. The merlon, however, in works designed with a purpose mainly military, is usually broader than the embrasure, and is itself pierced with a small arrow-loop, splayed internally. This may be seen in the town-walls of Aigues-Mortes (77) and Carcassonne (78), where the merlons are of great breadth, and in such triumphs of fortification as the castles of Carnarvon (246) and Conway.[1] The merlons, however, were not always provided with loops, even in the Edwardian period. The barbican at Alnwick (243), a work of the early fourteenth century, is battlemented with plain merlons and embrasures. In this case, there are two further points which deserve notice. The embrasures at Alnwick were defended by wooden shutters, which hung from trunnions working in grooves in the adjacent merlons. The shutters could be lifted out at pleasure, and the embrasure left free: the device may be noticed in some other instances.[2] Also,

[1] In the battlement of the donjon of Coucy, each piece of solid wall between the arched embrasures is pierced by an arrow-loop (177).

[2] Viollet-le-Duc, *La Cité de Carcassonne*, p. 27, has a drawing of a similar device with an upper and lower shutter (245): the upper shutter is propped open by iron guards: while the lower is hung in iron hooks fixed in the face of the wall.

ALNWICK : barbican

ALNWICK : gatehouse of keep

upon the merlons at Alnwick stand stone figures of warriors, sometimes called "defenders," and supposed to be designed to strike terror into the enemy. The present figures at Alnwick are comparatively modern ; but the fashion was not uncommon and was purely ornamental. Similar figures are seen on the gatehouse of the neighbouring castle of Bothal, and upon the gatehouses of York : among the figures on the merlons at Carnarvon was an eagle, which gave its name to the famous Eagle tower. An enemy who could be daunted by the illusion of a rather diminutive archer or slinger balancing himself on a narrow coping, must have had very little experience of warfare. The merlons were treated very plainly in many French examples, as at Avignon, Aigues-Mortes, and Carcassonne (242), where they are flat-topped and unmoulded, while the embrasures have flat sills. In England they were generally finished off by a gabled coping, as at Carnarvon, where the top of each is moulded with a halfroll to the field (246).[1] The sill of the embrasure has also an

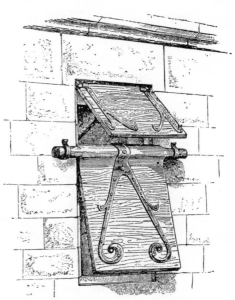

Shutter closing opening in wall or parapet

inner chamfer. It may be noted that the freedom with which machicolations were employed in the parapets of French castles and town-walls was unusual in England. Machicolated parapets were, as a rule, confined to the fronts of gateways, until the later part of the fourteenth century, when they began, as at Lancaster and Warwick, to show themselves in the towers of the gateway and curtain. They are very sparingly used in the Welsh castles, which are our noblest examples of military architecture ; and an *enceinte*, like the city wall of Avignon, in which

---

[1] *Cf.* sections of church parapets in Bond, *Gothic Architecture in England*, pp. 385-8.

27

the whole parapet is machicolated and built out on long corbels of considerable projection, is unknown in England.

What has just been said of the parapets of walls applies naturally to the parapets of towers. Towers on the curtain had, as we have seen, a double use. They flanked the wall, so that each pair could rake with their shot the entire face of the *enceinte* contained between them. They also commanded the rampart-walk, so that an enemy who scaled the wall was still exposed to their fire and confined to a limited area. A distinction, how-ever, must be drawn between the closed and open types of tower, as they may be called. The ordinary rampart tower was of two or three stages, divided into a basement and upper guard-room

Carnarvon Castle ; Crenellated parapet

or rooms. The basement was sometimes vaulted, as in the northern tower at Pevensey (247) or towers at Alnwick. Fire-places and garde-robe chambers are often found in the upper rooms,[1] the garde-robes being often placed at the junction of the tower with the curtain, and corbelled out over the outer wall.[2] At Carew, where there was no keep, but the castle formed a rectangular enclosure with drum-towers at the angles, all the

[1] At Kenilworth the Water tower, on the south curtain of the base-court, has a fireplace in the basement.

[2] Garde-robes built upon arches across re-entering angles of a wall occur on each side of a large buttress in the west wall of Southampton. A similar feature occurs at the junction of the north curtain of Porchester castle with one of the Roman towers. In both cases the addition was probably made in the fourteenth century.

towers were provided with garde-robe chambers, which, with the
passages leading to them, are roofed by lozenge-shaped slabs,
corbelled out one above another. In the south-east tower, the
first-floor chamber has a pointed barrel-vault, and is entered by
an outer stair from the ward. In the east wall are two garde-
robe chambers, entered by elbow-shaped passages. Each had
a door opening inwards, and was lighted by a separate loop.
The chambers were so planned that the seats were placed on
opposite sides of a partition wall, with a common vent.

The tower at Carew just mentioned is at earliest of
late thirteenth-century date, and has several advanced features.
Though its projection from the curtain is regularly rounded, its
inward projection is rectangular, so that its plan is actually an

Pevensey; Vaulting in basement of north tower

oblong with a rounded end. It seems to have been intended
to have been used in connection with the gatehouse: its first
and second floors had no direct communication with each other,
but both communicated with the gatehouse, and the ground-floor
of the gatehouse had a large lateral opening in the direction of
the first floor of the tower. The corresponding tower at the
north-east angle was used in connection with the domestic
buildings, and had a vaulted chapel (248) upon its first floor,
from the north wall of which open two rooms for the use of the
priest, with a garde-robe in the second. One tower, therefore,
was purely defensive, additional precautions having been taken,
no doubt, to guard a postern which opens from the basement
upon the scarp of the ditch; while the other was merely an
annexe to one of the two dwelling-houses within the enclosure.

The use of the eastern and south-western towers at Warkworth (49) was equally distinct. We have seen that the south-west tower (Cradyfargus) was used in connection with the domestic buildings: this may not have been its original purpose, but it was certainly thus employed early in the fourteenth century. The great feature of the east tower is the huge loop in each of its five outer faces, designed for a cross-bow 16 feet long: these loops, splayed throughout and fan-tailed at top and bottom, are the finest examples of cross-loops left in England, and declare the main purpose of the tower at once. In later years,

Carew; Chapel

when the cross-bow was out of fashion, the interior of the tower was somewhat altered, and a fireplace inserted.

The best examples of curtain-towers, both abroad and in England, form complete cylinders, like the angle-towers at Coucy, or polygons, like some of the towers at Carnarvon. But room was spared if the cylinder or polygon was left incomplete, and its inner face made nearly flush with the curtain. The two towers on the curtain of the inner ward at Pembroke projected with semicircular curves into the outer ward, but were flat at the back: the south tower covered the gateway of the inner ward, which was not in the face of the wall, but round an angle. The towers of the outer ward, on the other hand, are mostly complete cylinders: the stairs were vices contained in rectangular turrets on one side, the outer walls of which are curved to meet the circumference of the towers (181).[1] Marten's tower at Chepstow, and the towers of the curtain of the fine early fourteenth-century castle of Llanstephan, are cases in which the projection of the tower is only external. The tower which caps the eastern angle at Llanstephan is a half-cylinder, springing, not directly from the curtain, but from a broad rectangular projection on its face.[2]   The variations which might be noticed in the attachment of towers to the curtain are mani-

Door of main gatehouse

Stair to vaulted chamber in outer bailey

Chepstow Castle

fold ; but, as time goes on, the ordinary curtain-tower, where it was not placed at an angle of a ward, stood flush with the curtain on its inner side (228). Where the tower stood on the curtain by itself,

---

[1] These towers appear to be of the fourteenth century, and are therefore much later in date than the towers of the inner curtain.

[2] At Flint, Rhuddlan, and several other castles, the angle-towers were three-quarter circles, the face towards the bailey being a flat wall, on which, at Rhuddlan as at Harlech, the rampart-walk was corbelled out.

unattached to other buildings within the castle, there was usually an entrance to the basement direct from the bailey, on one side of which a vice in a turret attached to the tower rose to the upper floors and roof, communicating on the level of the first floor with the curtain.   The doorway opening on the curtain was fitted with a strong door, and, in Marten's tower at Chepstow castle, where the tower was of special importance, standing as it does at the lowest and most vulnerable point of the site, was provided with a portcullis.

There were cases, however, especially in walls of towns, where the curtain-tower, although projecting outside and above the wall, and covered with a timber roof, was left open at the gorge or neck, where it was flush with the curtain, so that it was

Fougères

simply an open tower, with a platform on the first floor, level with the rampart-walk, and a rampart-walk of its own at the level of its battlements.   Such a tower could be actively employed in time of war, and had all the advantages of the ordinary closed tower in flanking the wall and cutting the rampart-walk up into sections.   The numerous towers of the walls of Avignon, between the gatehouses, were arranged thus.[1]   At Conway, the

---

[1] These walls, pierced by seven gates and flanked by thirty-nine rectangular towers, were begun under Pope Clement VI. in 1345, and finished c. 1380.   The rampart is reached by stairs set against the inner face of the walls.   The walls of Aigues-Mortes, built 1272-5, and of Carcassonne, begun earlier and completed later than Aigues-Mortes, belong to an earlier period of fortification, corresponding to that of our Edwardian castles.   Of other well-known French examples, the walls of Mont-Saint-Michel are of

semi-cylindrical towers of the town walls, of which there are twenty, and the similar towers which flank the gatehouses, are open to the town: one tower only, on the south-west side of the town, where the wall turns to join the castle, is walled at the gorge.   The walls of Chepstow provide further examples of open towers.   At Carnarvon (251), the round towers on the face of the town walls are open, but the angle-towers were closed; and that at the north-west angle was entered through the town chapel, which was built against the curtain at this point.   The open tower was not, as a rule, used in castles: even the small towers which flank the outer curtain at Beaumaris have a wall continued across the gorge.

Every large castle was pro-vided with a postern or sally-port.   This was generally a small doorway, preferably in the base of a tower, but often in the curtain, opening on the least frequented side of the castle.   In time of siege, in a castle of the ordinary plan, a postern might easily be a source of danger; and its employment in the scheme of defence was incompletely under-stood at first.   But it was useful for the conveyance of provisions

Carnarvon; Tower of town wall

to the castle; and a postern, as at Warkworth, is often found in connection with a kitchen or store-room.   Where a castle stood near a river, a water-gate, communicating with a private wharf was made.   At Pembroke, where the castle stands between two water-ways, there were two water-gates, one in the south side of the outer ward, the other, as already mentioned, formed by wall-ing in the mouth of the cave below the great hall.   For the scientific employment of the postern, however, we have to look to the great castles of the later part of the thirteenth century, in which the means of defence described in this chapter were perfectly co-ordinated; and, with the introduction of a new plan, the last signs of a merely passive strength vanished from the castle.

various dates from the thirteenth to the fifteenth century : those of Domfront are partly of the thirteenth, those of Fougères (250) of the fifteenth century, and those of Saint-Malo chiefly of the fifteenth and sixteenth centuries. The thirteenth-century *enceinte* of Coucy has already been referred to.   A list of the numerous remains of town walls in France will be found in Enlart, ii. 623 *seq.*, under the name of each department.

CHAPTER X

THE EDWARDIAN CASTLE AND THE CONCENTRIC PLAN

CASTLES like Carew, enclosing a rectangular area with round towers at the angles, were the fruit of the transition in the course of which the fortified curtain wall took the place of the passive strength of the keep. At Carew the castle was protected upon its most exposed side by outer defences of stone; but on all other sides it presented a single line of defence, flanked by the four formidable angle-towers. A castle thus defended was, like the early stone castles at Richmond and elsewhere, a keep in itself; but its wall no longer depended merely upon its passive strength, but was calculated to resist attacks on which the builders of Richmond and Ludlow had no means of reckoning.

The castle of the latter half of the thirteenth century, the golden age of English military architecture, was, then, an enclosure within a strong and well-flanked curtain wall. The keep, where the site was new, was dispensed with: where an old plan was altered or enlarged, it took a secondary position. The castles of this age may be divided into three separate classes. First, there are castles without keeps, in which the flanked curtain wall forms the sole line of defence. Secondly, there are old castles, which, by extension of their site, have adopted a concentric plan of defence. And thirdly, there are castles newly planned, in which the defences are formed by two or more concentric curtain walls.

I. The grand examples of the first class are the castles of Carnarvon (253) and Conway (254). Conway was begun in 1285 by the orders of Edward I. Carnarvon, in which more architectural splendour is shown, was begun in 1283, and was not finished until 1316-22.[1] Both castles were built in connection with walled towns, and occupied an angle of the defences; and both stand on a point of land where a river meets the sea, so that two faces of the site were defended by water, while the base was separated from the town by an artificial ditch.

[1] Clark, i. 460, 312, 314.

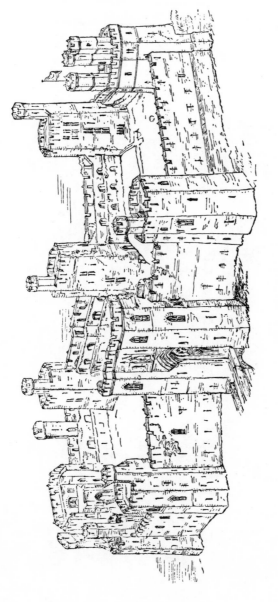

Carnarvon Castle

28

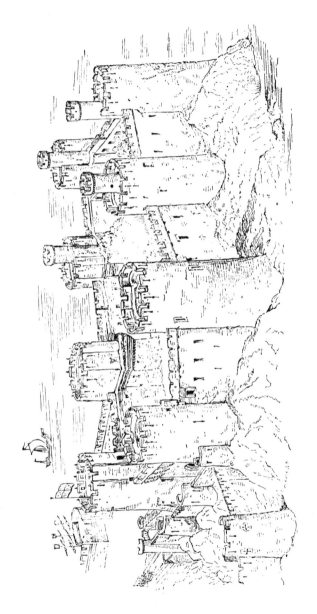

Conway Castle

Carnarvon, however, is situated on low ground, and commands the town only by the height of its curtain and its formidable towers ; while the promontory on which Conway stands is raised high above the greater part of the town and commands the whole (256).

The plan of both castles is very similar. The enclosure, in both cases an irregular polygon of an oblong shape, was divided into two wards by a cross-wall,[1] built at a point where the curtain is slightly drawn in on both sides, and the site is consequently narrowed. At Conway the main entrance is in the west or end wall of the lower ward, opposite the cross-wall. The lower ward, thus entered, is a hexagon in shape, flanked by six cylindrical or drum towers, one at each of the angles, and occupies about two-thirds of the enclosure. The remaining third is the upper ward, an irregular rectangle flanked by four drum towers, the two towers to the west being common to both wards. The whole enclosure is thus flanked by eight towers, four at the angles, and two on each of the sides.

The two wards at Carnarvon (253) were more nearly equal, the upper ward, placed, as in Conway, at the end next the confluence of the river and the sea, occupying about two-fifths of the site. The main entrance to the lower ward, the King's gateway, is in the middle of the side wall next the town, and the wall of division between the wards crossed the enclosure from a point close to the right of the inner entrance. The curtain of the lower ward was built in five sections, with a tower at each of the projecting angles between them. With these towers must be reckoned the two splendid gatehouses, the King's gatehouse at the north-west, and Queen Eleanor's gatehouse at the east angle of the ward. The curtain of the upper ward was built in four pieces, and this ward, with its cross-wall, forms an irregular pentagon, at the apex of which is the famous Eagle tower, at the point where the town wall joins that of the castle. . There are nine towers in all, counting the two gatehouses, and a turret on each of the north-east and south-east sections of the curtain. The towers are polygonal in shape, the straight faces being for the most part very broad, and the angles very obtuse.[2]

Of the two castles, Conway, which stands, as we have seen, on the better site, was the more economically defended. The leading features of the plan at Carnarvon are the two large

---

[1] The cross-wall at Carnarvon is gone.

[2] The polygonal towers which flank the great gatehouse at Denbigh had the same characteristic of obtuse angles, as can be still seen where the masonry has not been stripped from the rubble core.

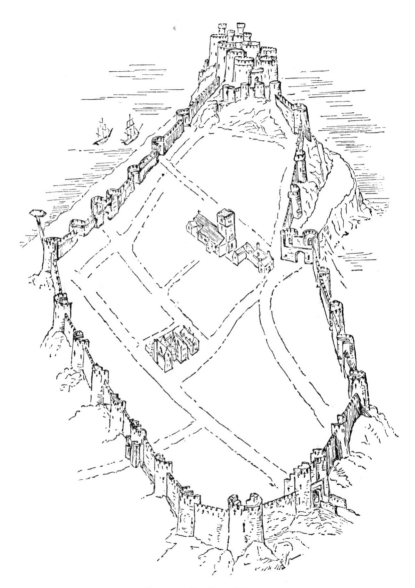

Conway Castle and Town

gatehouses and the Eagle tower at the western angle, which was virtually a strong tower or keep. The King's gatehouse formed the main entrance. Queen Eleanor's gatehouse stands at the highest point of the castle, and is now inaccessible from outside : when in use, it must have been approached by a steeply rising bridge across the ditch.[1]   There is also a postern, through which provisions were, no doubt, brought to the kitchen, in the basement of the Well tower, which caps the angle of the curtain between the King's gatehouse and Eagle tower.   At Conway, there was no separate strong tower, nor was there a real gatehouse : the gateway is in a narrow end-wall, and the towers on each side are in close connection with its machicolated rampart-walk.   There is also a second and smaller gateway in the wall at the opposite end of the castle, opening on a platform at the edge of the rock, from which a stair led to the water.

Where the curtain was so well defended as in these two castles, a double entrance was a source of strength rather than weakness.   The problem for the enemy was how to distribute his forces, so as to keep the whole *enceinte* under observation. To concentrate an attack upon one gateway was to run the risk of being outflanked and taken in the rear by a sortie from the other.   Strong as Château-Gaillard and other castles of the transition had been, they had simply met the prospect of attack with successive lines of defence.   Carnarvon and the castles of the Edwardian period generally were not entirely a refuge for a besieged garrison : they were shelters which provided a base of operations for offensive as well as defensive stratagem.   The most imposing feature of the defences of Carnarvon castle is the long irregular line of the south and south-west wall, fronting the river Seiont (258).   Here the curtain is pierced by three rows of loops, one above another.   The lowest open from a gallery in the thickness of the wall : the middle row from an upper gallery, which is now open internally, constructed on the top of the very massive lower wall ; while the top row is pierced in the merlons of the battlements (259).   The wall could be guarded simultaneously by three rows of archers, one above another—not an inviting prospect to a besieging force.   It is obvious that such a castle, large enough to shelter an army, could also be held by a relatively small body of men, so excellently was the area of defence concentrated, and so readily could every part of the curtain be reached from the interior of the fortress.

While the actual defences of the curtain at Conway were more simple than at Carnarvon, the isolation of the site was

[1] The threshold of the gateway was from 35 to 40 feet above the bottom of the ditch.

greater, and the possibility of active movement in and out of the
stronghold was less.   The attack was bound to be concentrated
upon the one main entrance; and consequently, next to the
flanking of the curtain, the chief object was the defence of the
gateway.   The end wall, in which the gateway was pierced, is
high above the adjacent town, and the level piece of ground
in front was broken short by a steep edge of cliff, at the foot of
which was the ditch.   The entrance was therefore approached
by a well-guarded barbican at right angles to the gateway.   This
outwork was reached from the town by passing along a rising
causeway with a drawbridge at the end, which gave access to

Carnarvon

the gateway of the barbican, standing in advance of the north-
west tower.   A short rising path then led through a doorway
closed by a wooden door to the platform in front of the gateway,
along the west side of which, above the ditch, was continued the
outer wall of the barbican, flanked by three small round towers,
open at the gorge.   The parapet above the gateway was machicolated, and the large corbels still project from the wall.[1]   Into a
narrow barbican like this, only a small detachment of an attacking force could venture; indeed, the position is practically impregnable.   The north-west tower commands every inch of the
approach; and the drawbridge, the portcullis and upper gateway

---

[1] The eastern gateway was defended in the same way.

CARNARVON CASTLE : towers and rampart-walk

CARNARVON CASTLE : interior

of the barbican, and the oblique entrance to the gateway of the castle, formed successive and intimidating obstacles. The main gateway was closed by a portcullis, which was worked from a mural chamber, between the crown of the arch and the rampart-walk. It may be noted that, while the oblique entrance at Conway has some likeness to the ingenious entrances at Beaumaris, the works of Conway have at least two points in common with Harlech—the corbelling-out of the rampart-walk against the interior face of the towers (261), and the carrying up of the

Conway Castle; Rampart-walk

stairs of the four eastern towers into turrets above the level of the roof. The lofty stair-turrets above the roof are also a prominent feature at Carnarvon.

The arrangements of the rampart-walks at Conway and Carnarvon were of the usual type. At Conway, where the cross-wall between the wards is still in existence, there is a walk along the top, so that no part of the curtain is really distant from another. The domestic buildings at Carnarvon unfortunately no longer stand; but the position of the hall and kitchen in the inner ward is still known. Probably, as at Conway, there was a large hall for the garrison in the outer ward. The domestic arrangements at Conway can be easily followed, although the kitchen, against the north curtain of the lower ward, is gone. The great hall, which is built against the south curtain, and follows the obtuse angle formed by it, stands above a cellar, but its floor was on a level with the surface of the ward. Its timber roof was built upon stone transverse arches, spanning the hall: the east end was screened off and formed a chapel. The buildings surrounding the smaller or upper ward formed a separate mansion, distinct from the great hall and its appendages. The chief features of this set of apartments were the smaller hall, against the south curtain, the separate withdrawing - rooms called the King's and Queen's chambers, and the small chapel or oratory in the northeast tower (263). This chapel was entered from the main stair of the tower, but a straight stair also led to it in the thickness of the east wall from the postern-gate, and communicated with a similar stair in the other half of the wall, leading to the King's chamber and the lesser hall. Water at Carnarvon was supplied from a well in the tower west of the kitchen: at Conway a cistern was made near the south-east corner of the lower ward.

Conway Castle; Fireplace in hall

II. There are old castles, however, which were adapted to the new form of fortification with an ingenuity equal to that shown on new sites at Conway and Carnarvon. In alluding to the lessons learned by the Crusaders in the east, we have noticed the concentric form of fortification which they saw at Constantinople. The city was girt by a triple wall, each ring of which was higher than the one outside it. The advantage of this was obvious : while three successive lines of defence were provided, the three could also be used simultaneously, each row of defenders discharging its missiles over the heads of the next. The Crusaders, the variety and ingenuity of whose castle plans deserve much admiration, profited by the concentric method of walling a stronghold ; and none of their fortresses is so remarkable as Le Krak des Chevaliers (176), rebuilt early in the thirteenth century, where the curtain of the inner ward rises high above the curtain of the outer *enceinte*.[1]   Approximations to the concentric plan were not unknown even in England at an early date. The earthen defences of Berkhampstead castle (42) are concentric, although no attempt was made to correlate them by giving the inner banks command of the outer.[2]

[1] Le Krak (Kala'at-el-Hosn) was rebuilt in 1202, and held by the Franks till 1271 (Enlart, ii. 536). It was a frontier fortress of the county of Tripoli in Syria, commanding the mountain country to the east, and must be distinguished from the great castle of Kerak in Moab, near the Dead sea, built about 1140, and surrendered in 1188, "the eastern bulwark of the kingdom of Jerusalem" (Oman, *Art of War*, 541).   The entrance to the castle of Kerak has been described above, pp. 240, 241.

[2] One feature of the defences of Berkhampstead is the series of earthen bastions, applied to the outer bank on the north side of the castle, probably at a date long after the foundation of the stronghold.

Conway Castle; Oratory

29

In the plan of the cylindrical tower-keep at Launceston, we have
a striking application of the concentric plan to a small area.
In France, Château-Gaillard, where the inner ward is nearly
surrounded by the curtain of the middle ward, was an approach to concentric methods ; but the leading idea was still
the exclusion of an enemy by lines of defence arranged upon an
elongated plan, with the donjon as the culminating point.   Even
at Coucy, where the defensive provisions are so elaborate, the
donjon is the great point of interest, and the castle is not
concentric in plan.   In fact, the concentric plan, although long

Carcassonne ; Plan

known in the east, was not
adopted as a basis of planning in the west until the
thirteenth century was far
advanced.   The fortifications
of Carcassonne, where the
plan was applied to a town
(264), were begun by St
Louis, and finished by Philip
III. : begun earlier than
Caerphilly, their erection
covered most of the time in
which our chief concentric
castles were built.[1]

The concentric plan may
be described as follows.   The
site on which the castle was
built was surrounded, as
usual, by a ditch.   The inner
scarp was crowned, and
sometimes partly reveted, by
a wall, flanked by towers at
the angles and, in the largest
castles, on the intermediate
faces.   Within this wall, and
divided from it by a narrow space of open ground, rose a second
and much higher wall, also flanked by towers at the angles and
on the faces.   This inner wall enclosed the main ward of the
castle, the intermediate space forming the outer ward or " lists."

[1] The breadth of the " lists " or intermediate defence of the town-walls at
Carcassonne varies.   On the steep western and south-western sides they
are very narrow, and in one place are covered by the rectangular Bishop's
tower.   The ground-floor of this was a gateway, which could be used to
shut off one part of the lists from each other.   Of the castle and its defences
more will be said later.

There was no keep: here, as in the plan of Conway and Carnarvon, reliance was placed on the curtains.   The entrances, however, were elaborately defended by large gatehouses and by sundry ingenious devices, as at Beaumaris, for perplexing a foe ; and the castle was sometimes reinforced, as at Caerphilly, by special outer defences both of earth and stone.   An enemy, attacking such a fortress, was exposed first to a double fire from the two curtains.   If he effected an entrance, he had to fight every step of his way into the inner ward ; while, if he was driven, by determined resistance at the gateway, into the narrow space of the outer ward, he was not merely in danger from the archers on the inner wa'l, but also might find his way blocked by one of the cross-walls which broke up the space in which he was confined.

Such a plan, although it might lack some of the advantages of a plan worked out on a new site, could be applied to the new defences of an old castle.   Both at Dover and the Tower of London during the reign of Henry III., additions were made which gave each castle a concentric plan.[1]   The effect at Dover was to ring the imposing keep about with a double wall : the inner circuit, however, is largely of the same date as the keep, and the outer is spreading and irregular in plan.   At London the defences were more closely planned in harmony, and one feature of the additions is that, when the buildings are examined close at hand, the White tower, originally the most important feature of the fortress, becomes comparatively insignificant in the defensive scheme.   The inner and outer curtains, with their towers, are of more than one date, from the end of the twelfth to the sixteenth century ; but the most important work was done in the reign of Henry III., during which the concentric plan of the fortress was developed.   The best idea of the fortifications can be obtained from the open space before the west front. Between the city and the castle lies the formidable ditch, which runs round three sides of the fortress, the fourth side being guarded by the Thames and a narrower ditch.   Dug by the Conqueror's workmen, the ditch was widened and deepened by Richard I.'s chancellor, William Longchamp : it originally seems to have admitted water at high tide.   The entrance to the castle is at the south-west angle.   A gatehouse, called the Middle tower, which was covered by an outer ditch[2] and outwork, stands

[1] At Newcastle the plan was nearly concentric ; but the curtains of the outer and inner ward met at one point, and the outer ward was a large space, containing the domestic buildings, while the inner was nearly filled by the keep.   The concentric scheme was therefore almost accidental, and no simultaneous use of both lines of defence was possible.

[2] *Cf.* the outer ditch constructed to cover the barbican at Alnwick, where there was possibly a further outwork next the town.

on the counterscarp of the great ditch, on this side 120 feet broad, and gives access to a stone bridge. This crossed the ditch to the Byward tower, a gatehouse at the south-west angle of the outer curtain. This curtain has been much altered, and its angles along the north face are capped by bastions which belong to the age when the cannon had taken the place of the catapult. Along its south face, towards the narrow ditch, the quay, and river beyond, it is flanked by towers, the chief of which is St Thomas' tower, the water-gate of the castle, well known by its name of Traitors' gate, and, like the Byward and Middle towers, originally a work of the thirteenth century.[1] From the bridge leading to the Byward tower, the curtain of the inner ward, flanked by three towers, the Beauchamp tower in the middle, the Devereux and Bell towers at the angles,[2] can be seen commanding the narrow outer ward. This approach was apparently defended by three rows of archers, like the south curtain of Carnarvon. The highest row occupied the rampart-walk and towers of the inner curtain. Loops were made in the face of the same curtain, below the rampart-walk, for a second row, on the raised ground-level of the inner ward; while a third row could be stationed behind loops in the outer curtain. The outer ward varies in breadth, but the passage to the gateway of the inner ward, along the south face of the inner curtain, is very narrow, and is flanked by the Bell tower and Wakefield tower.[3] The inner gateway is in the ground-floor of the Bloody tower, which joins the Wakefield tower; and is immediately opposite the water-gate in St Thomas' tower. At intervals the outer ward was traversed by cross-walls, so that an unhindered circuit of it was impossible: one of these crosses it on the east side of the Wakefield tower, and is continued across the ditch to the river bank.[4] The well-flanked approach from the Byward tower, arranged so that the gateway to the inner ward must be entered

[1] All these gatehouses, like the gatehouse at Rockingham and others of the same period, have a central passage, flanked by round towers towards the field. Traitors' gate, however, has an entrance of great breadth, wide enough to admit a boat from the river; and the interior is an oblong pool, without flanking guard-rooms. The round towers cap the outer angles, but are of relatively small importance in the plan. The interior pool is actually part of the ditch between the outer ward and the Thames, and the gateway is "a barbican . . . placed astride upon the ditch" (Clark, ii. 242).

[2] These angle-towers appear to belong in great part to the end of the twelfth century: the Beauchamp tower is generally attributed to the reign of Edward III.

[3] These and the adjacent curtain are largely of the twelfth century: the Bloody tower was added in the fourteenth century.

[4] Thus protecting the quay outside Traitors' gate. *Cf.* the spur-wall at Beaumaris.

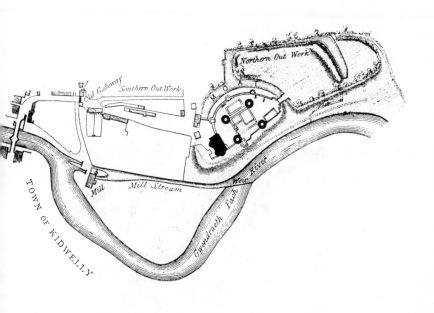

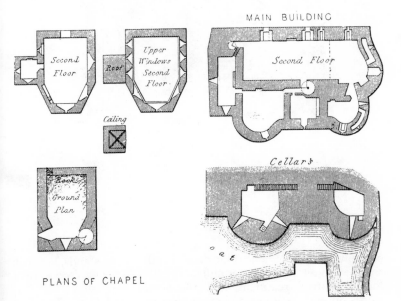

Kidwelly Castle; Plan

by a right-angled turn, may be compared with the entrances at
Conway and Beaumaris, or with the earlier approach to the main
bailey at Conisbrough.

In some respects, the alterations undertaken at Chepstow (104)
towards the end of the thirteenth century give it a place among

Chepstow ; Basement chamber

concentric castles. The ridge on which the castle stands, between
the town ditch and a sheer cliff above the Wye, was too narrow
for concentric treatment, and the actual plan shows us four
wards on end, each on higher ground than the last. The first
and lowest ward was the Edwardian addition. The second

ward formed the lower part of the bailey of the early castle. The third ward, at a very narrow point in the ridge, was almost filled by the great hall, which was virtually the great tower or keep of this castle; and there is only a narrow passage mounting the slope between the hall and the low curtain above the river. The fourth ward, at the highest point, and divided from the third ward by a deep rift in the rock, contains a wide gateway, which, as at Kidwelly—the nearest parallel—was the back entrance to the castle. We have only to imagine the ditch next the town filled up, and the outer curtain continued so as to embrace the second ward and great hall, and to unite the first and fourth wards; and we have what is virtually the plan of Kidwelly (267). Free ingress and egress for the garrison, so well studied in concentric plans, was provided by the two gateways at Chepstow. The exposed condition, however, of the lower ward, at the foot of the ridge, prompted an addition to the plan which recalls the Eagle tower at Carnarvon, or the strong towers at the later manor-castles of Raglan and Wingfield. Projecting from the lowest angle of the curtain, commanding the approach from the town, and covering the gateway, is the tower now called the Marten tower, rounded to the field and flat at the gorge. This tower, entered from the ground-level of the ward, had its own portcullised gateway, and a doorway, also portcullised, from the first floor to the rampart-walk of the curtain. Its three floors were very amply planned, and, projecting from the second floor, and partly built on the battlements of the curtain, is a small chapel or oratory, with an east window containing geometrical tracery. The Marten tower is a valuable example of the protection of a dangerous angle.. Its flanking capacities were improved by a spur or half-pyramid built against the base: this may be compared with the rectangular plinths of the two western angle-towers at Carew, from which spurs rise against the rounded surfaces of the towers themselves. The first ward at Chepstow contains a lesser hall and other domestic buildings on the side next the river: these, with the vaults below them (268), contain work of great beauty. All the Edwardian work at Chepstow has that simplicity and adequacy of design, admitting here and there of beauties of detail, which is found in the best military work of the age (249).[1]

III. The castles, however, of the last twenty years of the thirteenth century, planned with a system of concentric defences,

---

[1] The thirteenth-century work in the great hall (103) of Chepstow castle is unusually elaborate for military work of the period: nowhere in English castles have we such splendour and beauty of detail as that of which there remain many indications at Coucy.

may be taken, with Carnarvon and Conway, as reaching the
highest pitch of military science attained in medieval England.
The earliest of these, Caerphilly (270), which was begun before
the end of the reign of Henry III., was also the most elaborate.[1]
The castle proper was placed in the middle of a lake, formed
by the damming up of two streams; and in this respect the

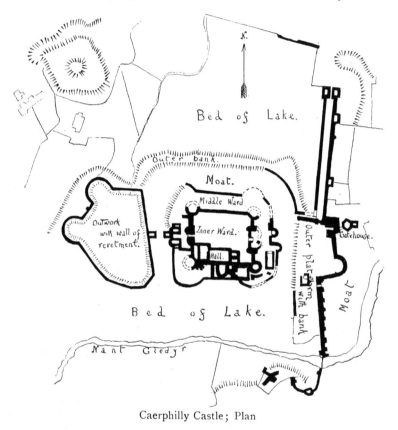

Caerphilly Castle; Plan

situation was not unlike that of Kenilworth, which was defended
on the south and west by an artificial lake, and was irregularly
concentric in the ultimate development of its plan.[2]　The sides

[1] It was begun about 1267 by Gilbert de Clare, eighth earl of Gloucester
and seventh earl of Hertford (d. 1295).

[2] The inner ward at Kenilworth lay at all points within an outer line of
defence.　The outer ward, narrow on the south and west, was very broad on
the east and north, and its western half was cut up into sections by cross-

of the island were enclosed within strong retaining walls, which rose to form the curtain of the outer ward. This curtain was low, and was flanked, not by towers, but by curved projections forming bastions at the angles. Within this outer defence rose the rectangular inner ward, the lofty curtain of which was flanked by drum towers at each angle, and by a very large gatehouse with two drum towers in each of the east and west sides. The outer ward had also a front and back gatehouse, flanked by small drum towers, in its east and west curtains: these were directly commanded by the inner gatehouses, and the entrance was not oblique. The inner ward was spacious and cheerful. In the centre is the well: the great hall (272), the excellent stonework of which is sheltered from the weather by

Caerphilly Castle

a modern roof, was built against the south curtain, and the chapel was at right angles to it at its east end. The kitchen was contained in a projecting tower south of the hall, which blocked the outer ward at this point: beneath the kitchen was a postern communicating directly with the lake. The place of the rampart-walk in the curtain next the hall was supplied by a gallery running in its thickness, and looped to the field. At the east end of the hall were apartments, through which the rooms in the first floor of the east gatehouse could be reached.

This plan, in which the military and domestic elements were

walls: it was also crossed by a ditch in front of the inner ward. The lake did not surround the castle, and on the north its outer defence was a very deep dry ditch.

so well combined, is interesting upon its own account. But more interesting still were the outer defences by which the castle was surrounded. The whole east face of the castle on the outer edge of the lake was guarded by an outer wall, which had in the centre, nearly opposite the inner gateways, a large gatehouse, and was returned at the ends into clusters of towers, the larger of which, on the south, covered a postern. A wet ditch divided this outer line of defence from the village of Caerphilly, and in its centre was a pier on which the two sections of the drawbridge met. North of the gatehouse, the outer curtain was defended simply by the rampart-walk : on the south side, however, there was a narrow terrace left in the rear of the curtain, by which

Caerphilly Castle ; Hall

access was obtained to the castle mill and other offices. These two portions of the curtain were separated from each other by the gatehouse and a dividing wall, which, in case of the capture of one part of the curtain by besiegers, gave the defenders a distinct advantage. The inner lake was crossed from the plat-form in front of the main gatehouse by a drawbridge, which probably was worked by a counterpoise from the island side.

The lake on the north side of the castle was divided into an inner and outer moat by a bank of earth which sprang from the platform of the outer gatehouse, and curved round the north side of the island. This bank ended at a second and smaller island, the sides of which were reveted by a stone wall, covering the west face of the stronghold. This horn-work or ravelin was

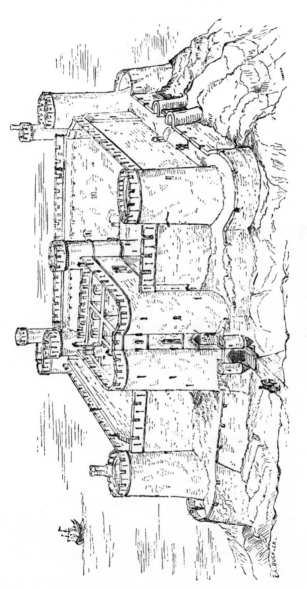

Harlech Castle

Harlech Castle; Gatehouse

connected by drawbridges across the outer and inner moats with the mainland and with the western gatehouses of the castle. It is evident that a fortress like this, in which every resource of the defenders' art has been brought into action, gave a besieger very few opportunities. Every entry was guarded: if he once effected an entrance, defence after defence had to be forced, while

Harlech; Inner side of gatehouse

the resources of the several lines of defence could all be used against him at once. Moreover, he had to be careful to cut all communications off from the rear entrance and posterns; and this was a difficult matter, where the defenders of the castle had so much freedom of movement and could assail him from so many different points. It is not surprising to learn that the impregnable fortress of Caerphilly is almost without a history. Constructed to defend the lower valley of the Rhymney and to cover the coast castles round Cardiff from an attack from the Welsh of the valleys which slope southwards from the Brecon Beacons, it endured no important siege;[1] and it was not until the civil war

[1] The partisans of the Despensers held Caerphilly against Queen Isabel in 1326: its defenders were granted a general pardon, from which Hugh, son of Hugh le Despenser the younger, was excepted, 15th February 1326-7 (Pat. 1 Edw. III., pt. 1, m. 29). One of the defenders, John Cole, received

that its military capacity was really tested—and then only in an age which had outgrown the methods responsible for its scheme of defence.[1]

Of Edward I.'s castles in North Wales, Harlech (273) and Rhuddlan, with lofty inner curtains and cylindrical angle-towers, have much in common with each other and with Caerphilly. The general plan of Harlech is nearly identical with that of the island defences of Caerphilly. Its situation on a lofty rock, however, does not call for elaborate outer defences. The rock was isolated from the mainland by a dry ditch cut across the east face. A causeway and a drawbridge led to the gatehouse of the outer ward, which was flanked by bartizans. The wall of the outer ward, like that at Caerphilly, is low, and has no towers : three of its angles form bastions, while the other, at the least accessible point, is simply curved. The unusually lofty curtain of the inner ward, some 40 feet high, towers above the comparatively slight outer defences ; while the centre of the east side is occupied by the great gatehouse (274), projecting far back into the inner ward. The entrance is flanked by two semi-cylindrical towers ; and in the rear of the gatehouse are two round turrets, rising high above the roofs. Rhuddlan, which stands on the right bank of the Clwyd, had a fairly broad outer ward defended by a deep and wide ditch on the three faces on which the site is fairly level. The inner ward had two gatehouses, of equal size and importance, placed diagonally to each other at the north-east and south-west angles of the curtain. Each of these was flanked by two large drum towers ; while each of the two remaining angles was capped by a single tower.

There were at Harlech a hall and other domestic buildings against the curtains; but the gatehouse was also a complete mansion in itself, with its own small chapel or oratory above the gateway. There was an outer stair to the bailey from the main hall of the gatehouse. Exactly the same arrangement occurs at Kidwelly, while the importance of the gatehouse as a dwelling reaches its climax in the hall of the northern gatehouse at Beaumaris.[2] The dual arrangement of a hall, kitchen, etc., for the garrison, and a private dwelling-house for the constable or the lord of the castle, has already been noticed at Conway, whilst its growth has been traced in connection with the castle of Durham.

a special pardon on 20th February (*ibid.*, m. 32). There is no record of a definite siege.

[1] The earthwork or redoubt on the north-west side of the castle is probably of this period : no definite details of the destruction of the castle are preserved.

[2] The inner buildings at Rhuddlan have entirely disappeared : traces of one or two fireplaces are left in the curtain.

Harlech presents two or three important points of interest. (1) The outer ward was not blocked at any point, as at Caerphilly, by projecting buildings, but was continuous: it was crossed, however, in at any rate one place, by a wall which barred an enemy's progress. (2) Owing to the nature of the site, only one gatehouse was built. But a small doorway in the centre of the north wall of the inner ward opened directly opposite a postern, flanked by half-round bastions, in the outer curtain. From this point an extremely steep path, now hardly to be traced, followed the edge of the rock, rounded the north-west bastion of the outer ward, and passed close beneath the west curtain to the south-west angle of the rock. Here, doubling on itself, it descended through a gateway into a long passage between the slope of the rock and the outer wall, and ended at the water-gateway of the castle, at the foot of the great crag and near the present railway station. The wall which protected the outer face of this tortuous passage, formed an outer curtain to the castle, descending the rock from the south-west angle of the outer ward, continuing round the foot of the rock on its north side, and climbing it again to meet the north-east bastion.[1] (3) The rampart-walk had no machicolations and, as at Conway (261), was continued round the inner faces of the angle-towers on corbelling. This left the interior of the towers free, while their doorways and stairs gave them ready command of the rampart-walk. The walls are not only lofty, but very thick. The section of the jambs of the hall windows and the small north postern points to the fact that the lower part of the walls was thickened, probably as an afterthought, when their present height was determined upon. The upper part of the walls is homogeneous, and is evidently a heightening. (4) Although vices in the angle-towers communicated with the rampart-walk, freedom of action was given to the defenders of the towers by the provision of a separate stair for those told off to guard the intermediate ramparts. This stair is reached through the basement doorway of the south-east tower, and, branching off from the internal stair a few feet above the entrance, reaches a small external platform. Here a narrow outer stair, with a rear-wall, is carried up the face of the flat gorge of the tower, and, turning along the south curtain, at length reaches the rampart-walk. The planning of this stair, with its carefully covered ground-floor entrance, is very interesting and curious.

Nowhere, however, can the beauty of the concentric plan be so well appreciated as at Beaumaris (278), one of Edward I.'s

---

[1] At Rhuddlan a passage, protected by an outer wall ending in a square tower, descended the river-bank to the water-gate.

latest Welsh castles.[1]   The site is flat and low, on a tongue of land at the northern entrance to the Menai straits.   There is no attempt at any elaborate outer system of defence, such as we see at Caerphilly.   The defences consisted of a ditch, filled with water at high tide, and an inner and outer curtain, the inner curtain, as usual, commanding the outer.   The inner ward is square: it has a drum tower at each of the angles, and another in the centre of each of the east and west sides.   The north and south curtains are broken by gatehouses, also flanked by drum towers.[2]   The north gatehouse was the largest, and upon its first floor was an imposing hall.   The curtain of the outer ward, surrounding the inner curtain, was adapted to the

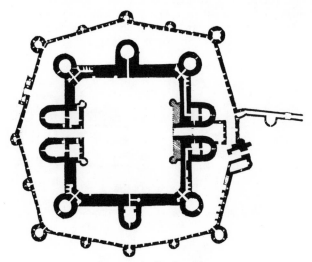

Beaumaris Castle; Plan

projection of the intermediate drum towers and the gatehouses of the inner ward by the construction of each face with a salient angle in the centre (277).   There are no traces of any cross-walls barring the passage of the outer ward.   The outer curtain, which, owing to the flat site, is not the mere low bastioned wall of Caerphilly or Harlech, has a drum tower at each angle.   On each of the north, east, and west curtains, there are three smaller

<hr />

[1] Clark (i. 217) places the date of foundation about 1295.
[2] The outer drum towers are large and imposing, though low: the inner angles are capped by smaller towers, which bear much the same relation to the gatehouses as the outer round towers to Traitors' gate in the Tower of London.

drum towers, the central one of which caps the salient. The plan is thus of a most symmetrical and uniform kind. The south curtain of the outer ward, however, has no intermediate drum towers, and its salient is nearly capped by the outer gateway. This gateway, however, flanked by rectangular towers,[1] is set obliquely to the wall. Entering the outer ward, immediately on our right is the small rectangular barbican, pierced with cross-loops, which covers the inner gateway, so that two right-angled turns must be made before the inner ward is entered (277).

This entrance, most carefully protected, shows even higher skill than the barbican of Conway and the elaborate passage from the water-gate at Harlech. But there are two further remarkable defences in this castle. We have seen that, as at Caerphilly, there is a large gatehouse at either end of the inner ward. The rear gatehouse, which, as already noted, is

Beaumaris Castle

the more important, has no barbican. The rear gateway of the outer ward is set obliquely to it, in the north curtain east of the salient, and is simply a large postern in the wall. Outside it, however, the wall is reinforced by four buttresses, each of which is pierced by a loop; the outer buttresses are looped to the field, the inner towards the gateway. The westernmost buttress projects beyond the rest, and it is clear that the design was intended to conceal and protect the postern from attack, and that the western side, in the direction of the interior of Anglesey, was that on which an attack was most to be expected. The

[1] Of these towers, that on the west has an outer salient or spur, on the sides of which two bartizans are corbelled out : these are united into one, so that the outer face of the upper stage of the tower is rounded into a semicircle. The eastern tower is smaller, with a solid base : the western part of the upper portion is corbelled off in the angle between the tower and a rectangular southern projection. The upper stages of the towers completely command the approach, while the projection just mentioned would conceal a small body of defenders posted between the gateway and the spur-wall (236).

other defence is the spur-wall, which, running almost at right angles to the south wall of the outer ward, shut off the main entrance and the beach on which it opened from the beach on the eastern side of the castle. The wall is pierced by a passage, is looped in both faces, and is flanked by a half-round tower on the west face.

Although, at first sight, the towers of Beaumaris, on its absolutely level site, look low and unimportant, and present an extraordinary contrast to those of Harlech, Carnarvon, or Conway, the area of the castle is actually large, and no other Edwardian castle presents so perfectly scientific a system of defence. The outer curtain, in addition to the rampart-walk, has loops pierced at regular intervals in its lower portion ; the rampart-walk is partly carried by continuous corbelling upon the inner face of the wall. The inner curtain, moreover, is pierced, on the level of the first floor of the gatehouses and towers, by a continuous vaulted passage, looped to the field. This extends round the whole ward, and is broken only at the north-west angle, where it meets the northern gatehouse. Everywhere in the walls of the castle where a loop could be of use, it was made. Of the points noticed, both the entrances are unusual, and the design of the postern at the rear seems to be unique. The spur-wall, though less elaborately treated, is found covering a main entrance at Kidwelly and elsewhere ; and the long passages in the thickness of the wall are found in portions of the defences at Caerphilly and Carnarvon. The towers at Beaumaris are entered by straight stairs from the gorge ; and throughout the castle, in the gatehouses, great hall, and basements of the towers, the method of carrying a wooden roof upon detached stone ribs prevailed, which is very noticeable also at Conway and Harlech.

Kidwelly castle[1] (267), another late thirteenth-century building, stands on a steep hill, the east side of which slopes abruptly to the Gwendraeth Fach river. The castle is on the opposite side of the river to the town of Kidwelly, and a long base-court, of which part of the gatehouse remains, descended the slope towards the bridge. At the head of this ascent a barbican and drawbridge formed the approach to a strong gatehouse, flanked by two battering towers, and further protected by a spur-

---

[1] This was not founded by the Crown, like the great castles of North Wales, but, like Caerphilly, was a private foundation. It passed by marriage, early in the fourteenth century, into the possession of the house of Lancaster. Some of the most important English castles—e.g., Kenilworth, Knaresborough, Lancaster, Lincoln, Pontefract, and Pickering—came at various times into the possession of this royal house, and, at the accession of Henry IV., became castles of the Crown as seized of the duchy of Lancaster.

wall across the end of the ditch. The gatehouse is in the extreme south-east angle of the outer ward, which, describing a wide curve, covers three sides of the nearly square inner ward, and is separated from the suburb of Kidwelly on this side the river by the ditch. The site was narrow, as at Chepstow, and the eastward slope so steep that the outer ward was not completed along this side, but its curtain was continued by the eastern drum towers and curtain of the inner ward. Three half-round towers were made in the curving curtain of the outer ward; at the opposite extremity to the gatehouse, near the north-east angle, a postern, flanked by small drum towers, gave access to a northern earthwork, which may be compared with the horn-work at Caerphilly, but had no retaining wall.

Kidwelly, with its outworks in front and rear, at once recalls Caerphilly. The irregularly concentric plan, with the inner ward on one side of the interior of the outer, is very unusual, but provides a link between the concentric plan and the extension of the early plan of Chepstow. The provision of both front and rear gateways is a feature of Caerphilly, Chepstow, Beaumaris, and Conway; and, as at Caerphilly, Rhuddlan, and Beaumaris, the inner ward also has front and rear entrances. These, however, at Kidwelly, are mere doorways in the wall. The inner ward was small, with very large and perfect drum towers at its angles: the domestic buildings arranged on either side of it left only a narrow passage through the middle. A tower, of which the two upper stories formed the chapel, was built out upon the east slope, from the corner of the ward next the south-east drum tower. The gatehouse, then, which here, as at Harlech and Beaumaris, contains a large hall and other apartments, and, in addition to a vice to the upper floors, has an outer stair and landing against its north face, was on the outer, not the inner, line of defence, and was protected by the ditch, the barbican, and the base-court beyond. There are remains of buildings, probably intended for the garrison, in the outer ward. The basement of the gatehouse, which is below the level of the ward, contains vaulted chambers. In one of these is a lower vault, which has had a domed roof, and may have been used for stores or a reservoir: in another there appear to be indications of the mouth of a well.

The defensive precautions taken at Kidwelly were not so thorough as in the other great Welsh castles of the time, and the chief reliance of the builders was in the strength of their walls and towers. The outer curtain has the peculiarity, rare in English castles of the date, of possessing a stair built against it from the level of the ward.[1]   The inner ward has several curious features.   The stair to the curtain was a straight flight of steps protected by the west wall of the main entrance from the outer ward.   A path along the back of the rampart of the south curtain led into the south-west drum tower, from the second floor of which the rampart-walk was gained.   The walk, though much overgrown by ivy and other weeds, still keeps its rear-wall, and is continued through the towers and round the inner ward. The two western drum towers are interesting.   The upper part of that on the north, where it faces the ward, is not a simple curve, but is broken into two convex curves, with a recess

Kidwelly Castle; Tower at south-west angle
of inner ward

between: the reason of this is not apparent.[2]   The south-west tower (281), standing at an angle from which it commands the inner face of the great gatehouse, has the most unusual peculiarity of having all its stages covered with vaulting : the vaults themselves are shallow domes, rather rudely constructed.   It is probable that the engineers may have intended to establish a catapult on the tower in time of siege.   The situation of the tower would have been excellently suited for that purpose, but

[1] The stair to the rampart-walk, built against the curtain, was, however, normal in the defences of towns (241).

[2] It may be compared with the division of the outer face of the polygonal tower at Stokesay into two smaller half-octagons (306).

its unusual strength may be due merely to its position in the line of attack. The basements of all the towers are vaulted, but that of this particular tower, instead of being entered from the ward or one of the domestic buildings directly, is entered by a long and dark passage in the thickness of the south wall, from the left-hand side of the doorway of the inner ward. The unusual precautions taken with regard to this tower and its entrances give it a prominent position in an account of the castle ; and, although it is no larger or loftier than the other angle-towers of the inner ward, it has something of the special importance of Marten's tower at Chepstow or the Eagle tower at Carnarvon.

Although the Edwardian castle in Wales has many points of interest, and provides a highly-developed scheme of defence, yet its devices are simple when compared with the highest achievements of French fortification. The elaborate care bestowed upon the outer defences of Caerphilly, and the variety of ingenuity manifested at Beaumaris, are exceptions to this general statement ; while the general plan of Carnarvon is as imposing as that of any castle in Europe. But such carefully contrived approaches as the barbican of Conway and the long ascent from the water-gate at Harlech take a second place when compared with such a work as the outer approach to the castle of Carcassonne, as restored with approximate faithfulness in the drawings of Viollet-le-Duc (283). The castle stood within the inner wall of the town, occupying a rectangular site on the south-west side of this masterpiece of concentric planning. The entrance from the town was guarded by a semicircular barbican ; but the approach which called for the most watchful defence was that from the foot of the hill, on the edge of which the city stands. Where the hill meets the plain, therefore, below the castle, a great barbican was constructed, within the outer palisade and ditch of which was a great round tower, not unlike the great tower on the mount at Windsor, surrounded by a wet ditch. The centre of this *châtelet* was open to the sky : the walls were pierced with two rows of loops below the rampart. This tower guarded the entrance to a walled and carefully protected ascent, which, after making a right-angled turn, led upwards in a straight passage,[1] commanded by the rampart of the outer

---

[1] Viollet-le-Duc's drawing (*La Cité de Carcassonne*, p. 75) shows a rampart-walk on each of the enclosing walls of this passage. He also shows the passage crossed by a series of looped barriers, so placed that each formed a separate line of defence, guarded by a few soldiers, and compelled an enemy to pursue a zigzag course through the passage. Much allusion has been already made to oblique and elbow-shaped contrivances for impeding an enemy's progress : the antiquity of these is evident from the entrances to earthworks like Maiden Castle (see Chapter I.).

Carcassonne

curtain of the town. Where it met the curtain, it turned to
the right, along the foot of the wall, and so reached a gateway
into the outer ward or "lists" of the town. But here the passage,
passing through a covered vestibule, turned back on its own
course, and entered an inner barbican, with two upper stages.
Not until this was passed, were the lists entered, and the chief
gateway of the castle, in the inner curtain, reached. As we
trace this passage, we recall the ascent at Harlech and the
traps set for an enemy at Beaumaris; but their combination
here is on a scale undreamed of in those fortresses, minutely
calculated though their planning was.

Domfront; Casemates

The wall-galleries, again, at Carnarvon and Beaumaris, are
a device of great utility, unusual in English castles, and are
planned at Carnarvon with exceptional skill; while, at Caerphilly,
the gallery in the south wall, between the hall and the moat, is
a solution of the defence of a point which the somewhat crowded
plan of the domestic buildings threatened to leave unguarded.
But the covered gallery below the ramparts was not a prominent
feature of medieval defence in England. On the other hand,
it was used freely in France. Two examples of the defensive
use of covered galleries may be given here. One is from
Domfront, where, as at Coucy, the castle was separated from

the walled town by a very formidable ditch. On the side next the castle, the rock was covered by a retaining wall flanked by two round towers at the ends, and a polygonal tower near the centre. At some time in the middle ages, probably late in the thirteenth century, the rock behind the wall was pierced by a long gallery, communicating with all three towers, and by stairs at intervals with the upper ward above. Loops were made in the retaining wall, so that the approach upon this side was thus provided with a line of defence below the level of the towers and curtain. The gallery is not on one level throughout, but forms a series of separate vaulted casemates, connected with one another by short flights of stairs [1] (284).

In the second case, at Coucy, we have a case of a closed gallery, without loops, which was designed as a counter-mine against the efforts of the sappers of an attacking force. Remains of such galleries exist in more than one part of the castle, forming a remarkable addition to defences which, by themselves, were strong enough to discourage attack. Towards the end of the fourteenth century, the curtain of the donjon, the strongest tower in Europe, was thickened by the addition of a talus or battering base, which was pierced by a passage. The main object of this work was to cover in a spring which had its source in the ditch at the foot of the curtain : the passage communicated at one end with an earlier and well-guarded passage leading from the domestic buildings to a postern in the wall which crossed the west end of the ditch, while, at the other, it communicated by a stair with the rampart-walk of the curtain and gatehouse of the inner ward. But it did not merely form a convenient means of access to the spring. It afforded an opportunity to the defenders of counteracting the miners of the enemy; while, if the miners pierced their way through the talus, they would be met by the thick curtain on the other side of the passage. The passage itself, well protected at both ends, would be commanded by the defence ; while the spring in the middle, to those not acquainted with the geography of the place, would form a dangerous barrier in the darkness.

To such finished achievements of military art as these, which have been quoted as specimen examples, our English castles can afford no exact parallel. In the military, as in the ecclesiastical architecture of France, principles were worked out with a logical precision and completeness, which, in its practical effect, provokes our wonder. The effort manifested in the Edwardian castle is

---

[1] Description and plan in Blanchetière, *Le Donjon . . . de Domfront*, pp. 59-63. The date there given is actually earlier than the probable epoch of construction.

more humble; the achievement more limited. This, however, is true rather of the scale of the castle and the details of its defence than of the general idea. The main object, of flanking the curtain effectually and completely, is as fully realised as in any foreign example; while it may be safely said that in no country were the advantages of concentric lines of defence better exhibited than in the Welsh castles, whose main features have been indicated in this chapter. The walls of Carcassonne may provide us with the concentric plan on its largest scale; but the Welsh castles show at least an equal understanding of the value of concentric fortifications. The difference lies in the fact that the French engineer proceeded to strengthen his defences by the addition of intricate refinements and subtle devices; while the Englishman stopped short at this point, and was satisfied when his aim of providing and combining adequate towers and walls of defence was achieved.

CHAPTER XI

MILITARY ARCHITECTURE IN THE LATER
MIDDLE AGES: FORTIFIED TOWNS AND
CASTLES

THE strengthening of the curtain of the castle was perfected in
the concentric plan, in which also was established, for the time
being, the superiority of defence to attack. But the very fact
that the castle had reached a point at which further development
in the existing condition of things was impossible, was fatal to
its continued existence as a stronghold. A castle like Caerphilly
did not put an end to local warfare : it merely warned an enemy
off a forbidden track. Its own safety was secured, because its
almost impregnable defences made any attempt at a siege
ridiculous. Other circumstances, however, combined to render the
castle obsolete. The rise of towns and the growth of a wealthy
mercantile class hastened the decline of feudalism. The feudal
baron was no longer the representative of an all-important class,
and his fortress was of minor importance compared with the
walled boroughs which were symbolical of the real strength of
the country. But, in addition to this social transition, there took
place a change in warfare which had a far-reaching influence
upon castle and walled town alike. Fire-arms came into general
use in the early part of the fourteenth century.[1] Missiles, for
which hitherto the only available machines had been those
involving discharge by torsion, tension, or counterpoise, could
now be delivered by the new method of detonation. This produced an artillery which could be worked with greater economy
of labour, and discharged the missiles themselves with greater
force. Not merely can a ball of stone or iron be projected with
greater impetus than can be given by the older methods ; but

[1] The progress of fire-arms in English warfare was slow. See the
various articles by R. Coltman Clephan, F.S.A., in *Archæol. Journal*, lxvi.,
lxvii., and lxviii. The earliest picture of a cannon is in a MS. at Christ
Church, Oxford, written in 1326 (lxviii. 49), while the earliest mention of a
hand-gun in England appears to be in 1338 (lxvi. 153-4). The long-bow
continued to be the popular weapon of the individual English soldier until
long after this date.

32

Gatehouse, Barbican, and Curtain wall of Town battered by cannon-shot

the direction which it takes is more nearly horizontal than that given to it by the mangonel and kindred machines. It is true that, at first, the power of cannon remained relatively weak ; but their gradual improvement made the old systems of defence useless. Lofty walls, which could resist the catapults of the past, were easily dismantled by cannon-shot (288). Harlech, with its lofty curtains and angle-towers, was an ideal stronghold, as long as explosives were not employed for attack and defence. But, when cannon are directed against such defences (273), and the surface of the walls is pounded with shot, the height of the fortifications becomes a danger ; and, in order to plant the cannon of the defence on the walls, those walls have

Alençon

to be as solid as possible to avoid the constant vibration arising from the discharge, and as low as possible to increase their stability and to place the enemy within range. The change is obvious, if we contrast the lofty and comparatively slender towers of Carcassonne or Aigues-Mortes with the massive drum towers of the French castles or walled towns of the fifteenth century, like those of the castle of Alençon (289) or of the town of Saint-Malo (290). Later still, the flanking of the walls of towns and castles shows a transition from the round tower to the bastion ; and we find massive projections like the Tour Gabriel at Mont-Saint-Michel (291), which rise little, if at all, above the level of the adjacent wall. The ultimate outcome of this transition is the bastion pure and simple, flanking the low and solid earthen bank with its reveting wall, as at Saint-Paul-du-Var, or, later, at our own Berwick-on-Tweed.[1]   A step further brings us to the scientific fortification of the seventeenth century, to Lille and Arras, and those magnificent fortresses which the progress of the nineteenth century has already made of historical, rather than practical, interest.[2]

With these modern developments we have no concern in this book ; and in these two concluding chapters we can trace merely the later history, from a defensive point of view, of that type of fortification whose advance we have hitherto pursued, and of the gradual amalgamation of the medieval castle with the medieval

Saint-Malo; Grande porte

dwelling-house.   The old distinction between the castle and the *burh* still asserted itself.   During the greater part of the middle ages, from the Norman conquest to the fourteenth century, the

[1] The ramparts of Saint-Paul-du-Var (Alpes Maritimes) are said to belong to the epoch of the wars between Francis I. and Charles V.   To the same period belong the fortifications of Lucca, Verona, and Antwerp.   The present walls of Berwick were begun somewhat later, in 1558, enclosing a space considerably smaller than the original *enceinte* of the town, as fortified by Edward I.

[2] Holes with embrasures for cannon were in many cases pierced in the walls of fortresses during the fifteenth century, or were formed, as in the eastern tower at Warkworth, by blocking the ordinary cross-loops through most of their height.

castle, the stronghold of the individual lord, was the highest
type of fortification, and the town, as at Berwick in the reign of
Edward I., or at Conway or Carnarvon, was, when walled, little
more than an appendage or outer ward to the castle.   With the
introduction of fire-arms, the town began once more to take its
place in the van of the defence.   Warfare, from the time of
the wars of Edward III. in France, and even earlier, ceased to
be an affair of sieges of castles.   Battles were fought more and
more in the open field, and the reduction of the fortified town,

Mont-St-Michel ; Tour Gabriel

not of strongholds of individuals, became the chief object
of campaigns.   The castle, relegated to a secondary place,
developed more and more on the lines of the dwelling-house ;
and, finally, as the castle disappeared, the town with its citadel
became all-important as the object of attack and the base of
operations.   In brief, the steps in the history of fortification
after the Conquest are these.   The timber defences of the
Saxon *burh* became of secondary importance to the timber
defences of the Norman castle.   These were subordinated to
the keep, the symbol of the dominion of the feudal lord.   The

keep reached its climax in the stone tower. At this point the revulsion began. The strengthening of the stone curtain made the keep obsolete ; and, finally, the perfection of the curtain of the castle once attained, military science applied itself to the strengthening of the wall of the town, until, aided by social changes and scientific improvements, the castle itself became altogether unnecessary.

The principles of defence of the walled town are those of the castle ; and hitherto we have drawn illustrations from both with little discrimination. In both cases the same methods of attack are provided against by the use of the same means. But it must be remembered that the area of the town is larger than that of the castle, and that while, in the castle, the bailey is the common muster-ground from which every part of the curtain can be easily reached, there can be no such open space enclosed by the walls of a large inhabited town or city. Thus, while the market-place, in or near the centre of the town, would serve as a general rallying-ground,[1] it was necessary also to keep a clear space at the foot of the inner side of the walls, so that free communication between every part might be preserved. From the continuous lane which was thus formed between the wall and the houses of the town, and was crossed at intervals by the main thoroughfares leading to the gates, access was gained to the rear of the flanking towers, and to the stairs by which, from time to time, the rampart-walk was reached. Most towns which have been walled retain traces of this arrangement. At South-ampton the *pomerium*,[2] as this clear space is called in medieval documents, survives on the east side of the town in the lane still known as " Back of the Walls." At Carnarvon it is nearly entire, except on the west side of the town. At Newcastle (293) it remains in a very perfect state on the north-west side of the enclosure, where the walls and their intermediate turrets are also fairly perfect ; and it can be traced in a paved lane on the west side, where the walls are gone.[3] Nearly the whole extent of the inner city walls of Bristol, of which little remains, can be easily

---

[1] This is very clearly seen in the fortified towns of Italy, or in the towns founded by Edward I. and by the kings of France in the southern districts of France.

[2] *Pomerium* = the space *pone muros*, *i.e.*, at the back of the walls. The word was at first applied to the sacred boundary of Rome and other towns, which limited the *auspicia* of the city.

[3] The re-erection of the rectangular wall-turrets at Newcastle, which are of very slight projection from the wall, appears to date from 1386 : a writ of aid was granted to the mayor and bailiffs on 29th November in that year for the repair of the walls and bridge of the town (Pat. 10 Rich. II., pt. 1, m. 8).

293

SOUTHAMPTON : town wall

NEWCASTLE : town wall

traced by the survival of the *pomerium* in a series of curved lanes. The line of the east wall of Northampton can be recovered in the same way; and although, as at York, modern encroachments have in many places removed the *pomerium*, it usually survived to mark the site of town walls, even long after those walls had been destroyed.

During the epoch at which fortification reached its highest point, the wall of a town was systematically flanked by towers, which, as we have seen at Conway and Avignon, were left open upon the side next the town.

Conway; Porth Isaf

Gates were made in the wall, where main roads approached the place. Thus the gates of Coucy were three, admitting the roads from Laon, Soissons, and Chauny. At Conway (256) there were three gates; but of these one communicated merely with a quay, while another gave access to the castle mill : the third or north-western gate alone was the direct entrance to the promontory on which the town and castle were built. At Chepstow, where the town also formed a *cul-de-sac*, there was only one main gateway, at the north-west end of the town. The main gateway of Carnarvon was on the east side of the town; while, opposite to it, in the west wall, was a smaller gateway opening, like the Porth Isaf[1] (295) at Conway, upon the quay. Not all towns, however, occupied positions like Chepstow, Conway, and Carnarvon, where water takes so large a share in the defence. Great centres of commerce like London and York, towards which a number of roads converged, had many gates, not counting the posterns in their walls. Four of the gates of York remain, Micklegate bar on the south-west, through which the road from Tadcaster entered the city, Walmgate bar on the south-east, admitting the road from Beverley

---

[1] *I.e.*, the lower gate. The north-western gateway is the upper gate, Porth Uchaf.

and Hull, Monk bar on the east, through which passed the road from Scarborough, Bootham bar on the north, which was the entrance from the direction of Thirsk and Easingwold. The gatehouses are all rectangular structures, the plan and lower portions of which are of the twelfth century, and recall the stone gatehouses of early castles : the upper stages, however, are of the fourteenth century, and have tall bartizans at the outer angles. The great Bargate at Southampton, through which the road from the north entered the circuit of the walls, is similarly a rectangular Norman gatehouse, enlarged and supplied with flanking towers in the fourteenth century : the outer face was further strengthened, within a century of these additions, by a half-octagonal projection, the battlements of which were machicolated. There was another gate on the east side of Southampton, which now has disappeared. In the west wall the rectangular water-gate and a postern remain ; while, on the quay at the south-eastern angle of the walls, there is another gate, covered by a long spur-work which projects from the wall at this point and crossed the town-ditch. For smaller gate-houses like the western gatehouses of Carnarvon and South-ampton, the old rectangular form was sufficient ; but the principal entries of towns needed effective flanking. As a rule, town gatehouses of the Edwardian period and the fourteenth century generally were flanked by round towers at the outer angles, like those at Conway (295), Winchelsea, or the West gate at Canterbury. In the fifteenth century, the warlike character of the defences of English towns was considerably lessened. The Stonebow or southern gatehouse at Lincoln, a long rectangular building with slender angle turrets of no great projection, had no special provisions for defence beyond the gates by which it was closed. Here and there, when the need of military defence ceased to exist, churches were built upon the walls and gateways of towns. Thus above the St John's gate of Bristol, on the south side of the city, rise the tower and spire which were common to the churches of St John the Baptist and St Lawrence ; while churches were built close to or immediately above the east and west gates of Warwick.

Where one of the main approaches to a town crossed a river, the defence of the passage was of course necessary. In the case of the St John's gate of Bristol, already mentioned, the course of the narrow river Frome, on which it opened, was defended by an additional wall on the other side of the stream ; and in this wall, covering St John's gate, was the strongly fortified Frome gate. The case of York, where the river nearly bisects the walled enclosure, is most unusual. In other instances, the town was

confined to one side of the stream, and the approach from the
river was protected by a barbican, which could take the form
either of an outer defence to the gateway itself, or of a *tête-du-pont*
on the opposite side of the stream, or of a fortified passage across
the bridge.   Of barbicans in general much has been said already ;
and we have seen at York and Tenby something of town
barbicans, while in the Porte de Laon at Coucy, we have had
an instance of a barbican acting as a *tête-du-pont* on the further
side of a town ditch.   The arrangement of the south-western
approach to Kenilworth castle is a good instance of the combination, in castle fortification, of *tête-du-pont*, fortified causeway,
and gatehouse with barbican.   Fortified bridges were not un-

Monmouth ; Gatehouse on Monnow bridge

common in the middle ages, but those which remain are few.
The finest example of all is the fourteenth-century Pont
Valentré at Cahors (Lot), a noble bridge of six lofty pointed
arches, divided by piers which are supplied with the usual
triangular spurs or cut-waters.   At each end of the bridge is
a massive rectangular gateway tower, battlemented, with pyra-
midal roofs, and machicolated galleries below the battlements ;
while in the middle of the passage is a third tower, the ground-
floor of which was gated and portcullised.   The brick bridge,
called the Pont des Consuls, at Montauban (Tarn-et-Garonne),
was somewhat similarly defended.   Examples from other
countries are the thirteenth-century covered bridge at Tournai,
the bridge of Alcantarà at Toledo, and the bridge of Prague,

33

which was defended about the middle of the fourteenth century
with a tall rectangular gate-tower at one end, and a gateway,
flanked by towers of unequal size, at the other.   In England
two small examples of fortified bridges remain.   Upon the
bridge at Monmouth (297) is a gatehouse with a machicolated
battlement and a gateway which was closed by a portcullis:
this stood well in advance of the Bridge gate of the town,
which was at a little distance from the stream.   At Warkworth,
on the side of the bridge next the town, is a plain rectangular
gatehouse, the arch and ground-floor of which remain intact.
The triangular patch of land, south of the Coquet, on which
Warkworth is built, was well defended on two sides by the
river, and on the third side by the castle, and the gatehouse
at the bridge was its only stone fortification.

The progress of the art of defence under Edward I. was
accompanied by the enclosure within defensive walls of areas
and houses not originally intended for military purposes.
Disputes between the cathedral priory and the citizens of
Norwich led to the enclosure of the monastery within a fortified
precinct :[1] the royal licence for the construction of the water-gate
bears date 27th July 1276.[2] On 8th May 1285, the dean and
chapter of Lincoln obtained their first licence for the enclosure
of their precinct with a wall 12 feet high ;[3] and ten days later
a similar licence was issued to the dean and chapter of York.[4]
On 10th June the dean and chapter of St Paul's,[5] and on
1st January following the dean and chapter of Exeter,[6] had
letters patent to the same effect.   Bishop Burnell had licence to
wall and crenellate the churchyard and close of Wells, 15th March
1285-6,[7] while he was busy building his strong house at Acton
Burnell.   Licence to crenellate the priory of Tynemouth, on its
exposed site, was granted 5th September 1295.[8] Bishop Walter
Langton had licence to wall the close of Lichfield, 18th April
1299.[9] Licence to the abbot and convent of Peterborough to
crenellate the gate of the abbey and two chambers lying between
the gate and the church was granted 18th July 1309.[10] At
Lincoln, where a large portion of the close walls may still be
seen, there was some delay in building.   Two licences, confirming

---

[1] Every monastery was, of course, surrounded by a wall ; but it was only
in certain cases and after a certain period that such walls were crenellated.
[2] Pat. 4 Edw. I., m. 12.   [3] *Ibid.*, 13 Edw. I., m. 22.
[4] *Ibid.*   [5] *Ibid.*, m. 15.
[6] *Ibid.*, 14 Edw. I., m. 24.   [7] *Ibid.*, m. 19 (sched.).
[8] *Ibid.*, 24 Edw. I., m. 8.   [9] *Ibid.*, 27 Edw. I., m. 29.
[10] *Ibid.*, 2 Edw. II., pt. 2, m. 25.   The abbot and convent of St Mary's,
York, had licence to crenellate their wall, except on the side towards the
city, 12th July 1318 (*Ibid.*, 12 Edw. II., pt. 1, m. 31).

WELLS : gatehouse of bishop's palace

the letters patent of 1285, were granted by Edward II. in one year.[1] On 6th December 1318, the licence was again renewed : the wall might be raised to a greater height than 12 feet, and might be crenellated and provided with crenellated turrets.[2] Further, on 28th September 1329, Bishop Burghersh received letters patent, permitting him, in the most liberal terms, to "repair, raise, crenellate, and turrellate" the walls of the bishop's palace.[3] Thus, in the reign of Edward III., there were no less than three fortified enclosures within the circuit of the walls of Lincoln—the castle, the close round the cathedral, and the bishop's palace. To-day, as we stand in the open space at the head of the Steep Hill, to our left is the gatehouse of the castle ; while to our right is the Exchequer gate, the inner gatehouse of the close. This is a lofty oblong building of three stages, with a large central archway, and a smaller archway on each side for pedestrians. On the west or outer side the face is plain, but on the eastern side it is broken by two half-octagon turrets, containing vices. There was also an outer gatehouse, some yards to the west.[4] The south-eastern gatehouse of the close, known as Pottergate, still remains, a rectangular building with an upper stage. At Wells, Salisbury,[5] and Norwich, the *enceinte* of the close may still easily be traced ; while at Wells, close by the gatehouse of the close, is the outer gatehouse of the bishop's palace. The palace itself retains its wet moat, and is still approached by its drawbridge and through a formidable inner gatehouse, which is flanked by two half-octagon towers (300).

Of gatehouses of abbeys and priories, many still remain, some of which, like those at Bridlington, Tewkesbury, and

[1] September 1315 (Pat. 9 Edw. II., pt. 1, m. 18), and 24th February 1315-6 (*Ibid.*, pt. 2, m. 31).

[2] *Ibid.*, 12 Edw. II., pt. 1, m. 7. No licence for crenellation had previously been given. The licences, here and elsewhere, explain that homicide and other crimes in the close by night made walling desirable. The gates were to be closed from twilight to sunrise.

[3] Burghersh also had licence to crenellate his manor-houses of Stow Park and Nettleham in Lincolnshire and Liddington in Rutland, 16th November 1336 (Pat. 10 Edw. III., pt. 2, m. 18). A comprehensive licence was granted, 20th July 1377 (*Ibid.*, 1 Rich. II., pt. 1, m. 26) to Ralph Erghum, bishop of Salisbury, to wall and crenellate the city of Salisbury and his manor-houses at Salisbury, Bishop's Woodford, Potterne, Bishops Cannings, and Ramsbury in Wilts, Sherborne in Dorset, Chardstock in Devon, Sonning in Berks, and his house in Fleet Street.

[4] There were four of these double gatehouses in the *enceinte*. The fifth gatehouse, Pottergate, was single.

[5] Bishop Wyvill had a grant, 1st March 1331-2, of the stones of the cathedral of Old Sarum and the old residential houses, for the repair of the cathedral and enclosure of the precinct (Pat. 5 Edw. III., pt. 1, m. 27).

Thornton Abbey; Gatehouse

Whalley,[1] are of great size, and were capable of offering defence, if necessary. But by far the most important of monastic gate-houses is that at Thornton abbey in Lincolnshire, a magnificent building of brick with stone dressings (260). The licence to the abbot and convent to "build and crenellate a new house over and beside their abbey gate" bears date 6th August 1382.[2] The gatehouse is an oblong of three lofty stages with half-octagon turrets at the angles. The single archway on the ground-floor is approached through a narrow barbican, set obliquely to the building (331). On each side of the entrance is a bold half-octagon buttress. The inner face of the entrance is flanked by half-

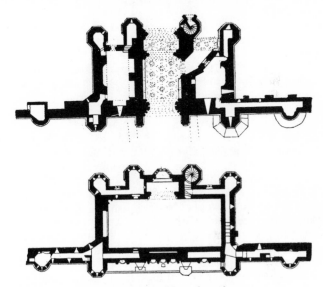

Thornton Abbey; Plan of gatehouse

octagon turrets, in the southern of which is the vice which gives access to the upper floors. There are no straight side-passages as in the Exchequer gate at Lincoln, where the porters' lodges are between the main and lateral entrances; but at Thornton an archway was built in the south wall of the central passage, and a diagonal side entrance constructed, with a wide inner archway. The outer entrance (303) was protected by a portcullis,

[1] Licence to crenellate Whalley, "the church and close," was granted 10th July 1348 (Pat. 22 Edw. III., pt. 2, m. 20).
[2] Pat. 6 Rich. II., pt. 1, m. 22 : a further licence to crenellate the abbey precinct bears date 1389, 6th May (Pat. 12 Rich. II., pt. 2, m. 13).

and the lodges and turrets on either side had loops to the field.
On the first floor of the gatehouse is a spacious room, which
communicates by mural passages with the first floor of the angle-
turrets and with galleries in the adjacent walls. These are all
provided with loops, so that the approach to the monastery was
effectually commanded. This gatehouse is nearly contemporary
with the West gate of the city of Canterbury, which was begun
by Archbishop Sudbury about 1379;[1] but the Canterbury gateway
takes the orthodox form of a central passage recessed between
two round towers, which are bold projections from a rectangular
plan, and its architecture cannot compare with the moulded
archways, elaborate ribbed vaulting, and canopied niches of
Thornton.[2]

Fortified closes, abbeys, and bishop's palaces bring us back
to the castle, in the history of which is the epitome of the art
of defence. The concentric plan displayed the resources of the
defenders in their most scientific form, but the concentric plan,
as we have seen, is not very common, and its systematic use
in English architecture was practically confined to a single period.
The site, as at Kidwelly, did not always allow of the full
extension of the outer ward, so as completely to encircle the
inner. As a rule, we find that the English castle of the fourteenth century consists, like Richmond and Ludlow in their
earliest form, or like Carew or Manorbier, of a single bailey
without a keep. This enclosure is flanked by towers at
adequate intervals, and is entered through an imposing gatehouse
between two drum towers. No English castle of this type can
compare with the fourteenth-century castle of Saint-André at
Villeneuve d'Avignon (307), which kept watch upon the castle
of the popes on the opposite bank of the Rhône, or with the
Breton castles of Fougères (250) and Vitré. The castle of
Caerlaverock (364), near Dumfries, not the famous castle besieged
by Edward I., but a castle founded in 1333 on a new site, is
a good instance of a simple plan, in which a single ward is
surrounded by a flanked curtain. The castle stands on low and
marshy ground near the Solway firth. An island, surrounded
by a broad wet ditch, which, in the rear of the castle, assumes
the proportions of a small lake, is enclosed by three sections of
curtain forming an equilateral triangle. A drum tower, low and
of rather slender proportions, covered each angle of the base;[3]

[1] Pat. 3 Rich. II., pt. 2, m. 10.
[2] The beautiful rectangular gatehouse of Battle abbey is earlier than
Thornton. Licence to crenellate was granted 9th June 1339 (Pat. 12
Edw. III., pt. 2, m. 28).
[3] One of these towers remains : the other, with the adjacent curtain, is gone.

STOKESAY : hall

STOKESAY CASTLE from south-west

while at the apex was a lofty gatehouse, flanked by drum towers, and approached by a drawbridge. The interior of the castle is somewhat confined, and the older domestic buildings were much enlarged in the sixteenth century by a mansion, somewhat in the style of the French Renaissance, which was built against the curtain to the left hand of the entrance. The old hall occupied the base of the triangle, while the kitchen offices were against the right-hand curtain.

Licences to crenellate mansions are common in the Patent rolls of the Edwards and Richard II. In this way, many private dwelling-houses reached the rank of castles, while still retaining

Villeneuve d'Avignon

strongly marked features of their domestic object. The fortified house of Stokesay (306) in Shropshire, which Lawrence of Ludlow had licence to crenellate, 19th October 1290,[1] is a case in point, where the moated manor-house, with its strong tower, well deserves the name of castle. At the same time, many of the houses for which licences of crenellation were granted were never more than manor-houses to which were added fortifications of a limited kind. This was the case with Henry Percy's houses of Spofforth, Leconfield, and Petworth, the licence for which bears date 14th October 1308.[2] Markenfield hall in Yorkshire, for which a

---

[1] Pat. 19 Edw. I., m. 2.   [2] *Ibid.*, 2 Edw. II., pt. 2, m. 19.

licence was granted 28th February 1309-10,[1] is still one of our most valuable examples of domestic, as distinct from military, architecture. Such fortifications as these houses had or still have were not designed to stand a siege, but to ensure privacy and keep off casual marauders. Even in the sixteenth century, dwelling-houses like Compton Wyniates in Warwickshire or Tolleshunt Major in Essex were surrounded by a moat or simply by a wall.

Against these minor fortifications, however, we must put the cases in which the process of crenellation definitely meant conversion into a castle. Dunstanburgh, which Thomas of Lancaster had licence to crenellate in 1315,[2] is a military stronghold of the most pronounced type. Its exposed position upon the Northumbrian coast was one reason of its strength : coast castles needed strong defences, and we find that, during the period of the wars with France and later, the fortification of castles like Dover was a constant method of precaution against invasion.[3] Dunstanburgh has much in common with the ordinary strong dwelling-houses of Northumberland. Its base-court is a very large enclosure, occupying most of the area of the promontory on which the castle is situated ; while the actual castle consists of a small and gloomy bailey. A wall, flanked at each end by a rectangular tower, shut off the enclosed space from the mainland. In the wall between the two towers rose the great gatehouse, which, standing in the front of attack, gave access to the smaller ward, and contained upon its upper floors the chief domestic apartments. Strongly defended as this gatehouse was, with two drum towers of great size flanking the entrance, the immediate access which it gave to the heart of the castle was evidently a source of danger. At a later date, the entrance was walled up, and a new gateway made in the curtain at a point near by. The gatehouse thus was practically turned into a keep, and the process which had taken place at Richmond towards the end of the twelfth century was virtually repeated, with this exception, that the actual fabric of the gatehouse remained, and was not superseded by a new form of strong tower. Precisely the same thing happened at Llanstephan in Carmarthenshire. This castle, one of the most imposing of Welsh strongholds, stands on a steep and almost isolated hill, where the Towy enters the Bristol Channel. It is divided by a cross-wall into a large outer ward and an inner ward which

---

[1] Pat. 3 Edw. II., m. 18.

[2] 28th August 1315 (Pat. 9 Edw. II., pt. 1, m. 25).

[3] See a commission to Humphrey, duke of Gloucester, to survey and repair defects in Dover castle, 22nd May 1425 (Pat. 3 Hen. VI., pt. 2, m. 17).

occupies the top of the sloping summit of the hill. The chief buildings were in the outer ward, and the finest of them was the great gatehouse, situated at the head of the landward slope of the hill, and concealed from the river by the convex curve of the curtain and by a large tower at the eastern angle of the enclosure. This gatehouse is of trapezoidal form : the gateway and its drum towers front the field, but the building spreads inwards, and has two much smaller round towers at its inner angles. It was undesirable, however, that the gatehouse, which, from the military and domestic point of view alike, was the principal building in the castle, should be the point on which the besiegers could concentrate all their force. Consequently, the gateway was blocked not long after it was built, and a new entrance was made beside it in the curtain. The way into the higher ward at Llanstephan was closed by a small rectangular gatehouse, built near one end of the dividing curtain.

Thus at Dunstanburgh and Llanstephan, castles in which the system of defence was not founded upon the concentric plan, but relied upon the strength of an adequately flanked curtain, gatehouses which are worthy of Caerphilly and Harlech, and stand upon the outer line of defence,[1] reverted to the condition of keeps. The possible use of a keep as an ultimate refuge never ceased altogether to have weight with castle-builders. The Percys, after their purchase of Alnwick early in the fourteenth century,[2] although there was ample room for a large mansion in one or other of the wards, built their dwelling as a cluster of walls and towers round a courtyard on the mount between the two wards. Some part of the substructure, the gatehouse with its octagonal flanking towers, and the curious triple-arched recess at the head of the well (310), are the most that remains to us of the early fourteenth-century mansion ; but with these is incorporated twelfth-century work, which shows that the Percys built their house upon the lines of an older house upon the mount.[3] Thus the dwelling-house at Alnwick is in reality a keep of unusual form, a large building with flanking towers built upon a mount which has been considerably levelled to allow of more room for the house and its internal courtyard (115).

[1] It will be remembered that the gatehouse of the quasi-concentric castle of Kidwelly, only a few miles distant from Llanstephan, is also situated upon the outer line of defence.

[2] Bishop Bek enfeoffed Henry Percy of the manor and town, 19th November 1309 (Pat. 3 Edw. II., m. 23).

[3] It has been already pointed out that this older house may have simply taken the form of a series of buildings against the encircling wall of a large shell-keep.

The strong tower, representing the survival of the keep, is found in another great northern castle of the fourteenth century, Raby, the castle of the Nevilles, where in other respects the domestic element is very prominent (311).[1] Raby, like Alnwick, is occupied to-day, but no such drastic changes as have converted the house on the mount at Alnwick into a comfortable modern residence were necessary here. There is an outer gatehouse slightly in advance of the north angle of the castle, which was surrounded by a moat and is nearly rectangular. The buildings are clustered round a main courtyard, the entrance to which is a gatehouse with a long vaulted passage behind it in the west block of buildings. At either end of the west front are two massive rectangular towers: Clifford's tower, at the north end, is almost detached, and covers the north angle immediately opposite the gateway. The remaining tower, known as Bulmer's tower, projects on five sides from the south angle of the building, and is the strong tower or keep of the castle. The kitchen, in the north block, is also contained within a strong tower, which

Alnwick Castle; Well-head

does not project, however, from the rest of the buildings. But it was in the north of England that the keep survived most persistently. Middleham castle received much alteration at the hands of its Neville owners in the fourteenth century; but the twelfth-century keep was retained as the central feature of the enclosure. The rectangular keep of Knaresborough is entirely of the fourteenth century: it stood between an outer and inner

[1] John, Lord Neville, obtained licence from Bishop Hatfield of Durham to crenellate Raby in 1378 (O. S. Scott, *Raby, its Castle and its Lords*, 1906, p. 47).

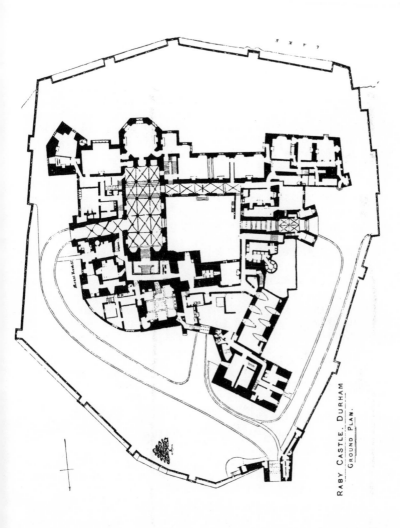

RABY CASTLE. DURHAM
GROUND PLAN.

ward, and its great peculiarity is that the only passage from one to the other was through the first floor of the keep.[1]

The tradition of the rectangular tower, however, was systematically preserved in the buildings known as pele-towers. These formed the chief defensive structures of enclosures called "peles," a word derived from the Latin *pilum* (a stake). The twelfth-century tower of Bowes, a large and important rectangular tower which guarded the pass over Stainmoor from the valley of the Eden to that of the Tees, is an early instance of the pele-tower; and probably a large palisaded enclosure or "barmkin" was attached to it. In the fourteenth century we find large pele-towers like those at Belsay (313) or Chipchase, or the great tower-house of East Gilling, the proportions of which recall the rectangular keeps of a century and a half earlier. Belsay, with its traceried two-light openings on the first floor, and large bartizans corbelled out at the angles of its battlements, is the most handsome building of its kind in the north of England. The ordinary pele-tower, however, is of a rather later date, and the large majority of Northumbrian examples are of the fifteenth, and now and then of the sixteenth century.[2] Halton tower, near Aydon castle, and the small tower in the corner of the church-yard at Corbridge,[3] are well-known examples; while one of the most imposing specimens is the oblong tower of the manor-house of the archbishops of York at Hexham. The normal elevation was of three stories. The ground-floor, in which was the doorway, was vaulted as a protection against fire; it may have been used as a stable, and certainly was used as a store-room. The door was of wood, but its outer face was

---

[1] At Middleham, where the plan of the fore-building is rather exceptional, there was a passage through the eastern part of the ground-floor of the fore-building: this, however, was not the only way from the northern to the southern half of the castle. The first floor of the tower at Knaresborough, which formed a great guard-room, is in a very ruinous state; but there are clear indications of the main entrance near the north-east angle, and the inner entrance in the south wall, at right angles to the outer, still remains. There is also a vice in the south wall, by which the inner ward could be reached when the gates were closed. This tower, of course, never contained the domestic buildings of the castle; but the kitchen was in the basement, to which there were three doors of entry from the inner ward. The approach to each gateway from outside seems to have been a rising causeway built on arches.

[2] The tower of Belsay measures $51\frac{1}{2}$ by $47\frac{1}{2}$ feet. The tower of Knaresborough, which is of the same period, measures 62 by 54 feet; while that of Gilling measures $79\frac{1}{2}$ by $72\frac{1}{2}$ feet.

[3] This is said to have been the medieval vicarage of the church, which was appropriated to the cathedral priory of Carlisle. A pele-tower forms part of the rectories of Elsdon and Rothbury and of the vicarage of Embleton, Northumberland.

BELSAY CASTLE

protected by a heavy framework of iron. The first floor, reached by a mural stair, was the main living-room. The second floor was a sleeping-room ; and the battlements at the top were generally machicolated. Garde-robes are usually found in these towers ; but they can hardly be called comfortable residences, and had all the disadvantages of the twelfth-century tower-keep, without its roominess. They are found, not only in Northumberland, but throughout the northern counties and the south of Scotland, while, in the hill country of Derbyshire, the pele seems to have been a favourite form of stronghold. The twelfth-century tower of Peak castle is one of those examples which allies the pele-tower to the normal tower-keep ; while Haddon hall gradually developed from an enclosure which was neither more nor less than a pele with a tower at one angle.[1]

In this connection a word should be said about the fortification of churches. Ewenny priory church in Glamorgan, with its crenellated central tower and transept, is our only important example of fortified religious buildings such as were common in the centre and south of France—the cathedral of Albi (Tarn), the churches of Royat (Puy-de-Dôme) or Les-Saintes-Maries-sur-la-Mer (Bouches-du-Rhône).[2] None of our abbeys is protected by a donjon, like that of Montmajour, near Arles. There are, however, a certain number of churches, in districts exposed to constant warfare, the architecture of which, if not exactly military, was yet possibly constructed with a view to defence. The massive structure of some twelfth-century towers, like Melsonby in north Yorkshire, is probably due to the idea that they could be converted into strongholds, in case of a raid from the Scottish border. In the fourteenth and fifteenth centuries, when Scotland was dreaded as a constant foe, the

---

[1] The term "pele-yard" is applied to the base-court of the castle of Prudhoe in Pat. 1 Rich. II., pt. 1, m. 1 ; where there is a licence to Gilbert de Umfraville, earl of Angus, to apply a rent to the augmentation of a chaplain's stipend in the "chantry of St Mary in le Peleyerde of Prodhowe."

[2] Enlart (ii. 623-753) quotes 242 examples of French churches which show remains of fortification. Most of the midland and southern departments of France contain a few ; but the thickest clusters occur near the northern frontier (15 in the Aisne, 10 in the Ardennes department), and on the coast of Languedoc and Roussillon, where inroads of pirates were common (Pyrénées-Orientales, 22 ; Hérault, 12). Among the larger fortified churches were the cathedrals of Agde, Béziers, Lodève, and Saint-Pons (Hérault), Elne (Pyrénées-Orientales), Pamiers (Ariège), Viviers (Ardèche), and Saint-Claude (Jura), and the abbey churches of Saint-Denis (Seine), Saint-Victor at Marseilles (Bouches-du-Rhône), La Chaise-Dieu (Haute-Loire), Moissac (Tarn-et-Garonne), and Tournus (Saône-et-Loire). The example of Ewenny was followed in one or two churches of the same district, such as Newton Nottage, and in the peninsula of Gower.

habit of giving additional security to the church towers in this district was common. Some otherwise simple church towers, as at Bolton-on-Swale and Danby Wiske in north Yorkshire, have their lowest stage vaulted, probably to minimise the danger of fire. The doorway to the tower-stair at Bedale was defended by a portcullis, and there are a fireplace and garde-robe upon the first floor. At Spennithorne, in the same neighbourhood, the battlements of the tower borrowed an ornament from military architecture, and are crowned with figures of "defenders." In border districts it is not unusual to find the ground-floor of the tower roofed with a pointed barrel-vault, as at Whickham in county Durham, where the church stands on a high hill near the confluence of the Tyne and Derwent. This is a very general custom in South Wales, where the towers are usually massive and unbuttressed, and stand upon a battering plinth.[1] In Pembrokeshire a more slender type of tower prevails, which usually batters upwards through its whole height : the ground-floor is vaulted, and in many cases the whole church, or, at any rate, the nave, is ceiled with a barrel-vault. It does not follow that the object of this form of construction is defensive : lack of timber, and the consequent employment of local stone for rubble vaulting, is partly responsible for it. But in no part of the country are military and ecclesiastical forms of architecture so closely allied. The barrel-vaults of Monkton priory church and St Mary's at Pembroke are similar to those of the chapel and its substructure which occupy the north-west corner of the inner ward of Pembroke castle : those of the church at Manorbier have their counterparts in the vaults of the castle chapel and the large room on its ground-floor.

If the pele-tower may be regarded as a direct survival of the rectangular keep in a simplified form, it is probable that the rectangular keep, with its angle turrets, also had a share in the origin of a type of castle or strong house, which became common, especially in the north of England, during the fourteenth and fifteenth centuries.[2] The plan of this species of castle is a rectangle, which, in the largest examples, as at Bolton in Wensleydale, has an open courtyard in the centre ; but its

[1] At Llanfihangel-cwm-Du, near Crickhowell, there was a fireplace upon the first floor of the tower until recently : the vent for the smoke remains in one of the corner turrets of the tower.

[2] The constant pressure of Scottish invasion upon the northern border is illustrated by the persistence of military architecture in the counties of Northumberland and Cumberland. Thus, as late as 1399, William Strickland undertook the building of Penrith castle "for fortifying that town and the whole adjacent country" (Pat. 22 Rich. II., pt. 2, m. 16 ; cf. pt. 3, m. 37).

distinguishing feature is the provision of four towers, each at an angle of the structure. Such keeps as those of Colchester and Kenilworth, where the turrets are of considerable size and projection, suggest this plan ; and some of the earliest examples, like Haughton on the north Tyne, the oldest parts of which are of the thirteenth century, have little to distinguish them from the ordinary rectangular keep. The angle-towers at Haughton are of no great prominence ; but, in the early fourteenth-century castle of Langley, to the west of Hexham, they are a striking feature of the building, and one is entirely devoted to a series of garde-robes, arranged in three stories, with a common pit in the basement. A building with a somewhat similar plan to these northern castles is the manor-house or castle which Robert Burnell, bishop of Bath and Wells, and chancellor of England under Edward I., built at Acton Burnell, in Shropshire.[1] Here, however, the building is of a thoroughly domestic type, with large two-light window-openings of great beauty, which at once remove any suspicion as to its military character. The castle of the Scropes at Bolton and that of the Nevilles at Sheriff Hutton represent the highest development of this quadrangular plan. The licence to crenellate Bolton was granted in 1379 :[2] the licence for Sheriff Hutton bears date 1382.[3] Both castles are large buildings with a central courtyard, and in both the military ideal was uppermost. Sheriff Hutton is now in a complete state of ruin, but Bolton is fairly perfect ; and from its structure one important fact may be deduced. While the usual precautions for defence were carefully preserved, and the outer openings in the walls interfered little with the general solidity of structure, the domestic buildings round the courtyard formed part and parcel of the fabric itself. They were not merely built up against or within the curtain, but the curtain was actually their outer wall, and not simply their defensive covering. In fact, the manor-house in these cases was not a separate building within the enclosure of the castle ; but the castle was also the manor-house. The same combination of military with domestic aims is noticeable in the contemporary castle of Raby (1378), of which the plan, already described, approximates irregularly to the type.[4] Castles akin to Bolton and Sheriff Hutton

---

[1] Bishop Burnell was building this house in 1284. He left the king at Conway on 25th July, to look after the progress of the works (Pat. 12 Edw. I., m. 7).

[2] 4th July (Pat. 3 Rich. II., pt. 1, m. 43). A contract is still preserved, of 14th September 1378.

[3] 26th April (Pat. 5 Rich. II., pt. 2, m. 21).

[4] The builder of Raby, John, Lord Neville (d. 1388), was also responsible for the fortification of Sheriff Hutton.

are Lumley, the licence for which was granted in 1392,[1] and Chillingham, the angle-towers of which are of a much earlier date than is usual in castles of this plan.[2] At Chillingham the medieval work is somewhat obscured by alterations made in the seventeenth century, but the original plan is retained. Survivals of the quadrangular plan may be traced in some of the great manor-houses of the early Renaissance period. It is not difficult to detect in the plan of Hardwick hall (1587), while the ground-plan of Wollaton hall (1580) is probably derived from a similar source. Smaller houses like Barlborough hall, near Sheffield, or Wootton lodge, near Ashbourne, have a kinship with it, although in these cases, and especially in the first, the elevation is more tower-like than is usual in medieval buildings of the type. It is needless to say that these Renaissance buildings are without any military character.

The traditional form of the rectangular keep was also responsible, no doubt, for the great tower-house which formed the principal feature, and is now the only portion left, of the castle of Tattershall in Lincolnshire. The discussion of this building belongs more properly to the last chapter of this book, for its general construction and architectural features are those of an age in which the military architecture of the middle ages was already little more than a survival. This age of transition begins in the last quarter of the fourteenth century; and, as already pointed out, castles like Bolton and Raby clearly show its influence. During the later half of the fourteenth and the fifteenth century, outside the north of England, it is rare to find a castle which actually deserves the name. The large private residence, with a certain amount of defensive precautions, became increasingly common; and, where alterations were made to existing castles, they were generally entirely in the direction of domestic comfort.

There are, however, a few striking exceptions which belong to the later part of the fourteenth century. The two polygonal towers, Guy's tower (319) and Cæsar's tower (321), which cover the angles of the eastern curtain at Warwick and flank the gate-house with its barbican, are cases in point. Few castles show features of the military architecture of all periods to such advantage. The plan is that of an early Norman mount-and-

---

[1] This date is given in the 43rd Report of the Deputy-Keeper of the Public Records, p. 71. The licence, as the castle was within the palatinate, was granted by Bishop Skirlaw.

[2] The licence to Thomas de Heton to "make a castle or fortalice" of Chillingham bears date 27th January 1343-4 (Pat. 18 Edw. III., pt. 1, m. 46). Some of the masonry in the angle-towers is, however, of a much earlier date than this.

WARWICK : Guy's tower

bailey castle, which has in course of time been surrounded with a stone curtain ;[1] while a magnificent residence, in the main a building of the fourteenth century, has grown up on the south side of the bailey next the river.[2] The most commanding

Warwick Castle ; Cæsar's tower

military features, however, are the towers just mentioned, 128 and 147 feet high respectively. The whole character of these

[1] The mount remains at the west end of the enclosure, but the shell-keep on its summit has been removed.

[2] The gatehouse and barbican in the east curtain, as well as the older portion of the dwelling-house, were the work of Thomas Beauchamp, earl of Warwick (d. 1369): Cæsar's tower and Guy's tower were the work of his son Thomas, who died in 1401.

35

towers is French rather than English. Their great height may be contrasted with that of the contemporary rectangular towers at Raby, the loftiest of which is only 81 feet high, and depends for its defence almost entirely upon the thickness of its walls. The nearest parallel to the Warwick towers, on the other hand, is such a building as the fifteenth-century Tour Talbot at Falaise, a lofty cylindrical tower built at an angle of the donjon, as is generally stated, during the English occupation of northern France.[1] The chief characteristics of the towers at Warwick are the bold corbelling out of their parapets, with a row of machicolations, and the provision of a central turret, rising some distance above the level of the rampart-walk—a feature common in France, but most unusual in England.[2] The vaulting of both towers throughout is also a French feature; and in every respect they bear traces of an influence which, beginning in the cylindrical donjons of Philip Augustus' castles and of Coucy, survived to a late date in France, and may have affected English military work in that country, but had little result in England itself. While, throughout the fifteenth century, the French castle maintained its character as a stronghold, and even kept that character when Renaissance influence was strong in that country, the military character of the English castle steadily diminished. The wars of the Roses were a succession of battles in open field, in which castles and walled towns played very little part. And while the military character of Warwick continued to be emphasised during the period of transition, the neighbouring castle of Kenilworth, in common with most English castles, was transformed, during the same period, from a stronghold into a palace.

The most imposing of our later castles, which may be considered primarily as military buildings, is Bodiam in Sussex (323). On 21st October 1385, Sir Edward Dalyngrugge had licence to crenellate his manor of Bodiam " by the sea," and " to make a castle thereof in defence of the adjacent country against the king's enemies." [3] The main object of this licence was evidently

---

[1] This is the usual date given for the tower, which is entered from the first floor of the great donjon, and from the lower floor of the " lesser donjon " attached to one side of the keep. E. Lefèvre-Pontalis, *Le Château de Coucy*, p. 82, departs from the usual date to assign the tower to Philip Augustus, two centuries earlier. The details certainly appear to be of a period much earlier than the fifteenth century.

[2] The turrets attached to some of the towers at Conway and Harlech are at the side, not in the centre. Such raised turrets were useful as look-out posts, and a watcher posted upon them could inform the defenders on the rampart-walk below of movements which they might not be able to follow for themselves.

[3] Pat. 9 Rich. II., pt. 1, m. 22.

HURSTMONCEAUX : gatehouse

BODIAM : north front and gatehouse

to provide against a French attack upon the ports of Rye and Winchelsea, at the mouth of the Rother: in the following March, Sir Edward was named first upon the commission appointed by letters patent to fortify and wall the town of Rye.[1] Bodiam stands upon the left bank of the Rother, some miles above Rye, and commands from its site, at some little height above the valley, a long stretch of marsh in the direction of the mouth of the river. The walls of the castle descend sheer into a lake, formed by the damming up of a stream. The castle is simply a rectangular enclosure surrounded by a lofty curtain. Each angle is capped by a cylindrical tower, and in the middle of each face is a rectangular tower: the great gatehouse, however, in the north face, has two rectangular towers, one on each side of the entrance. The tower in the centre of the opposite face is the lesser gatehouse of the castle. The plan bears a striking analogy to that of the castle of Villandraut (Gironde), built about 1250: Nunney in Somerset (1373) and Shirburn in Oxfordshire (1377) are coeval English examples. The interior is surrounded by domestic buildings. Against the south curtain were the hall and kitchen: the screens at the west end of the hall formed a passage to the lesser gateway. The wall dividing the screens from the kitchen still remains, with the three doorways which gave access to the kitchen, pantry, and buttery (326). The private apartments were returned along the east curtain, and at their north end was the chapel, which had the usual arrangement of a western gallery, entered from the chambers on the first floor of this range of building. Servants' quarters and barracks occupied the west side of the enclosure. All the buildings were plentifully supplied with garde-robes in the towers; and the upper portion of the south-west tower was arranged as a pigeon-house.

In spite of the ample space given to the domestic buildings, the defensive nature of the works at Bodiam is very clearly apparent, not only in the strength of the walls, the height of which (40 feet) is equal to the height of the walls at Harlech, but in the provision made for the defence of the approaches. The main gateway was protected by a barbican, which occupied a small island in the lake, some 54 feet in front of the gatehouse. A causeway, which is in part, at any rate, original, connected the gateway with the barbican; but it is probable that this had a bridge at one or both ends. A bridge, spanning a gap of 6 feet, connected the outer end of the barbican with an octagonal island in the middle of the broad moat. The straight causeway by which this island is now reached from the mainland does not

[1] Pat. 9 Rich. II., pt. 2, m. 24.

represent the original approach ; but a longer and more tortuous
approach was planned from a pier set against the west bank of
the moat and joined, probably by a double drawbridge, to the
octagonal island, which thus stood at a point where the road,
commanded throughout by the curtain and its flanking towers,
turned at a right angle towards the north gatehouse of the castle.
The approach to the smaller or south gate has now disappeared ;
but two walls project into the moat on each side of the entrance,

Bodiam Castle ; Courtyard

and against the south bank of the moat remains the pier on which
the outer drawbridge dropped.

The labour and pains which were taken to strengthen this
castle are shown by the revetting of the earthwork, not only of
the main island, but also of the lesser islands in the moat, and
of portions of the causeways of approach. The isolation of the
castle in the middle of a lake may have been suggested by the
plan adopted, at a much earlier date, at Leeds in Kent. The
great bàrbican of Leeds, however, divided by wet ditches into
three separate parts, forms the approach to the main bridge
across the moat. It is, in fact, the *tête-du-pont* of the castle, and

does not occupy a separate island, as at Bodiam, between the mainland and the gateway.

The gatehouse of Bodiam is an imposing building, and the castle-builders, from the days of Edward I. onwards, paid an attention to their gatehouses almost equal to that which the late Norman builders had given to their tower-keeps.[1] To the same twenty-five years within which Bodiam was built and the two great towers at Warwick were completed, belongs the greatest of English gatehouses, that of the castle of Lancaster.   It is known to have been built as late as about 1405 ; for the arms of Henry V. as prince of Wales appear on a shield above the gateway.   It is therefore one of the latest military works in the castles of the duchy, and the last of the series of gatehouses which owed their origin to lords of the house of Lancaster, and includes the noble structures at Dunstanburgh, Tutbury, and the great tower between the wards at Knaresborough.   The castle to which it was added was surrounded by a curtain, largely of twelfth-century date,[2] and contained a tower-keep and domestic buildings which appear to have been in the main of the thirteenth century.   Situated at the head of a very steep hill, and flanked by two huge octagonal towers, this gatehouse is the perfection of the type which is seen, with more slender flanking towers, at Bothal and in the keep of Alnwick.   The window openings towards the field are few and small : the battlements are boldly corbelled out, and machicolations of large size are left between them and the wall.   In a corner of each of the flanking towers rises a turret, the interior of which apparently served as a magazine for ammunition.   The interior of this gatehouse, although the space is ample, is fully in keeping with its sombre exterior.   Each of the two upper floors contains

---

[1] An interesting gatehouse, belonging to the later years of Edward I., is that of Denbigh, which was probably built by Henry de Lacy, the last earl of Lincoln (d. 1310).   Here a noble archway, flanked by two octagonal towers, gives access through a passage to an octagonal central hall, beyond which is a smaller octagonal guard-room.   The inner gateway to the enclosure is set in a side of the octagon, obliquely to the outer entrance.   The plan is apparently unique.   The upper portion of the gatehouse is badly ruined, and the walls have been much stripped ; but there is a statue, probably of the founder, left above the entrance archway, which is set in a niche and panel treated with a considerable amount of ornamental detail.

[2] The barrel-vault of a basement chamber in one of the curtain-towers retains the marks of the wattled centering on which it was built.   This is persistently asserted to be a mark of Roman origin.   As a matter of fact, no part of the present castle can be proved to be earlier than the beginning of the twelfth century, when Roger of Poitou may have moved the head of his honour here from Penwortham, south of the Ribble.   The castle, however, lies partly within, and partly outside the limits of a Roman military station.

three rooms, one in the central block of the gatehouse, the others in the towers at the sides. These rooms are large and lofty, and their original wooden ceilings still retain traces of colour; but they are gloomy and ill-lighted to the last degree. The apartments on the first floor communicate directly with one another, but those on the second floor are entered from an outer passage, which passes between them and the inner or west wall of the gatehouse. The guard-rooms on the ground-floor are approached in the usual way, by doorways near the inner entrance. The main stair is a vice in the south-west corner of building.

In the important additions made to the castle of Warkworth about 1400, the compromise attained between the requirements of defence and comfort is very striking. The plan of this castle, throughout its history, like the plan of Warwick, remained that of the original mount-and-bailey fortress. We have noticed already the addition of the stone curtain to the bailey, and the building of a large mansion against its western and southern faces. It is probable that a shell-keep was added to the mount, when the stone curtain was made; for the foundations of the present strong house on the mount are of masonry of an earlier and rougher character than the elaborately dressed stonework of the house itself. This house (221), which combines the features of keep and private residence in a most unusual way, appears to have been built by the first earl of Northumberland, who died in 1407.[1] The shape is that of a square with chamfered angles; but from the centre of each face projects a bold half-octagon, so that the ground-plan is a Greek cross with short arms and a large central block. The elevation consists of a basement and three floors. The basement contains tanks and a vault with a corbelled roof, which was certainly a prison, and bears a strong likeness to a similar vault in the inner gate-house at Alnwick. There is no basement stair, communication with the vaults being through trap-doors in the floor above. On this floor are a number of dark vaulted store-rooms, one of which was the wine-cellar, and has its own stair to the dais end of the hall on the floor above. The two upper floors are comparatively cheerful and well lighted: a shaft in the centre of the building gave light to the inner passage between the hall and kitchen. The main stair is in the south half-octagon, the chief doorway being in the west face of this projection, on the first floor. From

[1] This is the date proposed by Bates, *Border Holds:* C. H. Hartshorne (*Archæol. Inst.*, Newcastle, vol. ii.) proposed a later date, *c.* 1435-40. Mr Bates' date is more likely than the other: for neither is there any direct evidence.

the lobby on the second floor, at the head of the stair, two door-ways open. That on the right leads into the hall, which occupies the south-east angle of the central block, and is of the full height of the two upper floors. That on the left leads to the servants' quarters and the kitchens, which occupied the western part of the second floor, and communicated by separate doorways with the hall and chapel. The great kitchen filled the north-west angle of the central block, and, like the hall, was two stories in height. The north half-octagon and the north-east angle of the main block adjacent to it, were divided into two floors. The lower room in the half-octagon was probably the private room of the master of the house, communicating with the lower room in the main block, which was probably the common room of his immediate retinue. Similarly, upon the upper floor were a ladies' bower and a separate room for the countess of North-umberland's own use. Between the private apartments and the hall, occupying the centre of the east side of the main block and the half-octagon beyond, was the chapel. The chancel, in the half-octagon, was the height of both floors ; but the western part of the chapel was in two floors, the upper forming a gallery, with a doorway from the ladies' bower. From the south-east corner of this gallery, another doorway opened upon a narrow stone gallery, formed by the internal thickening of the lower part of the east wall of the hall : this may have served the purpose of a minstrels' gallery, or may have been used by the ladies of the house, when they wished to watch the festivities below. The wall beneath this gallery is pierced by a long vestry or priest's chamber, opening out of the south wall of the chapel, and built with a rising floor, in order to give head-way to the stair from the wine-cellar below. The ground-floor of the chapel also communicated with the hall and the men's apartments. In addition to the rooms already mentioned, there were third-floor rooms in the south-west angle of the main block and in the western half-octagon, which communicated with the gallery of the chapel. The area covered is not large, but the ingenuity of the plan is remarkable ; and the disposition of the various apartments must have required an amount of thought and skill, which no other medieval dwelling-house shows in so high a degree.

While the lower portions of the walls of the strong house at Warkworth are of great solidity and strength, the upper floors are lighted by large traceried window-openings, and the tall oblong windows of the hall, and those of the chancel of the chapel, convey no idea of the military purpose of the building. It is a curious fact that, in spite of the pains which were evidently expended upon this tower-house, the period of its employment as a residence seems to have been unusually short. The various lords of Warkworth were never satisfied with one residence for any length of time; and there is evidence that when John, duke of Bedford, was sent by his father, Henry IV., to pacify the north after Northumberland's rebellion, he took up his quarters at Warkworth in the gatehouse. Later in the fifteenth century, the old mansion, already described, in the bailey, was restored and altered: a porch-tower was made at the north-east end of the hall, and a stair-turret intruded in the south-east angle. The dwelling-house, which had been built within the castle about 1200, was converted, in fact, into a stately mansion; and the house on the mount was practically abandoned. No better instance could be found of the gradual weakening of the military ideal in favour of domestic comfort. All the castles of the later fourteenth and fifteenth centuries are examples of this in some degree. At Warwick the domestic buildings are at least of equal importance with the defences. The dwelling-house at Ludlow gradually increased in size and splendour, while nothing was added to its military defences. Even the outer walls of Bolton, a strong and well-guarded castle, are pierced with windows which admit a considerable amount of light. Bodiam and Raglan (331), relying on the great breadth of their moats, have large outward window openings. In all these instances, however, the dwelling-house, even at Raglan, is still regarded as a house within a castle. In the planning of the tower house at Warkworth the military and domestic ideals were both present to the minds of the builders. Neither can be said to prevail: the building was equally useful as house and castle. The hall at Warkworth, on the other hand, when it was rebuilt, was treated with an architectural splendour quite apart from any idea of its position within the walls of a place of defence. Those walls had become obsolete, and the house was the one object present to the aims of the restorers. A step further was taken at Hurstmonceaux (323), where the great brick house has the semblance of a castle, but little of its reality. At Carew in Pembrokeshire, three stages in the development of the domestic ideal as applied to military architecture can be studied in close proximity. On the east side of the ward are the earlier domestic apartments, somewhat cramped and gloomy, with outer windows which, wherever they occur, as in the chapel (248) and adjacent rooms, admit daylight very faintly. On the west side is the great hall built in the fifteenth century by Rhys ap Thomas, with its imposing porch-tower and entrance stair, a large and amply lighted room. On the north are the additions made in the sixteenth century by

RAGLAN CASTLE

THORNTON ABBEY: gatehouse and barbican

Sir John Perrott. The eastern rooms are those of a house within a castle: the western hall is that of a house which, although military considerations have had no part in its planning, is still confined within an earlier curtain. On the north side, however, the curtain has been broken through, and a series of apartments has been built out beyond its limits, proclaiming, with their long mullioned windows piercing the walls from floor to roof, that the day of castles is over, and that the dwelling-house has the field to itself.

CHAPTER XII

THE AGE OF TRANSITION: THE FORTIFIED
DWELLING-HOUSE

SOME account has now been given of the change which came over the English castle in the fourteenth and fifteenth centuries. The life of the feudal warrior in his stronghold gradually became the life of the country gentleman in a house whose fortification, such as it was, was of a merely precautionary character. It now remains for us to say something of those domestic buildings which are the principal feature of the English castles of the later middle ages, and of those houses which, while preserving the name and to some extent the appearance of castles, were designed primarily as dwelling-houses. In these examples the main lines of the normal dwelling-house plan, which have already been described, were preserved. The hall still formed the nucleus of the buildings and the centre of the life of the household: the kitchen, buttery, and pantry still took their place at the end of the hall next the screens, while the two-storied block, with the great chamber on the first floor, was found at the other end behind the dais. But, with the increase of comfort and splendour, came the desire for more space and greater privacy. The great hall at Ludlow (96), reconstructed in the early part of the fourteenth century, had a first-floor chamber at either end of the hall; and the additions made to these domestic buildings in the fifteenth century considerably increased the number of private apartments in a house which was already of great size. At Manorbier (208) the whole dwelling-house was enlarged and the number of rooms increased by a reconstruction in the second half of the thirteenth century. The dwelling-house in the inner ward of Conway, the hall and its adjacent rooms at Caerphilly, were planned on a more liberal scale than had been thought necessary in the castles of the eleventh and twelfth centuries. The essentially military character, however, of the Edwardian castle cramped the free development of domestic buildings within the precinct; and it was not until the middle of the fourteenth century that the plan of the dwelling-house in the castle had reached the stage at which it began to be considered for its own sake, apart from the curtain wall which protected it.

The development of the private mansion within the castle is well illustrated at Porchester. The outer defences of the castle, the twelfth-century great tower, the curtain of the inner ward, the fourteenth-century barbican, were all kept under repair ; for the French wars of the fourteenth and fifteenth centuries made the defence of Portsmouth harbour a desirable factor in English strategy, and the considerations which prompted the building of Bodiam also demanded that the military character of Porchester castle should be preserved. The barbican, however, was the last important addition to the defences. The later work included the remodelling of the twelfth-century hall against the south curtain.[1] This was in great part rebuilt, the hall on the first floor being supplied with large traceried windows towards the interior of the bailey : late in the fifteenth century, a porch with an upper floor was added at the end next the screens. Along the west side of the inner ward, between the great hall and the keep, a smaller hall was added late in the fourteenth century, the towers upon the east curtain were converted to domestic purposes, and a range of buildings was eventually added upon this side of the bailey (97).

Externally, Porchester castle is simply a fortress : internally, the domestic buildings rivet the attention, and only the imposing mass of the keep (131) reminds us of the military origin of the stronghold. Similarly, in the Cornish castle of Restormel, where the one ward is nearly circular in shape, and is surrounded by a deep ditch, the whole interior face of the curtain is covered by a series of domestic buildings, with partition walls radiating from the centre of the plan. The position of the hall, kitchen, and great chamber can easily be traced : the chapel was on the east side of the ward, separated from the hall by the great chamber, and the chancel, with a substructure, formed a rectangular projection from the curtain at this point. Here, too, as at Porchester, Ludlow, or Manorbier, the dwelling-house was masked by the fortress. But there are also castles in which the importance of the dwelling-house, as time went on, began to overshadow its military surroundings. At Tutbury the strong position of the castle, an entrenched stronghold which was probably ditched

---

[1] New works were begun at Porchester in 1386, when Robert Bardolf, the constable, was appointed to impress masons, carpenters, etc., and to take materials at the king's expense (Pat. 8 Rich. II., pt. 2, m. 23). This probably applies to the building of the barbican, but the hall may also have been remodelled at this period. There are considerable remains of twelfth-century work in the substructure of the hall, as already noted.

about for the first time long before the Conquest, the high mound raised by the Norman founder of the castle, and the fine four-teenth-century gatehouse[1] (237), approached by an ascent which was commanded by the whole length of the eastern curtain, strike the visitor far less than the remains of the great hall and its adjacent chambers. This beautiful work, often attributed, like so much else in castles of the duchy of Lancaster, to John of Gaunt, is probably of the middle of the fifteenth century: there is a remarkable similarity between the details of the stonework

Carew Castle; Entrance to great hall

here and at Wingfield, a house the date of which is well known to be somewhat later than 1441. As a whole, the castles which, like Tut-bury, became merged in the possessions of the house of Lancaster, and came to the Crown on the accession of Henry IV., furnish us with some of the best examples of castle dwelling - houses on a palatial scale. At Pontefract, for example, a range of buildings, known later as John of Gaunt's buildings, rose upon the site of the eastern mound. The drawings of Pontefract and of Melbourne in Derbyshire, preserved among the duchy re-cords, show us castles which have utterly changed their aspect, and have become palaces. Nowhere, however, is this more noticeable to-day than at Kenil-worth, where the erection of the great hall may be fairly attri-buted to John of Gaunt.[2] The whole of the north and part of the

[1] The stone gatehouse of the Norman castle appears to be incorporated in the fourteenth-century work, the outer archway, which was covered by a barbican, being merely a facing added to earlier work. The inner walls of the gatehouse were also lengthened, as part of the fourteenth-century enlargement.

[2] John of Gaunt was duke of Lancaster 1362-99. The gatehouse of

west side of the inner ward, on the summit of the raised ground on which the castle stands, are covered by a splendid series of late fourteenth-century buildings, chief among them the hall, probably the finest apartment of its date in England, West-minster hall alone excepted (337). Later still, just as at Carew, the transformation of the stronghold was completed by the addition, in Henry VIII.'s time, of apartments, which have now disappeared, along the south side of the ward ; and, in the reign of Elizabeth, the south-west angle was filled by a tall block of buildings erected by the earl of Leicester.

One may compare the growth of the domestic element at Kenilworth with that of the French château of Blois, where the military aspect of the building was obliterated by degrees. To the great hall in the north - east corner of the castle bailey[1] were added, first, the buildings of Charles of Orléans (1440-65) on the west face.[2] Then came the late Gothic work, on the east, of Louis XII. (1498-1502). In the six-teenth century the hall was joined to Charles of Orléans' block by the Renaissance pile of building raised under Francis I. and Henry II.

Kenilworth Castle ; Entrance to hall

The castle by this time had become a palace, and the trans-formation was completed in the seventeenth century (1635) by the erection of the tall range of Palladian buildings in the north-west angle, which is the most prominent feature in the

Lancaster castle, known as John of Gaunt's gateway, was not built until after his death. See p. 327.

[1] This hall was probably built late in the thirteenth or early in the fourteenth century.

[2] Charles also seems to have rebuilt the chapel on the south side of the enclosure.

northern view of the château.[1] A similar work of transformation took place at Amboise under Louis XII. and Francis I. In both these instances, however, the chief changes were made at a period when the Renaissance was exercising a powerful influence on French life and thought. As a rule, French castles of the fourteenth and early fifteenth centuries, while increasing in splendour, preserved much of the character of the feudal stronghold. The two splendid halls and the northern range of buildings at Coucy, built by Enguerrand VII., lord of Coucy, in the last quarter of the fourteenth century, were added without detriment to the strength of the fortress ; and to this same period belongs the talus covering the spring at the foot of the donjon curtain, a work of purely military character.[2] In the châteaux of Méhun-sur-Yèvre (Cher), built by John, duke of Berry, between 1370 and 1385, and Pierrefonds (Oise), built by Louis, duke of Orléans, between 1390 and 1420, the splendour of the palace was equally balanced by the strength of the fortress.

In tracing the development of the castle until it is merged in the manor-house, we must not forget that the fortified dwelling-house was not merely the creation of an age which was ceasing to build castles. Many of the strongholds to which allusion has been made, especially in the north and west of England, were dwelling-houses rather than castles. Acton Burnell, Aydon, Markenfield, Haughton, or those houses which, like Mortham in Yorkshire or Yanwath in Westmorland, have pele-towers attached to them, whether as part of their original equipment or as a later addition, are all fabrics in which military precautions had to be taken, but the everyday needs of the occupants were first considered. A castle is a military post which may include one or more dwelling-houses within its walls : the house which may be turned into a castle, when occasion requires, is on a different footing. Bishops' palaces, such as Auckland, Cawood, Wells, or Lincoln, are examples of the large manor-house in which fortification was merely a measure of precaution. The splendid houses of the bishops of St David's are not the least remarkable of the remains of medieval architecture, half-domestic, half-military, which are common in south-west Wales. Bishop Henry Gower (1328-47) developed at Swansea castle, and at his manor-houses of Lamphey and St David's, a type of architecture which deserves mention on account of its originality. The three houses mentioned are somewhat different from each other.

---

[1] See the drawing by Androuet du Cerceau and plans in W. H. Ward, *French Châteaux and Gardens in the XVIth Century*, Plates III., IV., and p. 11.

[2] See p. 285 above.

HADDON: upper courtyard and tower

Swansea castle is a large block of building, obviously military in character, and in general appearance not unlike the earlier castle which so nobly commands the town of Haverfordwest. Bishop Gower's hall at Lamphey is a plain building, the chief architectural feature of which is the great cellar on the ground-floor: this was covered by a pointed barrel-vault, originally strengthened by heavy transverse ribs, most of which have fallen away. The vast palace of St David's, on the other hand, displays in all its details, and especially in the ogee-headed doorway of the porch of its larger hall, a sumptuousness of decoration which is not often found in the domestic architecture of the time. The great hall on the west side of the courtyard, the

Lamphey Palace

smaller hall and private apartments on the south side, the vaulted cellars which occupy the whole of the basement in each range, are planned upon a scale equal to that of a castle of first-rate size. But, although these buildings differ so much in general character, they have a common feature in the parapet, pierced with a row of wide pointed arches, and corbelled out above the top of the walls. Comparatively rough and coarse at Swansea and Lamphey (341), this parapet at St David's is treated with much delicacy, and the jambs of the arches are furnished with slender shafting. Whether there was any thought of its employment in war is a doubtful point; although it might be useful in such a case, it was probably intended in the first instance merely as an ornament. The corbelling is very slight, without machicolation. The whole design of the parapet is a curious feature which deserves special notice. There is another and later hall at Lamphey, west of the earlier building; and adjoining this on the north is the handsome chapel, built by Bishop Vaughan early in the sixteenth century. The gatehouse at Llawhaden, another manor of the bishops of St David's, appears to be of the fifteenth century, and, with its flanking towers, rounded to the field, has a more distinctly warlike appearance than anything at Lamphey or St David's.

We may now take a few typical examples which illustrate the change from the fortified residence to the large dwelling-house, which was accomplished by the beginning of the sixteenth century. At a comparatively early date, a divorce between military and domestic architecture is manifest in such a house as Stokesay (306). Here the hall and its adjacent buildings are those of a private house pure and simple; and the defensive portion of the plan is confined to the polygonal tower at the south end of the range of buildings, which, in time of war, could be used as a separate stronghold, and was ingeniously planned and well lighted.[1] But at Stokesay (207) the tower appears to be a somewhat later addition to a thirteenth-century dwelling-house. Defensive precautions are added. Of the opposite case, in which they disappear, Haddon hall (340), the most attractive and most thoroughly preserved of English medieval houses, is the best example. In its earliest state, it appears to have been a mere pele, occupying a portion of its present site, with a tower at its north-east and highest corner. The chapel (343), in which large portions of twelfth-century work still remain, was probably built outside the palisade, as the parochial chapel of the hamlet of Nether Haddon. As time went on, the fortified enclosure enlarged its boundaries. A wall was built round it, and the chapel was taken into the line of circumference.[2] In the fourteenth century the present hall was

---

[1] The three principal features of the strong tower at Stokesay are (1) its isolation from the range of buildings adjoining it, its only entrances being from the outside, in the basement and on the first floor; (2) the division of its face towards the field into two small half-octagons; (3) the stairs carried from floor to floor in the thickness of the wall. The stair from the basement to the first and second floors crosses the entrance-lobby on the first floor; but, in order to reach the roof, the second-floor chamber has to be passed through, and a new stair entered in the embrasure of a window. This was planned partly, as at Richmond and Conisbrough, to give the defenders complete control of the stair, and partly to keep the stair within the wall of the tower which was least open to attack, and could therefore be lightened most safely.

[2] This was done towards the end of the twelfth century. The licence stated that the wall was to be without crenellations (*sine kernello*).

HADDON : chapel

built between the upper and lower courts.[1] At its north end were the screens, forming the communication between the two courts, with the pantry, buttery, and passage to the kitchen leading directly out of them. At the south end, behind the dais, was the cellar with the great chamber above. Later on, a porch with an upper chamber was built at the entry to the screens. During the fifteenth century, the upper courtyard was gradually surrounded by buildings; a new chancel and octagonal bell-turret were built to the chapel; and, at the end of this period, the old curtain wall, between the chapel and the great chamber, was covered by an outer wall on either side, and reduced to the state of a mere partition wall on which wooden upper buildings were carried. Wide windows were opened in the west walls of the cellar and the great chamber, and the cellar was turned into a private dining-room at the back of the hall. Early in the sixteenth century, the buildings round the entrance court were completed, and the timber stage east of the chapel was rebuilt in stone. Finally, in the reign of Elizabeth, came the addition which marks the last stage in this transition from pele to dwelling-house, when, on the south side of the upper court-yard, was built the long gallery, with its row of wide mullioned windows, and deep bays projecting towards the garden. While the manor-house at Wingfield, not many miles distant, is practi-cally all of one period, and illustrates a definite compromise between war and peace, Haddon is a growth of from four to five centuries, and from an early date showed a tendency to rid itself of its military character.

Wingfield manor is probably the most striking example of a later English manor-house with certain defensive features. It was begun by Ralph, Lord Cromwell, between 1441 and 1455. Its position is naturally strong. From an almost isolated hill, with steep slopes to the east, north, and west, it commands the valley in which it stands, but is itself commanded by the much higher hills which separate it from the Derwent valley on the west.[2] The buildings are arranged round two courtyards (346).

[1] The hall may be a little earlier than the fourteenth century: the windows seem to indicate the period 1290–1310. The great chimney and the heavy battlement were added when the porch to the hall was built.

[2] Such a position for a medieval stronghold was not unusual. Thus Richmond castle is commanded by much higher hills on the north and south-west. In medieval warfare, however, before fire-arms had received any full development, an enemy would have gained little advantage by occupying a commanding position at some distance from the place attacked. In 1644, the Parliamentary force which besieged Wingfield attempted to breach the walls from Pentrich common, on slightly higher ground to the south-east. This was found impossible, and the cannon had to be moved to a wood on the west side of the manor before any damage was done.

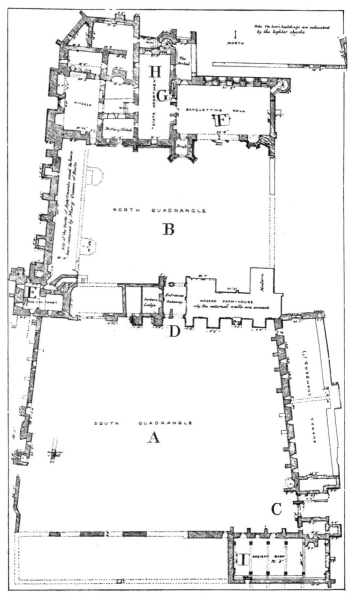

Wingfield Manor; Plan

The outer and larger court, which is entered by a wide gateway, with a postern on one side, at the south end of the east wall, contained store-houses and farm-buildings, with a large barn on the south side. This base-court, like the "barmkin" of a fortified house in the north of England, would be useful in time of war for the protection of tenants and their flocks and herds, who had no other means of defence. A gatehouse in the north wall gives admission to the second court, which was surrounded by buildings on all sides but the east. The whole length of the north side was covered by a magnificent block of buildings, which included the hall, kitchen, and chief private apartments (349). These buildings have not received the full attention which they deserve, but they obviously belong to two periods of work, the great kitchen block at the west end being added as an afterthought.[1] The plan is curious and unusual. The hall occupies the eastern extremity of the block. Although the roof and a large part of the south wall are entirely gone, and the north wall was mutilated by the later partition of the hall into two floors and a number of rooms, the porch, with its upper chamber, and the bay-window, at opposite ends of the south wall, are still fairly perfect. The hall was the full height of the block, and had a high-pitched roof, with large window openings in the gables: it is not certain whether the fireplace was in the centre of the room, with a louvre in the roof for the smoke, or in the south wall. The porch led into screens at the west end, over which was probably a minstrels' gallery. At the north end of the screens was a lobby, from which a vice led to the upper floor of the building dividing the hall from the kitchen; while a wide and well-moulded doorway opened upon a stair which descended into the garden behind the hall. On this side the slope of the ground is very abrupt, and the hall is built upon a very large and handsome cellar (348), divided into two longitudinal halves by a row of five columns. The aisles thus formed are vaulted in oblong compartments upon broad four-centred ribs. The bold wave-mouldings of the ribs and the carving of the bosses at their junction are carved with a masculine vigour of design which gives this cellar a place among the chief architectural masterpieces of its age. There is a short vice with broad steps at each corner of the cellar: those at the north-east and south-east corners communicated directly with the dais and sideboard of the hall, the entrance to the south-east stair being

---

[1] The additions at this end were possibly the work of John Talbot, second earl of Shrewsbury (d. 1460), to whom Cromwell sold the manor shortly before his death. The earl certainly did some building at Wingfield: see the short, but carefully compiled *Guide to Wingfield Manor*, by W. H. Edmunds, p. 11.

a lobby opening on the bay-window. The south-west vice was entered from the courtyard, while the north-west stair opened into a room on one side of the passage from the hall to the kitchen.

The kitchen and its offices were not entered in the usual way, directly from the screens. A block of buildings, with its main axis at right angles to that of the hall, intervenes. There are, however, three doorways, as usual, in the west wall of the hall. Of these, the middle and largest was that of a central passage leading to the kitchen. A smaller doorway, on either side of this, gave access to two ground-floor rooms, beneath which were

Wingfield Manor; Cellar of hall

cellars. The whole floor above these, entered by a vice from the large lobby at the garden end of the screens, was the great chamber, which had a high-pitched roof, and was lighted, towards the courtyard, by a large window-opening of four lights, with good rectilinear tracery and transoms, beneath a segmental arch. It need hardly be said that the position of the great chamber, at the entrance end of the hall, is most unusual. The best parallel example is found in connection with the hall of the thirteenth-century bishop's palace at Lincoln. Here the slope at the north end of the hall prevented the construction of a large block of buildings on that side. At the south end the ground fell away almost vertically, and here, upon a vaulted

WINGFIELD : bay-window of hall

substructure, was built a block of two stories, the lower of which contained the pantry, buttery, and passage to the kitchens, while the upper was the great chamber. The kitchen was contained in a detached tower, between which and the intermediate block was a bridge, with a covered passage on the first floor. The two-storied block has now been converted into the bishop's chapel, of which the windows of the great chamber form the clerestory ; while the passage across the kitchen bridge has been turned into a vestry.

At Wingfield the great chamber was evidently placed at the entrance end of the hall to avoid the type of construction which had been adopted as a *pis aller* at Lincoln, and the side of the hall was chosen where the ground was comparatively level. Nevertheless, at the dais end of the hall, where there is a fall of several feet in the ground, there are considerable remains of buildings on the lower level ; and it is possible that the first kitchen buildings may have been planned at this end. The position, with easy access to the large cellar, and, by a stair which still partly remains, to the hall, would not have been inconvenient, and expense in building would have been saved by this reversal of the usual arrangement, which placed the more costly great chamber block on level foundations, although at the far end of the hall. The four stairs of the cellar made it easy, whatever the position of the kitchen might be, to serve food directly to the dais, or through the screens to the lower end of the hall. However, whether this was the original arrangement or not, the kitchen block west of the great chamber was an addition made probably a few years after the original planning of the house.[1] The central passage below the great chamber was continued to the kitchen, passing between a large pantry and buttery. Its south wall, next the buttery, is pierced by two broad arched openings, forming a buttery hatch upon a magnificent scale, through which drink would be served. There were upper floors to the buttery and pantry ; but the kitchen itself, which contained three fireplaces, filled the whole west end of the block. Its floor is sloped and grooved, to facilitate drainage : the floor-drains were emptied through spouts in the west wall.

The use of the buildings on the south side of the inner court-yard, on either hand of the gateway, cannot be determined with certainty ; but the west side of the court is covered by an

---

[1] This can clearly be seen from the small open courtyard on the north-west side of the great chamber block. The kitchen block is there seen to have been built up against the west wall of the great chamber and its lower stage, without any bonding.

important range of buildings, between the kitchen on the north and the high tower at the south-west corner of the enclosure. Of these buildings, which belong to the original fifteenth-century work, little remains but the west and the foundations of the east wall, in which were two bay-windows. They were probably a suite of private rooms, containing a smaller hall or private dining-room, such as is found at Conway and Porchester, and in most of our castles from the later thirteenth century onwards.[1] At the south end of this block stands the one distinctively military feature of the manor-house, the tall tower of four stories, which, containing comfortable apartments in time of peace, could be isolated and converted into a stronghold in time of war.[2]

This provisional arrangement for defence is characteristic of the age. The primary object of the house at Wingfield was comfort and pleasure ; and its type is as far removed from the military perfection of Caerphilly or Harlech as it can possibly be. The need of a perpetual garrison was not felt ; for, in case of war, siege would be only the last resort of an attacking force. Consequently, the defences of the house, apart from the accommodation for barracks and the safety of refugees in the base-court, and from ordinary strength of the gateways,[3] were restricted to the provision of a tower as a last resource. The house, however, which the builder of Wingfield constructed at Tattershall in Lincolnshire between 1433 and 1443, on the site of an earlier stronghold, took the shape of a brick tower of four stages, with a basement half below the ground (356). There is an octagonal turret at each angle, the vice which leads from the ground-floor to the roof being contained in the south-east turret (357). The walls are of considerable thickness throughout, but are pierced above the basement with large two-light windows, two in each stage of the west wall. In the east wall are the chimneys of the fireplaces on the ground-floor and first floor ; but behind these the wall is pierced by mural passages, lighted to the field. The north wall on the first and third floor also is pierced by passages. These

[1] At Conway, Porchester, etc., however, the large hall was probably intended for the use of the garrison. The great hall at Wingfield was essentially the hall of a dwelling-house, in which the inner court is kept quite separate from the base-court, where possibly a common hall was provided for the men-at-arms who might be lodged there.

[2] This tower, like that at Stokesay, can be entered only by an outer door. This is at the foot of a turret containing a broad vice. The doorway had no portcullis, but was commanded by a slit in the wall from the stair, which ascends on the left of the entrance lobby.

[3] The gateways of the outer and inner courtyards each had double doors. There was no provision for portcullises. Each gateway has a small postern entrance on one side of the main archway. This would be used after the great doors had been closed for the night.

WINGFIELD : strong tower

communicated with chambers in the turrets and with garde-robes. The internal features, the vaulted stairs and passages in the thickness of the walls, and the stone fireplaces on the upper floors, with rectangular mantels ornamented with shields of arms,[1] are elaborate and sumptuous ; but the tower is a shell, and the floors above the vaulted basement are gone. A peculiar feature of the tower, however, is the covered gallery which is corbelled out on stone arches above each wall of the building between the turrets : the floor is machicolated between the corbels, and the gallery has rectangular windows opening to the field. Such a gallery is seen in French military architecture, as, for example, in the Pont Valentré at Cahors, but appears to be unique in England.[2] In the same part of Lincolnshire, and about the same period, towers of the type of Tattershall are not uncommon. Kyme tower, in the fens north-east of Sleaford, Hussey tower, on the north-east side of Boston, and the Tower on the Moor, between Tattershall and Horncastle, are cases in point : none of these, however, can compare with Tattershall in beauty and size, or can show anything like the same union of defensive with purely domestic arrangements.

Brick-work was employed in all these Lincolnshire towers : they lie in a district where stone was not abundant, and where brick-making on the spot was a more simple process than the conveyance of building-stone from Ancaster or Lincoln. In the fifteenth and sixteenth centuries, brick was very freely used for domestic architecture in the eastern counties ; and houses like Oxburgh in Norfolk or the rectory at Hadleigh in Suffolk, with their gatehouse towers, are prominent ex-amples of late fifteenth-century work.[3] The old hall at Gains-borough in Lincolnshire is a large mansion of the fifteenth and sixteenth centuries. This again is chiefly of brick, but with a considerable amount of timber and plaster employed in the hall and one of the wings ; while the bay-window of the hall is of the grey Yorkshire limestone in large blocks, which was much used in the churches of the lower Trent valley. At one corner, however, is a polygonal tower entirely of brick, with cross-loops in the walls of the ground-floor, and battlements at the top. These battlements are corbelled out, so as to give an impression of machicolation : there is, however, no machicolation

---

[1] These have recently been removed, to the great detriment of this noble tower.

[2] The high tower at Wingfield is not machicolated, and affords a curious contrast in this respect to Tattershall.

[3] The late thirteenth-century hall at Little Wenham, near Hadleigh, is an early example of a brick house in this district.

at all, and the spaces between the corbels are arched and filled with simple tracery. The principle here is the same as that at

Tattershall Castle

Wingfield and Tattershall: the residence is provided with its strong tower, which, at Tattershall, as at Warkworth, is identical with the residence itself. But while, at Warkworth, considera-

tions of safety and comfort were fairly balanced, with perhaps a
slight inclination of the scales to safety, at Tattershall, in spite

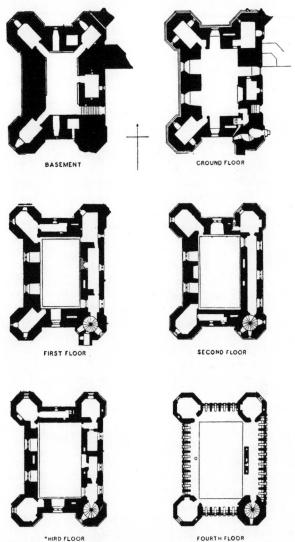

BASEMENT

GROUND FLOOR

FIRST FLOOR

SECOND FLOOR

THIRD FLOOR

FOURTH FLOOR

Tattershall Castle; Plan

of the covered gallery with its machicolated floor, the balance is
on the side of comfort. Both at Tattershall and Wingfield the

38

splendid residence is studied in the first instance, while the defensive stronghold is a secondary idea. The tower at Gainsborough is simply an imitation of the strong towers of the past, conceived in admiration of their strength and conservative love of their beauty, but with no serious idea of practical utility.[1]

The fine manor-house of Compton, in a secluded Devonshire valley a few miles west of Torquay, was probably built about 1420 by one of the family of Gilbert. The main entrance, in the centre of the east front, beneath a tall archway including the ground-floor and first floor in its height, is flanked by bold rectangular projections finishing in corbels some feet above the ground. It does not lead, however, into a vaulted passage barred by portcullises and flanked by guard-rooms, but into one giving direct access to the hall. This no longer exists, and a modern building covers part of the site, but the weathering of the high-pitched roof still remains, and at its south end we can still see the entrances of the kitchen and buttery, and the stair-door of the minstrels' gallery. The courtyard and domestic buildings are enclosed by a wall with a continuous rampart-walk, from the parapet of which are corbelled out at intervals machicolated projections which are so arranged as to be directly above doorways and windows, and thus to protect the most vulnerable points of the house, such as the large four-light east window of the chapel, north of the hall. The house was not surrounded by a ditch; but the space between it and the road probably formed a base-court, although any remains of fortification have disappeared. The whole building is a good example of the reversal of the usual process. The dwelling-house has not grown up within a castle, but has been converted by a very thorough process of walling and crenellation into a fortified post to which the name of castle may well be applied. The situation is anything but commanding, but the house lying hidden in its valley, might be a formidable obstacle, like the neighbouring castle of Berry Pomeroy, to marauders pushing their way inland from Tor Bay.

The character of house first, and castle afterwards, which is remarkable at Wingfield, is also prominent in two of the great Yorkshire residences of the house of Percy, Spofforth and Wressell, princely manor-houses dignified by the name of castle. But perhaps the best example in England of a castle which is one only in name is the brick house of Hurstmonceaux in Sussex. This splendid building was begun about 1446 by Sir Roger

---

[1] Other Lincolnshire examples of brick-work are the gatehouse of Thornton abbey (1382), already described, and the early sixteenth-century manor-house on the Trent above Gainsborough, known as Torksey castle.

Fiennes. Its position, in a sheltered hollow at the head of a small valley, has no military advantages : it may be compared with the secluded site of Compton Wyniates, or with the low sites, within easy reach of water, which the builders of Elizabethan houses were fond of choosing. The house was surrounded by a wet ditch—a feature shared by Compton Wyniates, Kentwell, and other Tudor houses.[1] The imposing gatehouse is in the

centre of the south front, a rectangular building flanked by tall towers,[2] with its portal and the room above recessed beneath a tall arch which at once recalls the machicolated archways that guard the entrance to castles like Chepstow and Tutbury. The gatehouse has certain military features : its rampart and that of the towers is machicolated, and the entrance was closed by a portcullis (323). If cannon had made the curtain of comparatively little importance, it was still advisable to defend the gatehouse. There was no base-court, like that at Wingfield, in advance of the main buildings. The castle was simply a collection of buildings arranged round a series of courtyards, none of which was of any great size, or cor-

Hurstmonceaux Castle; Chapel

responded to that distinctive feature of the military stronghold—the open ward or bailey, which served as the muster-ground for the garrison. The hall was in its usual position, on the side of the first court opposite

[1] The ditch at Hurstmonceaux is now dry. That at Compton Wyniates has been partly filled up. The moat of Kentwell, an Elizabethan house, is still perfect.

[2] The upper stories of these towers only are semicircular. The two lower stages are half octagons. The towers have circular upper turrets like those at Warwick.

the main entrance.   Most of the private apartments were against
the east wall, from which the chancel of the chapel (359) projected in a half-octagonal apse.

An unrivalled opportunity for studying the progress of the
castle in England is provided by a comparison of Hurstmonceaux
with its neighbours at Pevensey and Bodiam.   Pevensey, taking
us back, in its outer circuit, to the Roman era, is, so far as the
actual castle area is concerned, a Norman mount-and-bailey
stronghold, with stone fortifications chiefly of the thirteenth
century.   Bodiam represents one of the last and highest efforts
of perfected castle building in England.   Hurstmonceaux is a
house designed for ease and comfort, but keeping something of
the outer semblance of the stronghold of an English landowner.
A further step was taken at Cowdray, near Midhurst.   Here the
house, nominally a castle, was built about 1530 by Sir William
Fitzwilliam : the battlements of the great hall and its beautiful
porch-tower are the only relic of military architecture which it
retains ; and these are really no more military in character
than the battlements of a church tower or clerestory.   The
comparison and contrast between these Sussex buildings may
be further extended by including in the list the early fortresses
of Lewes and Hastings, and the episcopal castle of Amberley.[1]
In these, with what remains of the early castle of Arundel,
we have as perfect an epitome of the history of the rise and
decline of castle architecture in England as any county can
afford.

Castle building, after the fitful examples of later Plantagenet
times, ceased altogether under the powerful monarchy of the
Tudors, when prominent subjects were made to feel the reality
of the influence of the Crown.   Only once again, during the civil
wars of the seventeenth century, were castles generally resorted
to as strongholds.   The three sieges of Pontefract, the operations
of the royal troops in the Trent valley, between the castles of
Newark and Belvoir and the fortified house of Wiverton, the
defence of Denbigh, Rockingham, and Scarborough, show that
the private fortress could still be used on occasion ; while such
a mansion as Basing house proved itself capable of stubborn
resistance.   To this belated castle warfare we owe much destruction : it was followed by the "slighting" of defences, and the
general reduction of castles to their present state of picturesque
ruin.

[1] The castle of Amberley was built about 1379 by Bishop Rede of
Chichester, and is therefore nearly contemporary with Bodiam.   It is
rectangular in shape, with lofty curtains, and has a gatehouse flanked by
round towers.

In concluding this account of military architecture, it may be useful to gather, from some of the surveys drawn up in the reign of Henry VIII., the state of some of our principal castles at a period when medieval ideas were disappearing. The coloured drawings, already mentioned, of castles among the duchy of Lancaster records, which probably belong to the early part of the reign of Elizabeth, may owe something to fancy. But of the general accuracy of these verbal surveys, apart from inadequate measurements, there can be less doubt. They all show clearly that castles, as military strongholds, were obsolete, and that not merely their defences, but even their domestic buildings, were allowed to go to decay in time of peace. A survey of Carlisle castle, returned 22nd September 1529, is eloquent of the neglect of the fortress by its constable, Lord Dacre. The wooden doors of the gatehouse of the base-court had rotted away : the lead of the roof had been cut away, probably with an eye to business, so that the rain soaked through the timber below, and had leaked through the vault into the basement, which was at this time used as the county gaol. The gatehouse of the inner ward was in a not much better state ; but the gates were of iron and offered more resistance to the weather. The domestic buildings, on the east side of the inner ward, had been roofed with stone slates : the roof of the great chamber had fallen in, and the gallery or passage between the great chamber and hall was "clean gone down." The chapel and a closet adjoining were partly unroofed : the closet chimney had fallen, and the parlour beneath was in a ruinous state. The hall itself was "like to fall" : the kitchen and some of its offices had fallen, and the bakehouse and pantry were on the point of falling, while rain had gone through the pantry floor into the buttery, which in this case was apparently on a lower level. The great tower, "called the Dungeon," was, through the decay of the leaden roof, open to rain, and the floors of its three "houses" or stages were gradually rotting. The castle was supplied with artillery, but this was of "small effect and little value." It included twenty-three iron serpentines or small cannon, six of which were provided with iron axletree pins or trunnions for use on gun-carriages ; a small brass serpentine, a foot long ; nine other serpentines ; forty-five chambers ; one iron sling for discharging stone shot ; four "hagbushes" (arque-buses or hand-guns) ; and two bombards or mortar-shaped cannon. The ammunition for the serpentines and arquebuses consisted of 560 leaden bullets : there was also some stone shot and gunpowder. Some gun-stocks, bows, and arrows complete the list of artillery.[1]

[1] *Lett. and Pap. Hen. VIII.*, vol. IV., nos. 2,655, 2,656.

Sheriff Hutton castle in Yorkshire, surveyed during the same year, was better off as regards its dwelling-house ; for this, as we know from contemporary history, had been occupied with little intermission from the end of the fourteenth century onwards. There were three wards, the outermost being evidently a large base-court, and the middle ward probably, as at Carew, a small court in advance of the inner gatehouse. The hall, kitchen, buttery, pantry, bakehouse, chapel, and lodgings for the lord were in the inner ward. In the base-court were the brew-house and horse-mills, with stables, barns, and granaries. The lead on the roofs was in a generally bad state, and the gutters and spouts wanted mending ; but the timber of the inner roofs was still fairly good. The walls and towers of the inner ward, the plan of which, as we have seen, was akin to that of the contemporary Bolton castle, were "strong and high, but must be mended with lime and sand." Three tons of iron were required to mend the gate of the inner ward. The "mantlewall" of the middle ward was defective and partly in ruin ; while the base-court was "all open," its walls decayed, and its gates gone. In the inner ward was a well, and ponds "for baking and brewing" were near the outer walls. The artillery included "six brass falcons with their carts " and twenty-one arquebuses, for which six barrels of powder and ten score iron shots were provided, bows, bowstrings, and arrows, and two bullet moulds.[1]

After the attainder and execution of the third duke of Buckingham in 1521, two royal escheators took a survey of his lands and houses. Their return, contained in a book of eighty-eight pages,[2] supplies details as to eleven manor - houses and castles. Of these, Caus castle, in west Shropshire, was a mere ruin. Huntingdon castle was decayed, but a tower was reserved for prisoners. The description of Oakham castle might be repeated at the present day. It was "all ruinous, being a large ground within the mantell wall." The hall, however, was in excellent repair, "and of an old fashion ": the escheators recommended its preservation, because the courts were held there. The three towers of the castle of Newport next the Usk are mentioned, with the water-gate below the middle tower, "to receive into the said castle a good vessel ": the hall and other lodgings were decayed, especially in timber, but the stone could be renewed with a quantity of freestone and rubble stored in the castle. Here, as at Carlisle, Launceston, and elsewhere, the basement of the gatehouse was used as a prison ; and its maintenance is therefore insisted upon. The hall at Brecon castle had a new

[1] *Lett. and Pap. Hen. VIII.*, vol. IV., no. 1,089.
[2] Calendared *ibid.*, vol. III., no. 1,186.

CAERLAVEROCK CASTLE

MAXSTOKE CASTLE

and costly roof with pendants: it was "set on height," with windows at either end, and none upon the sides. As a matter of fact, the remains of this hall stand above a twelfth-century substructure, which was vaulted from a central row of columns: the south side wall still remains, and is pierced with a row of lancet windows, so that the statement of the survey may refer to a newer hall which has disappeared. There was a new hall in the inner ward at Kimbolton, which had been built some sixty years before by the duke's great-grandmother. The old curtain against which it stood was in a bad way, and threatened to ruin the hall. Round the inner ward was a moat: the base-court on the outer edge was overgrown with grass, but the barn and stables were in good condition.

"The strongest fortress and most like unto a castle of any other that the Duke had" was the castle of Tonbridge, a mount-and-bailey stronghold whose shell-keep is still one of the finest examples of the type. The keep or "dungeon"—no mention of the mount is made—was at this time covered with a lead roof, half of which was gone. Otherwise, the castle and its curtain were in good repair, the rampart-walk keeping its battlemented outer parapet and rear-wall. The gatehouse, on the north side of the castle, was "as strong a fortress as few be in England": on the east curtain was a square tower called the Stafford tower, and at the south-east corner, next the Medway, was the octagonal Water tower. The river constituted the chief southern defence of the castle, and there was no south curtain: the sub-structure of the hall and lodgings, 26 feet high and built of ashlar, was on this side, but the buildings themselves had never been finished.

Castles of a later type were Stafford, and Maxstoke (364) in Warwickshire. Stafford castle at this time consisted of a single block of lodgings with two towers at either end and another in the middle of the south front. The hall was in the centre of the block, with the kitchen, larder, buttery, and pantry beneath it: at one end of the hall was the great chamber with a cellar below, and at the other was a "surveying chamber," or service-room, to which dishes would be brought from the kitchen. Each of the five towers contained three rooms, in each of which was a fireplace. The towers were machicolated, "the enbatelling being trussed forth upon corbelles." Outside the house were the chapel, gatehouse, and another kitchen; but this front court was apparently without defensive walls. Maxstoke, originally a castle of the Clintons, which was built and fortified in or after 1345,[1] had been largely repaired by the duchess Anne,

[1] Pat. 19 Edw. III., pt. 1, m. 25.

the builder of the hall at Kimbolton. There was a base-court with a gatehouse, stables, and barns, which were walled with stone and covered with slate. Round the castle, "a right proper thing after the old building," was a moat. The house, with a tower at each corner, was built round a quadrangle, and in the side next the bridge over the moat was a gatehouse tower, with a vaulted entry. The hall, the chapel, the great chamber, and the lodgings generally were in good condition, although they were not entirely finished and much glazing was still necessary. The provision of fireplaces is specially mentioned, as well as a point in the planning of the house—the convenient access to the chapel, or, rather, to its gallery or galleries, from the various first-floor rooms at "the over end" of the hall and great chamber.

The moated manor-house of Writtle in Essex can hardly be counted among castles: it was a timber building round a cloistered quadrangle. There was no hall, but "a goodly and large parlour instead." Thornbury castle in Gloucestershire, however, which was in great part of the duke's own building, was one of those houses in which some semblance of military architecture was kept. There was no moat, but a base-court and an inner ward. The buildings of the base-court itself had been set out, but were in a very incomplete state, and little had been finished beyond the foundations of the north and west sides. The entrance to the inner ward was in the west face of the quadrangle; but of the west and north blocks only the lower story had been completed. This was of ashlar, while in the base-court ashlar had been used only for the window openings, doorways, and quoins. The hall and kitchen offices formed the east block, "all of the old building, and of a homely fashion"; but the south block, of the newer work, was "fully finished with curious works and stately lodgings," and from it a gallery of timber cased with stone, with an upper and lower passage, crossed the south garden to the parish church and the duke's chapel therein. A magnificent feature of this house, which became more and more characteristic of the palaces of noblemen of the age, were the great parks to the east of the castle, and the gardens on its east and south side. Between the east garden and the New park was the orchard, "in which are many alleys to walk in openly," and round about the orchard were other alleys on a good height, with "roosting places," covered with white thorn and hazel.

Thornbury castle had reached this degree of unfinished splendour only a few years before the survey was made. The gateway of the outer ward still bears an inscription with the date 1511, while at the base of the moulded brick chimneys of the south block is the date 1514. Remains may still be seen of most of the buildings mentioned in these surveys. Thornbury and Maxstoke are still occupied, and of Thornbury in particular the details of the survey still hold good. The great value of these descriptions is the fact that they tell us something, on the eve of the Renaissance period, of the state of a series of fortresses which represented almost every type of an architecture that had grown up under the influence of conditions rapidly becoming obsolete. At Tonbridge we see the mount-and-bailey fortress of early Norman times, built to meet needs which were purely military, and strengthened with a stone keep and walls and towers of stone as those needs became more pressing. At Carlisle we have the fortress with its compact inner ward and great tower, approached through the spacious base-court which served the needs of the garrison and might shelter flocks and herds in time of war. No castle of the most perfect type, planned in the golden age of military architecture, is represented. At Brecon, however, we can study the growing importance of the domestic buildings of the castle. At Sheriff Hutton we have the quadrangular castle of the fourteenth century with its angle-towers, and its walled base-court serving the purposes of a farm-yard. Stafford castle, the plan of which has been imitated in the modern house on the site, is a fortified residence built in a single block, to which some of the strong houses of the north of England are analogous. The moated house of Maxstoke preserves the quadrangular plan, and has its provisions for defence ; but its domestic character was the first aim of its builders, and its walls and towers are without the formidable height and strength of Sheriff Hutton and Bolton. Here and at Thornbury the base-court was still retained ; but at Thornbury the energy of the builders was concentrated in the beautiful mansion, and the idea of the defensive stronghold had almost departed. The day of the castle and the walled town was over, and, in the face of methods of attack of which the builders of Norman castles had never dreamed, military engineers were beginning to move along new lines to which architectural considerations were no longer a matter of great importance. An architecture which, developed from earthwork in the beginning, reproduced in stone, at its height, the disposition of the concentric earth-works of primeval times, gave place in its turn to a science in which the employment of earthwork and the natural resources of a defensive position played an increasingly prominent part.

INDEX OF PERSONS AND PLACES

N.B.—Illustrations are denoted by numbers followed by the name of the photographer, draughtsman, or source from which the picture is derived.

INDEX RERUM

A

Adulterine castles, 56, 57, 89
Adulterinus, 56
Agger, 11, 60
Alatorium, 89
Allure, 89
Angle, dead, in fortification, 162
Angles, reduction of, in fortification, 165
Arbalast, 73 ; *see* Cross-bow
Arx, 22, 32, 53, 65 ; *arcem condere*, etc., 38
Attack, science and methods of, 66-79
Aula, hall or manor-house, 197, 198
Aula principalis, 56 ; *see* Hall

B

Bailey, 40, 43, 44, 45, 46, 50, 51, 55, 56 ; *see* Castles, plan of
Ballista, 16, 63, 67, 73, 74
Ballium, 40
Barbican, 215, 229, 230, 233-6, 239-41
Barmkin, 189, 229, 312, 347
Bartizan, 187, 235, 236
Base-court, 40, 96
Basse-cour, 40
Bastille, 236
Bastion, 289, 290
Battering ram, *see* Ram
Bayeux tapestry, 36, 38, 45, 46, A. Thompson ; 36, 38, 44, 45, 46, 52, 66, 190, 192
Belfry, 72, Viollet-le-Duc ; 67, 70, 71, 78
Berfredum, 67
Berm, 5, 11, 60
Bishop's palaces, fortified, 301, 338, 341, 342
Bore, 70, Viollet-le-Duc ; 61, 64, 68
Borough, 30
Bourg, 26
Bower, 192, 193
Brattice, 79, 187
Bretèche, 79, 187

Brick-work in eastern counties, 355, 358
— tower of, at siege of Marseilles, 62
Bridges, fortified, 297, 298 ; London bridge, 64 ; bridges at Paris, 63
Burg, 25, 26
Burgus or *burgum*, 30, 41
Burh, 25 ; *burhs* in Saxon England, map of, 31, A. Thompson ; 25-27, 28-33, 35, 38, 41, 42
Byzantine military science, 59, 61, 67, 73

C

Cabulus, 76
Carfax, 22
Castel, 35, 37, 42
Castellum, 35, 55, 60, 66 ; *castellum construere*, etc., 38 ; *castellis, vastata in*, 42
Castles, dwelling-houses in, 188-211
— in England, Norman, earthworks, 26, 30, 32, 33, 35-57 ; mount-and-bailey plan, 42-47, 48-52, 55-56, 112, 113, 160, 161 ; relative date of, 56, 57 ; importance in warfare, 65, 66, 83-7 ; stone fortifications, 47, 89-107
— in relation to plan of walled towns, 87-89
— plan of, with successive baileys, 162, 163, 164 ; concentric, 7, 164, 264, 264-82, 304 ; mount-and-bailey, *see* Castles in England, Norman
— strategic position in North of England, map illustrating, 84, A. Thompson ; 83-87
— Syrian, *see* Crusaders
Castrum, 35, 53
Cat, 68
Catapult, 73, Viollet-le-Duc ; 16, 17, 51, 67, 70, 71, 73-6 ; *see Ballista, Mangana*, etc.
Centering of vault at Lancaster castle, 327
Cervi, 60
Chamber, great, 54, 205, 206, 207
Chapels in castles, 107-9, 209-11 ; *see* also Keep
Châtelet, 236